POETRIES *of* AMERICA

Essays on the Relation
of Character to Style

1920  1985

IRVIN EHRENPREIS

POETRIES
OF
AMERICA

Essays on the Relation of Character to Style

Edited and with an Introduction by DANIEL ALBRIGHT

UNIVERSITY PRESS OF VIRGINIA
Charlottesville

THE UNIVERSITY PRESS OF VIRGINIA
Copyright © 1989 by the Rector and Visitors
of the University of Virginia

First published 1989

Design by Janet Anderson   Frontispiece photo by Dave Skinner

Library of Congress Cataloging-in-Publication Data

Ehrenpreis, Irvin, 1920–
  Poetries of America.

  1. American poetry—History and criticism.
I. Albright, Daniel, 1945–   . II. Title.
PS305.E35   811'.009   88-10699
ISBN 0-8139-1203-2

Printed in the United States of America

CONTENTS

ACKNOWLEDGMENTS

No editor could hope for better fortune than mine. Every difficulty that might hinder this book's appearance—rights and permissions, clerical support, and so forth—has been swept aside. I am extremely grateful, for personal as well as professional reasons, to the executors of Professor Ehrenpreis's estate: E. D. Hirsch, Jr., and David Ehrenpreis. The University of Virginia, the University Press of Virginia, and *The New York Review of Books* also deserve special praise; but many people who knew Professor Ehrenpreis have been eager to make this book possible.

In most cases, the essays here collected had no sources specified for quoted material. It was difficult to trace obscure passages from interviews, early drafts of poems, uncollected letters, and so forth, cited in Professor Ehrenpreis's texts. Patricia Welsch of the University of Virginia and Wendy Bashant of the University of Rochester have helped greatly in the thousand small exasperations that attend a project such as this. I must also thank Lawrence Garretson of the University of Virginia, who risked his eyesight and his sanity poring over microfilms, manuscripts, and so on—indeed anyone who enjoys this book is in his debt. His discretion, wisdom, and sheer will to get things right are reflected on many pages of this text. Finally I thank her whom I always thank, and never thank enough, Karin Larson.

DANIEL ALBRIGHT
Rochester, N.Y.

INTRODUCTION

The world agrees that the biographies of monks, imbeciles, and literary critics do not need to be told. Yet I think that many readers of this book would like to know something about its author.

Irvin Ehrenpreis was born in Manhattan in 1920, the son of Jewish immigrants from Poland and White Russia. As a child he was small and attractive; he was treated well and encouraged to develop his remarkable intellectual gifts. He attended a school for bright children, where he did not receive excellent grades; by his own account he had no great ambition when young. His father was the owner of a boys' clothing store who went bankrupt in the Great Depression; afterwards he operated a newsstand. There, after school, Irvin sold newspapers and magazines; in later life he was pleased to think that some of his articles were published in magazines he had himself once vended. He graduated from the City College of New York at the age of eighteen—but he regarded this acceleration as a great error, and would fly into a rage when he heard about children who were promoted beyond the grade appropriate to their age. After his graduation he had no strong sense of direction. He applied to several medical schools but was rejected by all. He taught English, Latin, and history at a rural high school, to students not much younger than himself. Then he attended Columbia Teachers College, from which he received a Ph.D. in education in 1944. He spoke of his years at Columbia as an exhilarating time: he took courses in physics as well as literature, he read *Finnegans Wake* as it appeared, he became involved with various left-wing political activities. These last were, I think, a slight embarrassment to him as an adult—he remained politically liberal but became a strong anti-Communist.

His first college teaching position was at the University of Indiana, where he stayed for many years, until he joined the faculty of the University of Virginia in 1964. Both Charlottesville and Bloomington offered a pleasing contrast to New York City. He spoke of Bloomington, Indiana, in the same idyllic tone that Theocritus used to describe Sicily, and liked to call Charlottesville "the Athens of Albemarle County," with a mocking but affectionate grimace. Virginia offered several advantages over Indiana, not all of them immediately apparent. First, the chairman of the English Department in those days was Fredson Bowers, a bibliographer for whom Irvin Ehrenpreis had great respect, and who was eager to recruit him. Second, his wife Anne was struggling with cancer, which required medical facilities beyond those easily available in southern Indiana. Third, the landed gentry of Albemarle County offered a delicious spectacle of extravagance and squirearchical affectation. Fourth, Virginia was beginning to attract a number of fine graduate students. As a teacher Irvin Ehrenpreis was famous for a somewhat terrifying classroom presence: he would call on students by name, transfix them by his gaze, and demand specific answers. Even bright students who adored him sometimes felt wrung dry by the end of class.

He had a striking presence out of class as well. Most extremely intelligent people find ways of softening themselves to the world at large: every academic knows a distinguished chemist who plays in a Dixieland band, or a historian of Roman law who can reel off the batting averages of the whole starting lineup of the 1967 Red Sox, or someone similar. But Irvin Ehrenpreis had none of these mollifying ways. He was always intense—his brother once said that Irvin would have been intense even before the age of one, if there had been anything to be intense about. Short and thin, fidgety, abrupt, he rarely walked if he could find an excuse to run. He spoke rapidly in a carefully modulated voice, in correct, organized sentences and paragraphs; during the several hundred hours that I heard him speak, he committed perhaps three grammatical errors. His face typically seemed to express surprise, as if he were perpetually startled by the wickedness and folly of men. In his company, other people seemed half-asleep by comparison.

This book is a collection of essays on American poetry. Most of these essays were book reviews, either of poets' biographies (Whitman and Dickinson), or of literary criticism (Pound and Eliot), or of original books of poetry as they appeared. In 1982 Irvin Ehrenpreis prepared a typescript of eighteen of these essays, carefully arranged and edited, with the title *Poetries of America: Essays on the Relation of Character to Style*. He talked of publishing it; I do not know why he never did so. I have added a nineteenth essay, "Eliot III," a review published in 1984 that I am confident he would have wished to include here. I have also appended some published replies to those who objected to his comments.

As a book reviewer he lived by a code. Among his tenets were (1) do not write a wholly negative review of an original book of poetry; (2) always hold something back. The rationale for the first tenet was that an altogether bad book of poetry should not be reviewed in the first place. To errant scholars he felt no need to show mercy; but to misguided poets he tried to be kind (the reader may judge for himself the degree of success). The rationale for the second tenet was that some particularly shameful error should be left unmentioned in a review, so that, if the reviewee objected to the reviewer's treatment, a bludgeon was readily at hand. In general, his reviews—of Augustan studies as well as of modern poetry—are somewhat cautious. In private conversation he often made much more severe complaints than the reviews declare. But in his replies to objections, he let himself go— more of his wit and vivacity are manifest.

In almost every essay in this book, certain aspects of the poems are shown to be congruent with biographical details of the poet's life. Thus we are told that the hymnlike stanza that Emily Dickinson used in most of her poems is related to the disarming facade of her public character—a plain and childlike exterior that hides a bold inner content. Perhaps I can show that the theory of poetry advanced in this book is congruent with the biographical details of Irvin Ehrenpreis's life.

The central assumption of his critical method was that content is prior to form—that poets have something to say, and then choose a literary style either as an appropriate, or as an ironically inappropriate, expression. This assumption is anti-Romantic in that it contradicts the belief of Coleridge and Walter Pater that form and content are ideally inseparable; but both Dryden and T. S. Eliot would have found it congenial. It is in no way strange that the child of Eastern European immigrants, with little early participation in high culture, whose vivid personality must have been developed consciously and carefully, would have thought that style was not inherent in a man but a kind of artificial constraint. Irvin Ehrenpreis's handwriting showed the labor he expended to achieve a personal style. He wrote slowly, in a perfect italic script—his son once said that his father used to madden him (when he needed money) by taking what seemed like hours to sign checks. But when hurried, his handwriting degenerated suddenly into sheer scrawl—there was no middle ground between the unintelligible and the overintelligible. I take this as a sign of a kind of chaos underlying the achieved persona. Excited, he could resemble Albert Einstein as played by Jack Nicholson.

Again and again in these essays we find the assumption that poetic form is a bulwark against the chaos of the poet's feelings. In "Berryman II," for example, we are told that the poet's stanza form, though loose, is "rigid enough to make significant barriers to the waves of feeling." In "Lowell I," the critic complains of the arbitrary, seemingly purposeless contrast in Lowell's early poetry between the tight stanza form and the violence and bitterness of feeling. In the essay on Elizabeth Bishop—possibly the finest piece in this collection—we are shown how the poet assuages grief and loss by arranging colorful bits and scraps into a design. This is the Ehrenpreis model of the poetic act: dangerous, overwhelming feelings are tamed and clarified by meter, rhyme, metaphor, art. Perhaps this is clearest in his essay "The Powers of Alexander Pope" (*New York Review of Books,* 20 December 1979, not included here), where he described how Pope's neat couplets arise from creative wells of "pain, confusion, misshapen birth and growth, delusive transformation"—the unborn forms in the Cave of Dulness, the phantasmagoria of the Cave of Spleen.

One of these essays, "Poetry and Language," is in fact a kind of polemic, urging poets not to abandon the traditional resources of art through an impatient desire to do away with all that impedes free expression, or through a wish to imitate the authentic shapelessness of reality. But in fact Irvin Ehrenpreis was a less conservative critic than this essay suggests: he (like all men of an Augustan temperament, valuing the clear, the agreeable, the spruce) was fascinated with chaos, and wrote sympathetically about poets who present raw feeling, feeling unmediated by poetic form. Indeed he considered highly cooked poetry slightly un-American. Thus he described Whitman as achieving great success by rejecting conscious artifice:

> It is a mistake to measure rhythms or to trace pattern of sound in his lines. Whitman deliberately held back from the forms that Tennyson and Longfellow relied on.
>
> There is a level of intuitive expression, just above the dark chaos from which all creation starts. At this level Whitman found he could trust his genius.

Similarly, Irvin Ehrenpreis thought that Stevens's predilection for nonsense syllables arose from his desire to give a voice to reality before it had been digested, shaped by the conscious mind, or from his desire to express the unconscious self: "The inmost self is subrational and prelinguistic. It holds the feelings and tastes that move us to speech, not those that issue from speech. Stevens's nonsense syllables bypass the conscious, literary, reflective mind. . . . [A certain memory] takes us back to ancestral impressions, first impressions, the primordial response to the world, without myth, symbolism, human associations." In "Heaney, Ammons, Strand," we are offered a contrast of the formal European Seamus Heaney with the formless American A. R. Ammons, whose poems are so radically enjambed that it is difficult to see any reason behind his line breaks: "Often, Heaney writes in conventional forms. Ammons does not. . . . The American tends to confront the universe directly. As an artist, he gets little support from liturgical forms or from the songs and hymns that often provide patterns for Irish and British verse. . . . It may be significant that Lowell [who influenced Heaney] was at one time drawn to the Roman Catholic Church, for which mediation is far more important than it is for Protestantism." And in the final essay, on Sylvia Plath, Irvin Ehrenpreis regarded her poems as the speech of an infant self incapable of establishing a secure position in the universe, a fragmentary, jejune, easily dismembered being. In all these cases the critic attempted to understand a poem as a record of the poet's unconscious and immediate responses to the world. Sometimes we hear a note of disapproval of the poet who, instead of writing a poem, simply offers to his readers the verbal equivalent of dough or protoplasm; but often there is respect for the ingenuity of poets who can gesture imaginatively toward what Wallace Stevens called the World without Imagination, reality uninflected by human thought.

Irvin Ehrenpreis's preoccupation with biography is part of a general preoccupation with the imaginative prehistory of poetry: what is the nature of a poem before it is actually written? He used biography as a tool for reconstructing the inner dialogue that led to a poet's choice of theme and form—few critics in any age have achieved such brilliant results with this method. He laid more emphasis on the process of composition than on the finished product—he had little interest in the poem as verbal icon or well-wrought urn. He liked to speak of the poem as an enactment of the process of insight (this phrase occurs in the Pound essay): "Poems like Elizabeth Bishop's 'Poem' . . . Robert Lowell's 'Skunk Hour,' . . . and James Merrill's 'The Thousand and Second Night' are suitable models [for poets today], not because they reveal any scandal about the poet but because they involve world and self in the fascinating, funny, terrible work of connecting and disconnecting the immediate sensibility and the experiences that produced it. A group of such poems is the grandest epic we can use" ("Warren I"). The poet's life and his poem are beheld as mutually sustaining, mutually nourishing, delicately groping at each other's truths. A poem is less an end than a means of inquiring into the meanings of experience. Although Irvin Ehrenpreis insisted that many questions of interpretation could not be settled by biographical evidence, he often preferred those lyric poems in which the poet's persona differed little from the self inferred by biographical information. He did not usually enjoy poems of rhetorical self-inflation, or poems excessively ambitious in scope. Indeed a continual theme of these essays is the crusade against the long narrative or epic poem: "the stronger the narrative, the weaker the verse" ("Merrill").

No critic is universally sensitive, pan-empathic, and there are weaknesses to be found in this book. I am uneasy about Irvin Ehrenpreis's lack of curiosity about the poetic or philosophical theories of the poets he criticized. He insisted again and again (I think correctly) that an author's "persuasive theoretical grounds for his literary practice" do not prove "that what the man writes is good" ("Ashbery and Justice"); and that "a coherent design is not necessarily a mark of literary value" ("Eliot I"). And I respect him deeply for his attempt to take an "independent point of view" ("Eliot I") in evaluating Eliot's achievement, instead of judging Eliot by principles derived from Eliot's critical essays. And yet I believe that his essays on Eliot and Pound would have been better if better informed by knowledge of Eliot's dissertation on F. H. Bradley, or Pound's theory of vorticism, and so forth. A poet's ideas are also part of his total effort. The Pound essay is the least impressive in the book: Irvin Ehrenpreis's revulsion against Pound's anti-Semitism distorted his responses to the poetry. In this case the direction indicated by the subtitle (*Essays on the Relation of Character to Style*) led to the too easy conclusion that a poor character makes for a shapeless and vulgar style. (Distaste for less accomplished poets, however, could be more productive. The last pages of "Poetry and Language" contain a denunciation of Gary Snyder that is a miracle of invective, worthy of *The Dunciad* itself.)

Some readers of this book will object to its treatment of John Ashbery and Mark Strand. Irvin Ehrenpreis did not have great respect for the work of either poet. This was perhaps inevitable, since he believed that lyric poetry was essentially mimetic in character and communal in purpose: "It is . . . this turning on itself, the movement toward solipsism, that weakens Strand's work. Many of the poems seem written to exemplify designs . . . but not to illuminate an experience so that readers might match it with their own. If I recommend the short lyric of self-definition as the proper modern poem, it is not because the character of a poet is the most important focus of a literary work. It is because through this frame the poet can describe human nature and the world" ("Heaney, Ammons, Strand"). Irvin Ehrenpreis believed that lyric poetry had a moral mission, to unite mankind in shared responses to experience. He could not easily approve of poets whom he judged to be morally defective (like Pound and Snyder), or of poets whose work was so involved and private that it had no public, moral aspect whatsoever. If Irvin Ehrenpreis erred in this matter, it was the error of a generous and grave man who believed in the importance of art.

I regret that he never wrote a preface to this collection. I can, however, try to supply one from an unusual source. During the mid-1980s, Irvin Ehrenpreis spent his summers at the University of Münster, Germany (the home of an institute of Swift scholarship now named in his honor), where he and a German colleague, Dr. Heinz Vienken, decided to compile an anthology of German translations of modern American poems. He undertook this project with great zeal, and by the time of his death he had carefully annotated a good number of poems and had left notes toward a preface. This preface, if completed, could have easily served for this collection as well as for the anthology. I offer here a construction of these notes—the last paragraph is very doubtful, but most of the rest is clear.

The history of American poetry can be discussed in terms of three traditions. The first is conventional didactic verse in which the poet uses familiar forms and correct language in order to convey moral implications that challenge common attitudes. Some of the subtlest, most disturbing poets belong to this line: Dickinson and Frost, for example.

The second tradition is that of high, aesthetic literature embodied above all in the Symbolist tradition. The poets avoid didacticism, celebrate the creative imagination, strive for musical versification, and are not afraid to be difficult. Poe (especially in French translation), Hart Crane, and Wallace Stevens are examples of this line.

Finally, a strong tendency, starting early in the country's history, is the effort to elaborate native themes opposing America to Europe, to use American images and speech. This tradition found its best-known expression in the work of Walt Whitman, whose use of free verse and a bold vocabulary went along with a delight in the American landscape, pride in the potentialities of his countrymen, but disappointment with their political and cultural institutions. From Whitman the line to W. C. Williams is direct, and Williams has had an incalculable influence on poets of the last forty years.

Behind these developments stand certain representative figures whose thought may not have been familiar to all modern American poets but whose works embody fundamental elements that keep reappearing in the poetry. The most important is Emerson, a deliberately unsystematic thinker who directly inspired Whitman. Emerson, William James, and John Dewey were formative influences on American education and helped to shape the view of human nature most characteristic of the country, a view to which the poets respond with strong sympathy or hostility, though they are not always conscious of its sources. The themes of personal identity and national and private self-definition are typical of Western literature during the last seventy years but especially of American poetry, in which they rival the old themes of death, love, and religious faith.

The essays in this book illustrate the concern with self-definition that lies behind the best work of American poetry. One can relate the various forms of the impulse to Emerson, who inspired and first recognized the greatness of Whitman. Other poets may not always have admired Emerson. But for a nation of immigrants, self-definition is always a peculiar obsession, and the forms in which Emerson explored it provide a natural frame for a survey of American poetry.

In "The Poet," "The American Scholar," and his journals, Emerson dwelled on the dangers of an imposed culture, a canon of books to be mastered, a set of moral laws to be learned and obeyed. He knew better than most men how much evil resides in the heart of man, but he also believed that no good was reliable if its roots started elsewhere.

Clearly Whitman profited from the notion of a national culture that could be developed afresh, without the dead hand of the past; and Whitman's free verse, where form is determined by meaning, might have been more difficult to achieve without the example of Emerson's ideas and his rapturous prose. But the other two traditions also owe much to Emerson, who was both a moralist and a kind of aesthete. When Emerson said, in "Nature," that "beauty is the mark God sets upon virtue," he invited moral poets to find the Good in the American landscape. Another passage from "Nature" shows that Emerson anticipated the Symbolist line as well: "Such is the constitution of all things, or such the plastic power of the human eye, that the primary forms, as the sky, the mountain, the tree, the animal, give us a delight *in and for themselves;* a pleasure arising from outline, color, motion, and grouping" (Frederic I. Carpenter, *Ralph Waldo Emerson,* p. 15). This is an expression of the mood of much of Wallace Stevens's poetry. Like Stevens, Emerson could see the world around him as a painting, as if there were some pressure toward design in nature herself. George Santayana, who taught at Harvard when Stevens attended the university, wrote of Emerson, "Imagination is his single theme. . . . Emerson traces in every sphere . . . the self-expression of the Soul in the forms of Nature and of society" (Carpenter, p. xl). The high aesthetic tradition, the moral tradition, and the native American tradition are all comprehended in Emerson's thought.

This sober preface does not prepare the reader for the energy or the authority of this book. Running through these pages there is an undercurrent of feeling that sometimes seems in excess of the provocation offered by the texts under discussion. In the foreword to the third volume of his masterpiece, the biography of Swift, Irvin Ehrenpreis wrote: "The one who would have felt the strongest pleasure in the completion of this book is dead. But readers who follow my account of Swift's response to the loss of Esther Johnson may wish to know that I could not help thinking of Anne, my wife, as I wrote." This covert grappling with personal emotion through literary research is not rare among critics. The fond, lingering, elegiac summaries of Emily Hale's role in T. S. Eliot's life (in the Eliot essays) may indicate that the critic was reminded of some person in his own life. Similarly, the outbursts of bitterness and aggressiveness may suggest a spirit that seeks an occasion to vent itself. In his lecture "Why Literature Should Be Taught" (1958), he said that "as far as I can judge, essential human nature is neither good nor neutral."

One of the reasons why this collection of essays has unique force is that Irvin Ehrenpreis knew and consulted with some of the most distinguished poets discussed in these pages. Robert Lowell seems to have valued his opinion when revising poems; and Elizabeth Bishop was a friend of his. I once had lunch with her and Irvin in a seedy cafeteria, of the sort that bears a certificate of commendation from *McCall's* magazine, 1956, and I can testify to their warmth and ease in each other's company. There was a sort of game, not to make any conversation inappropriate to the decor of the restaurant: so they talked, deadpan, about the weather and the difficulty of gardening in warm climates and the rest, with only the faintest gestures of irony.

Conversation with Irvin Ehrenpreis was unlike conversation with other men. Even when wholly relaxed, he spoke in periods, as if he were wrapping birthday presents, proffering his matter in a beautiful gift box with a bow on top. Here is a specimen—I had just complained about some astonishing mistake I had found in a scholar's annotation to a novel:

> The standards of annotation are high these days. Soon scholars will be providing footnotes to conjunctions and prepositions as well as to nouns. On the other hand, it is difficult not to make mistakes. When Anne [his wife] was editing [Charlotte Smith's] *Emmeline* she added a gloss to *Côte Rôti,* noting that it meant a rib roast. You know better, don't you? *You* are a connoisseur. After the edition was published, we spent the summer in France. No one knew where we were but Cecil Lang [our friend, the scholar of Swinburne and Tennyson; he lived a few houses away from Irvin]. In a small country inn we were surprised to learn that someone had sent to our table a bottle of wine. It was from Cecil. It was a bottle of *Côte Rôti.* He had written to the innkeeper from America.

After hearing such a story, you were expected to present a similarly prepared gift in exchange. Like most Americans I had grown up believing that all conversation was stichomythia, and it took time to adjust to this style.

It was good to know him. He was not the sort of man who liked to expound a philosophy of living, but I remember a time when he said that, even though he was a Jew by birth, there were some parables in the New Testament that meant more to him than any in the Old: the parable of the Talents (Matthew 25:14), for one, and the parable of the man who instructs his servant to scour the streets and byways looking for strangers to invite to the feast (Luke 14:16). I think that that parable, more than anything else, explains what he hoped to be as a teacher. He would sometimes startle his students and friends by asking them personal questions—as if he were trying to memorize the father's occupation and the mother's maiden name, a body of facts about everyone he met. But this was his way of issuing his own passport, of extending an invitation to the intellectual feast over which he presided. As this book of essays shows, he was a democrat of the intellect: "The old humanistic ideal [is] sometimes imagined to be aristocratic, but [is] really available to anyone with the mind and the will: this is intellectual and aesthetic culture, comprehending poetry and the other arts, history, and philosophy. A mark of this culture was that (contrary to some snobbish illusions) it could be passed on from Greek to Roman, from slave to noble, from antiquity to Renaissance. . . . It united men over the barriers of social institutions" ("Pound"). I think that this belief had the intensity of religious conviction. He was not a religious man: during his wife's terrible, interminable dying, he used to refer to God as The Blunderer. Yet perhaps it is not surprising that, a little before his unexpected death—he fell down a staircase at the University of Münster, after a long weekend of work on the German-American anthology—he had begun to attend Roman Catholic Mass. My first thought, when I learned that he had died, was that the world's intelligence quotient had measurably sunk; but in fact, through his network of students and admirers, he succeeded in populating the world with people who try to emulate his intelligence, alertness, and generosity.

He was not Falstaffian in temperament—he was far too judicious and agile—and yet, like Falstaff, he was not only witty himself, but the cause that wit is in other men.

DANIEL ALBRIGHT

POETRIES *of* AMERICA

Essays on the Relation
of Character to Style

1

WHITMAN

It was Walt Whitman, at the age of forty-five, who finally took his elder brother Jesse to a lunatic asylum in Brooklyn and left him there. As Justin Kaplan reports in his brisk and accurate biography of Whitman, Jesse had an unstable, violent nature, and Walt early became their mother's favorite child. Even when she was dying, Mrs. Whitman singled out her "dear beloved Walter" by name for a particular leave-taking.[1]

Jesse died after five years in the asylum and received a pauper's burial, with no member of the family at hand. Kaplan reminds us of the line in *Song of Myself* that foreshadows the poet's management of his brother: "The lunatic is carried at last to the asylum a confirm'd case" (p. 41).[2]

Not only did Walt displace this rival for parental love. He also won the contest with their father. Mr. Whitman was a philoprogenitive

This essay was first published 2 Apr. 1981 under the title "All American Bard" as a review of Justin Kaplan, *Walt Whitman: A Life* (New York: Simon and Schuster, 1980). Reprinted with permission from *The New York Review of Books*. Copyright © 1981 Nyrev, Inc.

1   Horace Traubel, *With Walt Whitman in Camden* (Philadelphia, 1953), 4:514.

2   All quotations from Whitman's poetry are taken from *Leaves of Grass*, Comprehensive Reader's Edition, ed. Harold W. Blodgett and Scully Bradley, in *The Collected Writings of Walt Whitman* (New York: New York Univ. Press, 1965), and they will be cited in text by page number.

carpenter who succeeded in little besides the fathering of a large brood. Hard-working, short-tempered, and laconic, he quarreled with his literary son. It is easy for us to believe that the lines about a father in "There Was a Child" are autobiographical: "The father, strong, self-sufficient, manly, mean, anger'd, unjust, / The blow, the quick loud word, the tight bargain, the crafty lure" (p. 365). Scholars have noticed how often Whitman's early stories deal with the injustice of a father toward a son.

The poet wished to live by no discipline but the promptings of his genius. He would refuse, his brother George said, "to do anything except at his own notion."[3] The young Whitman came late to meals; and while other sons were rising betimes to work normal hours with hammer and saw, the poet loafed and invited his soul. In the preface to *Leaves of Grass* he sneered at the "abandonment of such a great being as a man is to the toss and pallor of years of moneymaking."[4] In a fragment of verse addressed to poor people, he wrote:

> The road to riches is easily open to me,
> But I do not choose it
> I choose to stay with you.—
>
> ("To the Poor—"; p. 677)

About the time the poet began to conceive *Leaves of Grass,* his father's health began to fail. Mr. Whitman sank eventually under a paralytic stroke that left him bedridden. It was Walt who took the invalid for a visit to the family homestead on Long Island. When Mr. Whitman died, a week after *Leaves of Grass* came out, his widow commented on the length of time he had been ill, and the "many bad spells" he had suffered.[5]

---

3   Horace Traubel, Richard Maurice Bucke, and Thomas Harned, eds., *In re Walt Whitman* (Philadelphia, 1893), 33.

4   "Preface 1855," *Leaves of Grass,* ed. Blodgett and Bradley, 723.

5   Gay Wilson Allen quotes this letter from a transcription made by Clifton J. Furness in *The Solitary Singer: A Critical Biography of Walt Whitman* (New York: Macmillan, 1955), 151.

One might have expected the prolonged sickness and the death to stir feelings of guilt in a son who took over the father's position in the family. But Kaplan quotes another anticipatory passage from the preface to *Leaves of Grass*. Speaking of his countrymen's attitude toward history, the poet says that America does not repel the past but accepts the rightful place of successor—"perceives that the corpse is slowly borne from the eating and sleeping rooms of the house . . . that its action has descended to the stalwart and well-shaped heir who approaches."[6]

Whitman says so much in the very first sentence of the preface; and one is tempted to speculate that the poetical son gained creative energy from the decline of the parent. Selfhood and its coming into being are the characteristic subjects of Whitman's best poems. A reaching for identity is the process that underlies his work. He strove to form his personality in opposition to that of Mr. Whitman: for Walt devoted himself to speech as his father had done to silence; he liked to appear as genial as his father was irritable; he celebrated his own health while his father's was fading. Mr. Whitman's shrinkage drove his son (I think) to define himself more positively, and not merely in contrast to a rejected model. The father's absence left room for the poet to expand imaginatively and re-create the world.

Yet the world of men stirred ambitious responses in the younger poet. American politics, American civilization, human nature, his own nature, less often pleased than troubled him. Close at home there was his brother Andrew, consumptive and alcoholic, chained to a slatternly wife who walked the streets (Andrew died miserably a year before Jesse was put away). There was his brother Eddy, youngest in the family, feeble-minded from birth, with a crippled arm and leg. Although Eddy was sixteen years younger than the poet, they often shared the same bed.

The family had shallow roots. During Whitman's early years they moved constantly from house to house on Long Island or in Brooklyn, while the mother bore child after child. It seems clear that the stable term in young Walt's development was Mrs. Whitman's love. Only

6 "Preface 1855," *Leaves of Grass*, 709.

through her was he able to connect himself with his siblings; and among these, the two girls whose birth followed his own were inevitably rivals who kept the infant poet from absorbing an eager mother's attention.

He had himself displaced the one elder son. The other children, including the girls, he treated as domestic responsibilities, objects of a surrogate maternal impulse; for he helped Mrs. Whitman look after them. The poet's much younger brother George said it seemed "as if he had us in his charge," and added that "now and then his guardianship seemed excessive."[7]

When he was a young man, Whitman often took short-term jobs as a schoolmaster. The evidence is that he was easygoing and not a severe disciplinarian. Although he kept order, he disapproved of corporal punishment and did not encourage learning by rote. He would play games with the children and gave special attention to the younger ones.

In the columns Whitman wrote for the *Long Island Star* (1845–46), he liked to give parental advice to youthful readers. Here, moral improvement obsessed him. So far from sounding manly and permissive, he habitually condemned vulgarity and coarseness: "Swear not! Smoke not! and rough-and-tumble not!"[8] If *King John* was one of Whitman's two favorite plays by Shakespeare, the reason was probably Mrs. Kean's harrowing rendition of maternal woe.

John Burroughs, who knew Whitman intimately, compared his look and eyes with those of "the mother of many children."[9] Whitman celebrated maternity and called his mother "the most perfect and magnetic character, the rarest combination of practical, moral and spiritual, and the least selfish, of all and any I have ever known."[10] Her letters do not bear out this description. Twice when he made a will, Whitman left his property to his mother in trust for the care of Eddy, the most

7   *Correspondence,* ed. Edwin Haviland Miller, in *The Collected Writings of Walt Whitman* (New York: New York Univ. Press, 1969), 5:73.

8   *Long Island Star,* 4 Dec. 1845, as quoted in Allen, *The Solitary Singer,* 72.

9   Burroughs, as quoted in Clara Barrus, ed., *The Heart of the Burroughs Journals* (Boston: Houghton Mifflin, 1928), 42.

10   Whitman, as quoted by Emory Holloway in *Whitman: An Interpretation in Narrative* (New York: Knopf, 1926), 267.

dependent of his surviving brothers and sisters. Such a testament seems to me an odd blurring of filial and maternal characters, with Whitman trying at the same time to serve his mother and to push her offstage.

Certainly the family was not the sort on which one could comfortably establish one's identity—there was so much more to reject than to accept. For an imaginative boy drawn to music, literature, and self-contemplation, the community of the nation seemed no better disposed. Whitman was ten years old when Jackson became president; and the two decades that followed were periods of national obsession with growth, productive industry, and material wealth. Whitman recorded his disgust in the preface to *Leaves of Grass,* where he denounced the accumulation of riches as "the great fraud upon modern civilization."[11]

In verse and prose over the next ten or dozen years he reiterated his condemnation of American politics and culture: "Smother'd in thievery, impotence, shamelessness, mountain high; / Brazen effrontery, scheming, rolling like ocean's waves around and upon you, O my days! my lands!" ("Respondez!"; p. 591). The virulence of his attack on the presidential campaigns of 1856 was unrelenting. Every "trustee of the people" said Whitman, "is a traitor, looking only to his own gain, and to boost up his party." Public office was a mark of criminal character: "The berths, the Presidency included, are bought, sold, electioneered for, prostituted, and filled with prostitutes."[12]

In an essay on democracy (1867) he broadened the attack. All the branches of American government were, he said, "saturated in corruption, bribery, falsehood, mal-administration." American civilization was "a sort of dry and flat Sahara . . . crowded with petty grotesques, malformations, phantoms, playing meaningless antics." The American character, he said, was quintessentially hypocritical: "Confess that everywhere, in shop, street, church, theatre, barroom, official chair, and pervading flippancy and vulgarity, low cunning, infidelity—every-

11   "Preface 1855," *Leaves of Grass,* 723.

12   "The Eighteenth Presidency," in *Walt Whitman's Workshop: A Collection of Unpublished Manuscripts,* ed. Clifton J. Furness (Cambridge: Harvard Univ. Press, 1928), 95.

where the youth puny, impudent, foppish, prematurely ripe—everywhere an abnormal libidinousness . . . shallow notions of beauty, with a range of manners, or rather lack of manner . . . probably the meanest to be seen in the world."[13]

Yet American character was only an instance of the general failure of humanity:

> The devilish and the dark, the dying and diseas'd,
> The countless (nineteen-twentieths) low and evil, crude and
>   savage,
> The crazed, prisoners in jail, the horrible, rank, malignant,
> Venom and filth, serpents, the ravenous sharks, liars, the
>   dissolute;
> (What is the part the wicked and the loathsome bear within
>   earth's orbic scheme?)   (*Goodbye My Fancy;* p. 554)

From the general condemnation he did not exclude himself:

> I own that I have been sly, thievish, mean, a
>   prevaricator, greedy, derelict,
> And I own that I remain so yet.
>
> What foul thought but I think it—or have in me
>   the stuff out of which it is thought?
> What in darkness in bed at night, alone
>   or with a companion?[14]
>   . . . . . .
> Inside these breast-bones I lie smutch'd and choked,
> Beneath this face that appears so impassive hell's
>   tides continually run,

---

13   *Democratic Vistas,* in *Prose Works 1892,* ed. Floyd Stovall, in *The Collected Writings of Walt Whitman* (New York: New York Univ. Press, 1964), 2:370.

14   Whitman, "You Felons on Trial in Courts," in *Autumn Rivulets,* ed. Blodgett and Bradley, 384n (ll. 5–8 of eight-line opening published in *Leaves of Grass* 1860 and removed from all succeeding editions).

Lusts and wickedness are acceptable to me,
I walk with delinquents with passionate love.

("You Felons on Trial in Courts"; p. 386)

Such reflections are not anomalies but rise from a poem as central to Whitman's accomplishment as "Crossing Brooklyn Ferry":

I too knitted the old knot of contrariety,
Blabb'd, blush'd, resented, lied, stole, grudg'd,
Had guile, anger, lust, hot wishes I dared not speak,
Was wayward, vain, greedy, shallow, sly, cowardly,
    malignant,
The wolf, the snake, the hog, not wanting in me.   (p. 163)

A sign of Whitman's displeasure with the culture and people of his own age is the way he turned to youth and the future for his ideals to be realized. In a letter of 1852 he urged a man about to become a presidential candidate to "look to the young men."[15] Speaking of New York, he says there are "tens of thousands of young men" who yearn for political reform. "In all these, and behind the bosh of the regular politicians, there burns, almost with fierceness, the divine fire which more or less, during all ages, has only wanted a chance to leap forth and confound the calculations of tyrants, hunkers, and all their tribe."[16]

In the essay on democracy he declares that America counts for her justification "almost entirely on the future."[17] And so (much later) he described his "Song of the Redwood-Tree" as celebrating the Pacific half of the country, which he called "the future *better half*."[18] So also among social classes, Whitman did not interest himself in those who

---

15   Whitman, letter to John Parker Hale, 14 Aug. 1852, in *Correspondence,* 1:39–40.

16   Ibid.

17   *Democratic Vistas,* 362.

18   Whitman, letter to Rudolf Schmidt, 4 Mar. 1874, *Correspondence.*

could not use his guidance: members of the established order, the higher professions, families deeply based in old wealth.

Instead, he strove to identify himself with young, semiliterate workingmen, the class to which he was sexually drawn and which he exalted in poetry as in love. Through these "offspring of ignorant and poor— boys apprenticed to trades" he could—I think—narcissistically cherish the boy who lived on in the poet ("A Song for Occupations"; p. 213). With them he could play the role of attentive mother; and to them he wished to entrust the government of his country.

If Whitman's constant invocation of unknown, future readers suggests his disenchantment with those at hand, so also his constant shifts from one casual boyfriend to another suggest his disappointment with each. The poet regularly attributed his own feelings and character to strangers (including posterity). Sometimes he thought they were staring suggestively at him; they wanted his companionship. He created an imaginary milieu of this sort, a community for himself, to replace the alien, hostile body of his contemporaries, the nation to which languor and poetry were offensive.

Close up—I suspect—the boys who accepted him showed themselves finally to want the qualities he sought. Their lack of definition was genuine, their lack of commitment, or fixed place. But they were not after all Whitmans in embryo and had little sympathy with his aesthetic tastes.

He pursued those who were teasingly accessible but equivocal. Motion was important. Young men who worked on streetcars, railways, ferries, whose very work suggested undefined potentiality, lured him particularly. He loved movement without destination, action without commitment, journeys that were infinitely renewable and returned him to his starting point. So also he established no proper residence but lived in ill-furnished, obscure rooms for transients, leaving himself free to move along, keeping all options open.

During the Civil War, when he busied himself as a hospital visitor and volunteer nurse, he could feel deeply satisfied with the wounded soldiers. Passive in their invalidism, the boys took his kisses with his gifts. Again and again they could not disappoint him because they died, leaving the ideal relationship unspoiled. If they recovered, they went home or back to camp; and Whitman could enjoy fantasies of renewing the intimacy.

The tendencies that directed Whitman's social doctrines and sexual habits also appear in his poetry. Here, self-definition is the pervasive theme. The poet could not happily blend his own nature with that of his family or nation. Yet he wished to be a national poet with praiseworthy antecedents.

An attractive solution was to evade the problem by embodying pure potentiality himself, by representing an amorphousness that suited the usual description of his country. In the land of boundless possibility, the poet who rejected definition could speak for all. When Whitman assumed his public, heroic posture, this was the character he promoted.

Yet his best poems do evoke distinct personalities, and one of them is the liberator of natural enjoyment. I think we may connect this with the deep separation, in Whitman's development, between morality and imagination. Authoritarian didacticism pervaded the early writings of Whitman—his journalism, poems, and stories—until he conceived *Leaves of Grass*. I suspect that moral principle, self-discipline, and materialistic ambition all were tied, for Whitman (as for most boys), to the figure of his father; and that self-indulgence, pleasure, and the aesthetic impulse were tendencies blessed by the mother. The physical decline of Mr. Whitman may have driven the poet to establish a more independent personality. If so, I think one way he met the challenge was by profiting from a split he felt in his consciousness.

"I am always conscious of myself as two," Whitman said, "—as my soul and I."[19] The soul would normally be the seat of morality; the "I" would then be the body, vessel of sensuous pleasure. It is clear from Whitman's poems that yet another person was involved, a permissive observer before whom the poet engaged in his free acts.

To escape from self-condemnation, Whitman could find the true self in the body and declare from his own experience that the dangers of alleged misconduct were illusory. In this comic phase he could substi-

---

19 *The Uncollected Poetry and Prose of Walt Whitman* ed. Emory Holloway (Garden City, N.Y.: Doubleday, Page, 1921), 2:66.

tute physical well-being for moral integrity and defy the communal, fatherly shibboleths of industry, virtue, and duty. The true poet, he said, had "the soundest organic health."[20]

So we find Whitman, in poem after poem, cherishing the body and its voluptuous pleasures as if they would carry him to salvation. "I . . . receiv'd identity by my body," he said ("Crossing Brooklyn Ferry"; p. 162). In private life he was ostentatiously indifferent to the walls and furniture around him; but he cared for his body as if it were an infant nourished, bathed, and rubbed down by a proud mother.

Here is the liberated poet who bounds through *Song of Myself.* He is a protagonist in whom the artificial conscience has given up the effort to control the flesh. Instead, it now yields authority to creative genius, which operates by opening a route from the depths of undifferentiated sensation to the forms of art. Hence the climactic, central section 24 of *Song of Myself,* exalting the hidden parts and secret sensations of the body.

In this phase the poet escapes from immediate, routine reality, abandons the society of conventional adults, and withdraws to a hidden life in a natural setting along with likeminded comrades. Here he does not feel isolated, for the encounters with landscape become narcissistic deeds of sex-tinged voyeurism. The looseness of Whitman's syntax allows the episodes to seem a boy's sex-play with a boy, or childish self-exposure to the caresses of nature herself. Amazingly, Whitman combines innocence with sexual titillation:

> I will go to the bank by the wood and become
>   undisguised and naked,
> I am mad for it to be in contact with me.
>
> The smoke of my own breath,
> Echoes, ripples, buzz'd whispers, love-root,
>   silk-thread, crotch and vine.   (*Song of Myself;* p. 29)

20   "Preface 1855," *Leaves of Grass,* 723.

Nature is both observer and participant, blessing the occasion. The poet cherishing his own body is parent and infant at once; and in this spirit he offers to liberate the reader: "Long enough have you dream'd contemptible dreams, / Now I wash the gum from your eyes" (*Song of Myself;* p. 84). This comic dismissal of danger, and free indulgence in sensual gratification, is magnificent. Whitman's fiat reverses the direction of conventional American poetry in his generation. But he cannot always sustain the mood; and when it goes, beaten down by reality, he must confront the pathos of dependence. Without a lover, the poet sees his bold fantasy fade and loses his confident buoyancy. Comradeship assuages his guilt, frees the will to act on the body's sensual momentum. Rejected by those to whom he has offered love, the poet drops his insouciance:

> Who pensive away from one he lov'd often lay
>   sleepless and dissatisfied at night,
> Who knew too well the sick, sick dread lest the one
>   he lov'd might secretly be indifferent to him,
> Whose happiest days were far away through fields, in
>   woods, on hills, he and another wandering hand in
>   hand, they twain apart from other men.
>
> ("Recorders Ages Hence"; p. 122)

Without a lover the achieved self comes apart, and pathos takes charge.

Both these phases, the comic and the pathetic, are means of giving shape to an undeveloped personality. They are private resolutions of private conflicts. But the other way also existed, the publicly heroic; and this was, ignoring the inner selves, to identify the poet with his nation. By assuming the role, Whitman really evaded the problem of selfhood and clung to unfocused potentiality. If we consider the reservations the poet had concerning the nation, and his tendency to replace the present by the future, we can understand why self-definition was no obvious feature of Whitman as American bard.

To veil his reservations, he merely associated his own voice with all the voices of the people. Instead of being a person who contemplates the world, the poet becomes the belvedere from which the world is seen by others. To the extent that this heroic poet has shape, it is in terms of things that impose themselves on him.

Hence Whitman's catalogues. If the poet is to have no character distinct from that of his world and people, he cannot describe himself with a sharp outline. The infinitude of the universe is evoked by the length and randomness of the catalogues, and the poet dissolves into a list of sympathies:

> O race of the future! O women!
> O fathers! O you men of passion and the storm!
> O native power only! O beauty!
> O yourself! O God! O divine average!
>
> ("Apostroph"; p. 600)

In his theories of poetry as in his achievements of selfhood, Whitman made his first principle the acceptance of carnal indulgence. Sexual passion was the best food of the sympathetic imagination. "Doubtless I could not have perceived the universe, or written one of my poems, if I had not freely given myself to comrades, to love." Sometimes he describes his book as if it were either a phallus or his own phallicized body, offered to the reader's hand.

But without a lover he has only a weak feeling of selfhood; and without an identity of his own, he has no position from which to make the impressions of his senses coherent and reliable. A powerful poem, "Of the Terrible Doubt of Appearances," makes the process clear.

Yet if the insecure self finds the external world unreal and menacing, the secure self welcomes and encompasses it. Through the imagination the poet not only tames but sanctifies the things he can conceive. Whitman yearned to give his imprimatur to the book of creation.

A shining instance of his attitude is the note he made in 1852 on a sentence by an unknown literary critic. The essayist had said, "The mountains, rivers, forests, and the elements that gird them about, would be only blank conditions of matter, if the mind did not fling its own divinity around them." Whitman commented, "This I think is one of the most indicative sentences I ever read."[21]

In *Song of Myself* he wrote, "Divine am I inside and out, and I make holy whatever I touch or am touch'd from" (*Song of Myself,* p. 53). Again and again his catalogues are sacraments of praise. By naming and consecrating, the poet transformed the workaday world into an imaginative experience.

The enormous variety of items in an eruption like section 33 of *Song of Myself* reveals the poet's pride, surprise, and joy in the scope of his imagination. The point of the passage is not the substance of the articles enumerated but the sudden leaps and transitions from one to another; it is the fact that he can conceive and find words for such diverse material.

Whitman's best poems spring from a rejection of the usual schemes of conscious art. It is a mistake to measure rhythms or to trace pattern of sound in his lines. Whitman deliberately held back from the forms that Tennyson and Longfellow relied on.

There is a level of intuitive expression, just above the dark chaos from which all creation starts. At this level Whitman found he could trust his genius. In his early career as journalist, storyteller, and versifier, before he produced *Leaves of Grass,* Whitman discovered how weakly he wrote when he followed conventional models.

Yet the intuitive style that Whitman discovered does not lend itself to large structures. It calls for lyric forms and revelations of the self shifting its moods while the poet watches. This method of composition might seem to simplify the character of the speaker in a poem. But it does not. The suffering self, the triumphant self, and the observing self hold the center by turns as the reader is invited to share their experience.

One of the least fortunate pieces of advice that Whitman ever received came from his friend Hector Tyndale, who told the poet to strive for "massiveness, breadth, large, sweeping effects, without regard to

---

21   Whitman, *Notes and Fragments,* Richard Maurice Bucke, ed. (London, Ontario, 1899), 77.

detail."²² Tyndale used a cathedral—York Minster—to suggest the impression he had in mind.

This sort of counsel only aggravated Whitman's epic yearnings. It encouraged him to be vague and repetitious, to give many examples where a handful would suffice, to move back and forth among themes and images without deepening them, to anticipate conclusions ponderously and to declare them pretentiously.

Poems like *Song of Myself* and "Crossing Brooklyn Ferry" can easily be treated as collections of lyrics on related themes, like the *Calamus* sequence. Some of these lyrics we may wish to put aside while we linger over others. By giving too much attention to "Passage to India" and "When Lilacs Last in the Dooryard Bloom'd," critics leave too little for short masterpieces like "Patroling Barnegat." Here the poet evokes the depths of his own creative power from the features of the storming ocean, and he suggests the emergence of poetic images from the turmoil of inchoate, dark feelings:

> Wild, wild the storm, and the sea high running,
> Steady the roar of the gale, with incessant
>   undertone muttering,
> Shouts of demoniac laughter fitfully piercing
>   and pealing,
> Waves, air, midnight, their savagest trinity
>   lashing. . . .
>   .   .   .   .   .
> Steadily, slowly, through hoarse roar never
>   remitting,
> Along the midnight edge by those milk-white
>   combs careering,
> A group of dim, weird forms, struggling, the night
>   confronting,
> That savage trinity warily watching.
>
> ("Patroling Barnegat"; pp. 262–63)

22   Hector Tyndale, as quoted ibid.

In his compact and excellently written biography, Kaplan touches on the topics I have been handling. But he does not examine them closely. The triumph of the book is its cunning, dramatic design. Instead of beginning with the poet's birth and proceeding to his death, it opens with the start of the final era in Whitman's life, his acquisition of the house in which he spent eight disease-ridden years and in which he died. This period is minutely documented, and Kaplan can give us a sharply detailed impression of the old man's character. Then he returns us to Whitman's origins and goes on to the time of the opening pages.

The arrangement is not only ingenious but more instructive than the normal plan would be. We have incalculably more information about Whitman's closing years than about his childhood. Kaplan can supply us with vivid and reliable anecdotes of the aging poet's intimate life. When we then review his beginnings, we are so well orientated that the paucity of details hardly troubles us.

Even more important is the way Kaplan's approach reveals Whitman's obsession with self-presentation. The poet put immense energy, into the manufacture of his reputation—the construction of a visible personality that he believed was appropriate to a national poet. The story of his career is, to an alarming extent, the story of how Whitman created his public self. We can observe the process close up during the final period when several admirers boswellized him; and this knowledge alerts us to the many aspects of the process that are less obvious during Whitman's maturity and middle age.

Kaplan has also gone through the scholarship on his subject. His mastery of a century of research appears in the many corrections and fresh details he has been able to add to the much longer biography published by Gay Wilson Allen in 1955, *The Solitary Singer*.

And yet, for all its virtues, Kaplan's biography does not much alter the view of Whitman presented by Allen. The new book constantly illustrates the homosexual character of the poet. We get perhaps more information than we need about Whitman's attachments to miscellaneous young men. But the nature of his sexuality was made clear both by Allen and by Roger Asselineau (among others) decades ago. It is probably a step backward for Kaplan to intimate that Whitman may have visited prostitutes when he was in his early twenties, and for him to describe Whitman's attitude toward boys as fatherly.

On the poetry Kaplan does not try to be adventurous. He connects the life with the works chiefly by suggesting that passages in the poems allude to experiences of the poet. Like Allen, he shows how consistently Whitman refused to weaken his poems in order to accommodate conventional moralists or uneasy publishers. He demonstrates the poet's admirable integrity in retaining provocative sexual material against strong opposition. But he seldom offers new judgments or interpretations of the poems.

The price of Kaplan's brevity is his omission of much important information. So the fascinating account of Lincoln's reading of *Leaves of Grass* does not appear here. Neither does the masterly analysis of Whitman's character by his disciple Edward Carpenter—an analysis more penetrating than anything to be found in Kaplan's study. I am afraid that Allen remains indispensable.

2

DICKINSON

 Looking at the Dickinsons in love, one gets some useful insights into the meaning and power of a difficult poet. Emily Dickinson was a reticent woman with a habit of passionate attachment to married men. She called the Reverend Charles Wadsworth her "closest earthly friend," though she could have met him only two or three times, and may never have heard him preach. For the last of her recorded fixations, she settled upon an old justice of the Massachusetts Supreme Court. "The Air is soft as Italy, but when it touches me, I spurn it with a Sigh, because it is not you," she wrote to him when he was a recent widower of seventy and she was fifty-two. A few years earlier, she had told him, "I am but a restive sleeper and often should journey from your Arms through the happy night, but you will lift me back, wont you, for only there I ask to be."[1]

Meanwhile, her brother Austin was diving into the magic fire of concupiscence. "I love you, love you, love you with all my mind and

This essay was first published 23 Jan. 1975 under the title "Dickinsons in Love" as a review of Richard B. Sewall, *The Life of Emily Dickinson* (New York: Farrar, Straus, & Giroux, 1974). Reprinted with permission from *The New York Review of Books*. Copyright © 1975 Nyrev, Inc.

1   Dickinson to T. W. Higginson, in *The Letters of Emily Dickinson,* ed. Thomas H. Johnson, 3 vols. (Cambridge: The Belknap Press of Harvard Univ. Press, 1958), 3:737, 728, 617.

heart and strength!"[2] he wrote to Mabel Todd, wife of an astronomer. She was born the year Austin was married. He was treasurer of the college in which her husband held a professorship. Both lovers were parents. "Oh! my love, my king! My star and guide and heaven-sent light," Mrs. Todd wrote to Mr. Dickinson as he neared sixty. "Do you not know that my soul is knit to yours by an Almighty hand?"[3] Professor Todd used to whistle a tune from *Martha* on his way home, so he should not embarrass everyone by surprising his wife and her guest behind closed doors. (Yet when the elderly admirer died, the husband wrote in his diary, "My best friend died tonight, and I seem stranded.")[4]

These are deceptive fragments, torn from their ground, but they do not misrepresent the noisy power of the feelings that produced them. Neither the poet nor her brother was so simple as to follow passion with action. They kept their bodies out of their romantic adventures: the flames burned on words alone for the sister; on secret walks, drives, and domestic conversations for the brother.

The sire of these improbable siblings was the first citizen of Amherst, Massachusetts, a very small town thronged with descendants of the primordial Dickinson, who reached our country two hundred years before the poet was born. When Mr. Dickinson senior wooed his bride, he described himself to her as "quick & ardent in my feelings ... decided in my opinions ... hard to be persuaded that I am wrong ... have a little personal irritability in my constitution."[5] Underneath, he was obviously gentle and devoted; during at least one period when he

---

2   Austin Dickinson to Mabel Loomis Todd, in *Austin and Mabel: The Amherst Affair and Love Letters of Austin Dickinson and Mabel Loomis Todd,* ed. Polly Longsworth (New York: Farrar, Straus, & Giroux, 1984), 185–86; Sewall, *The Life of Emily Dickinson,* 182. Professor Ehrenpreis's source for some of the family correspondence was undoubtedly Sewall's citation of the unpublished manuscript collections of the Yale University Library and the Houghton Library at Harvard. The letters of Mabel and Austin have subsequently been published. Any quotation of currently unpublished manuscripts will be ascribed to the place where it appears in Sewall's biography.

3   Sewall, 182.

4   Ibid., 179 n. 7.

5   Ibid., 50.

was away from home, we have a letter from his wife thanking him for writing to her daily.

But I doubt that the three small children—Austin, Emily, and Lavinia, all born within a span of four years—would have peeked behind the facade. A niece said he rarely smiled. A visitor who saw him in old age found him "thin dry and speechless," and supposed that as a parent he had been not severe but remote.[6] Commenting on the father-daughter connection, the visitor said, "I saw what her life has been." Emily Dickinson said her father "never played."[7] (Elsewhere she said, "Blessed are they that play, for theirs is the kingdom of heaven.")[8]

A consequence of so much affection frozen into solicitude was mentioned by the young poet in a letter to her brother. After tea one day, she paid some visits, stayed too long, and returned home at nine, finding her father in "great agitation at my protracted stay—and mother and Vinnie in tears, for fear that he would kill me."[9] The drama is deliberately overplayed, and meant to amuse, not scare, her brother; but the hint of Mr. Brontë and Mr. Browning remains. When she was older, Emily sometimes refused invitations on the pretext that her father was "in the habit of me."[10]

Austin's Platonic mistress, who never knew his parents, opined that the father had discouraged the daughters' suitors; and of course neither Emily nor Vinnie married. When Austin himself was young, he told his fiancée that he had never received tenderness "from any *body*."[11] Emily wrote to him while he was a law student, "I do think it's so funny— you and father do nothing but 'fisticuff' all the while you're at home, and the minute you are separated, you become such devoted friends."[12] Austin thought of leaving home to settle with his bride in Chicago, but

6   Ibid., 45.

7   *Letters,* 2:486.

8   Ibid., 3:691.

9   Ibid., 1:111.

10   Ibid., 2:450.

11   Austin Dickinson, draft of a letter to Susan Colbert, in *The Years and Hours of Emily Dickinson,* ed. Jay Leyda, 2 vols. (New Haven: Yale Univ. Press, 1960), 1:315.

12   *Letters,* 1:231.

Mr. Dickinson overruled his objections to Amherst, made him a partner in the law practice, and built a handsome house for the young couple next to his own.

As for the mother, all accounts agree that though she (like Emily) was excellent in the kitchen, she was strong in neither body, character, nor intellect. Emily herself said she never had a mother. Cheerful loving-kindness does not seem to have been identified with membership in this family. Loyalty, duty, possessiveness, a serious concern for one another's welfare—these are the attributes that joined the generations. But it is one thing to be accepted with anxious concern, and quite another to be cherished with delight. What was meant as devotion may have been felt as rejection.

As children, Emily and Austin paired themselves off against their father and sister. Austin was literary and moody. He loved to botanize and to contemplate landscape; he wrote verse as well as elaborately composed letters. Emily once told him, "I think we miss each other more every day that we grow older, for we're all unlike most everyone, and are therefore more dependent on each other for delight."[13] Austin may have succeeded his father as the Pericles of a provincial Athens, but his inner character was no compound of strength and force. According to a perceptive memorialist, "His nature was all gentleness and refinement, and there were a shyness and reserve in his composition, coupled with an intensity of feeling, that were almost pathetic at times."[14] This nature appeared in the furiously uncertain appeals he had made to the girl he finally married: "I love you Sue up to the very highest strain my nature can bear—the least tension would snap my life threads—as brittle glass—more—you could not ask—more man could not give—Love *me*, Sue—*Love* me—for its my life."[15]

But she was not the sedative type, and his life threads endured more tension than he had thought possible. So far from acting motherly and

---

13   Ibid., 239.

14   Obituary in the *Springfield Republican,* 20 Aug. 1895. Quoted by Sewall, 127.

15   Sewall, 109.

protective, Sue (daughter of an innkeeper) became a brilliant hostess, competitive and demanding, who felt rapture when she took the "transcendental arm" of her guest, R. W. Emerson, as he walked her home after delivering a public lecture in Amherst.[16] One professor at the college recalled her as a "really brilliant and highly cultivated woman of great taste and refinement, perhaps a little too aggressive, a little too sharp in wit and repartee, and a little too ambitious for social prestige."[17] Among the several articles the Dickinsons possessed in abundance was of course social prestige.

I suppose Emily Dickinson had the powers of genius in her observation of people, her understanding of them, her imaginative sympathy and responsiveness. I suppose the remoteness of her father and the weakness of her mother threw the children back on themselves; and Austin, whose sensibility matched her own, became Emily's bulwark. I suppose that with others she veiled the boldness of her mind behind a disarming, childlike exterior. Secured by this screen, by her brother's devotion and the family's solidarity, she could let herself reflect searchingly upon the baffling elements of our difficult life: the impersonality of nature, the existence of pain and evil, the mysteries of death and immortality, the character of God. At the age of fifty she wrote to a family friend, "Austin and I were talking the other Night about the Extension of Consciousness, after Death and Mother told Vinnie, afterward, she thought it was 'very improper.' . . . I dont know what she would think if she knew that Austin told me confidentially 'there was no such person as Elijah.'"[18]

The poet required not only Austin but his wife and their children— as if she were trying to remedy in their generation what had gone wrong in her parents'. Years before Austin married Susan, Emily was infatuated with the bright, bookish, strong-willed girl, and wrote her

16   Ibid., 115 n. 7.

17   John W. Burgess, *Reminiscenses of an American Scholar* (New York: Columbia Univ. Press, 1934), 60.

18   *Letters,* 3:667.

love letters. After the marriage, Emily still clung to her sister-in-law; and though, as usual, immediacy produced difficulty, the overburdened filament never quite broke. Plain, little, and shy, the poet could not attract the kind of suitor whom she might take seriously, the kind whose charms could master her fear of sexuality. She retreated into presexual roles, into elaborate fantasies about older, tutorial, inaccessible figures whom she pursued in letters and poems; their death would both terrify and free her, as she felt guilty for half-willing it but relieved from the pressure of imaginary duties. When the discord between Austin and Susan grew too loud to be ignored, she blamed herself (I think) for having encouraged the match against the vacillations of her brother. Cleaving to both sides, she was torn as they pulled apart.

Emily Dickinson always disliked to be away from home; her father, she claimed, "likes me to travel with him but objects that I visit."[19] But during her thirties she began to withdraw even from the streets of Amherst. As she saw fewer people, I suppose she expected more of those she met. Some must have bruised her by their failure to respond; a few who were tactful and sympathetic would have fed her fantasies; a few others, by their final candor, would have destroyed the web of reverie and shocked the poet. The drift toward seclusion seems to have quickened sharply after some lacerating emotional crisis, still unknown; and I assume that the savagery of the Civil War entered into casual conversations, making them harder to endure. There was also the hateful side of her dependent love. At the age of twenty-one she refused to spend a week with a friend and wrote, "I look at my father and mother and Vinnie, and all my friends, and I say no-no, cant leave them, what if they die when I'm gone."[20]

Before she was forty, Emily Dickinson could declare that she never crossed the limits of her father's land. It looks as if she were exaggerating his own influence and wounding herself to wound him. Eventually, she hardly left the house, and saw only her family, the Irish

19   Ibid., 2:453.
20   Ibid., 1:197.

servants, a few children, and some chosen friends. She would fail to meet even persons she had encouraged to visit her. When she did appear, her conversation was riddling, witty, and aphoristic. Like her poetry it suggests a rhythm of hide-and-seek appropriate to someone who feared and courted rejection. "I never was with any one who drained my nerve power so much," said Colonel Higginson.[21] She would normally wear a white piqué dress and often carried a flower or two as a gift. Whether she struck one as a child or a nun, her feature was virginal innocence. Critics who pay great attention to her Puritan heritage might consider that she not only rejected every distinctively Calvinist doctrine but behaved like a Roman Catholic recluse, cherished her Roman Catholic servants, and asked that her pallbearers be Roman Catholic laborers who worked on her father's grounds: all this when she certainly was not attracted by the religion of Rome.

To those who read her best poems with care, the mark of her literary style is not innocence but a constant acquaintance with the most profound experience. It is no paradox that such a woman should write such poems. Probably, the bitterness of her wisdom has the same ironic relation to the hymn form of her verses that it has to her disarming appearance. One thinks of Hardy, whose versification also plays against his meaning; he might almost have written this:

> I shall know why—when Time is over—
> And I have ceased to wonder why—
> Christ will explain each separate anguish
> In the fair schoolroom of the sky—
>
> He will tell me what "Peter" promised—
> And I—for wonder at his woe—
> I shall forget the drop of Anguish
> That scalds me now—that scalds me now![22]

21   Ibid., 2:476.

22   Emily Dickinson, in *The Poems of Emily Dickinson,* ed. Thomas H. Johnson (Cambridge: The Belknap Press of Harvard Univ. Press, 1955), no. 193.

The scrim of conventional form and language will mislead the superficial reader as the nunlike appearance and seclusion misled the villagers. Responding as powerfully as she did to the anxieties, illnesses, and deaths that threatened whomever she loved, the poet had to defend herself against fresh demands and save time to deal with the awesome questions that her trials provoked. Emily Dickinson wrote not about immortality but our hope of immortality, not about nature but our separation from nature, not about God but our belief in God. Those who imagine she was deeply troubled by the apparent clash between natural science and religious faith mislead us. It was the defeat of love by circumstance—by jealousy, egotism, illness, death—that drove her to doubt the existence of God and to yearn for a trust in immortality. She often quarreled with the language of Scripture; she never believed in hell and could not bear the linkage of godhead to punishment. The common suffering imposed on mankind is bleak enough; but the slow provocation of attachment and the wanton destruction of it give our evanescent lives their most monstrous aspect.

In *The Life of Emily Dickinson* Professor Sewall has really produced three studies, issuing from decades of painstaking scholarship. One is of Emily Dickinson's connections with the people of most importance to her: relations, friends, and the men who became the vessels of her ambiguous affection. This study, based mainly on her letters, is sober, comprehensive, and elaborately documented from old and new sources. Much of the author's energy goes into the analysis or disproof of doubtful anecdotes; much goes into the cautious reconstruction of backgrounds. The results have fundamental value for professional scholars, although nonspecialists will find them less absorbing. The second study, scattered through the first, deals with the intricate story of the publication of the poems, many of which receive meticulous explications. Since few of the texts can be easily fixed, any serious critic must grasp the information surveyed by Professor Sewall if he is to know how to read them.

Finally, we are given an account of the way three households wore on one another: the Homestead, where the poet lived with her father, mother, and sister; the Evergreens next door, where her brother lived with his wife, sons, and daughter; and the family of David Todd, his wife Mabel, and their daughter. The hostility between Susan Dickinson and her in-laws; the scandalous intimacy of Austin Dickinson and Mabel Todd; the impact of the lurid affair upon their spouses and children—all make a history that easily breaks through the body of the book and overflows into appendices.

Although Professor Sewell produces new material everywhere, it is in the account of the scandals that he has the most startling abundance, much of it in the form of primary documents. One may differ with him in the interpretation of the facts he has gathered for all three topics; but one must thank him for the fullness and impartiality of his presentation.

3

STEVENS

Stevens's best poems are those that draw and hold us by their surface. The charm and mystery of the sounds and turns of phrase, the drama of the leaps from one point of view to another, the subtlety and irony of the changing moods, the flickering of the language between refinement and coarseness—all these produce delight before we are aware of doctrine. For such elements, the nonsense syllables in the poems provide an enveloping air of freedom and comedy. The author apparently lets himself go, abandoning his voice to cheerful or satirical impulse. Yet when one examines them, these irrational sounds seem to embody remarkable aspects of the poet's meaning.

In his best poems, Stevens keeps several subjects going at once. "Depression before Spring" (CP 63) shows how he does it.[1] Here, on the level of common human experience, a man tired of winter looks for a sign of spring. On the level of a theory of the imagination, the poet in a barren season waits for inspiration that does not come. At

This essay was originally published under the title "Strange Relation: Stevens' Nonsense," in Frank Doggett and Robert Buttel, eds., *Wallace Stevens: A Celebration.* Copyright © 1980 by Princeton University Press. Excerpt reprinted by permission of Princeton University Press.

1   *The Collected Poems of Wallace Stevens* (New York: Knopf, 1971), hereafter referred to as *CP.* All reference to poems from this volume will be cited in text by page numbers.

the same time, in Stevens's myth of a romance between the mind and reality, an observer makes love to the world, but the world does not respond: it remains untouched by the imagination. In the course of this poem Stevens gives himself several forms. He appears first as a cock crowing and waiting for a hen that never appears. He is also a potential king who cannot claim his throne until an absent queen accepts him. He is at the same time a lover who fails to find his mistress.

The story of the poem comes out in several modes: third-person narrative, dramatic speech, and nonsense. To start with, the author speaks as a narrator telling a story: "The cock crows / But no queen rises." In line 3, the character's voice is heard directly. But instead of crowing, the character speaks, praising the beloved in mockery: "The hair of my blonde / Is dazzling." The speech ends in onomatopoetic ejaculations, "Ho! Ho!" suggesting the laughter of self-ridicule. Then the narrator returns and continues his story on the level of cock and hen: "But ki-ki-ri-ki / Brings no roucou." In the last lines Stevens climbs back to the metaphor of royalty and the reference to the seasons: "But no queen comes / In slipper green"—the world in springtime being a princess wearing green slippers.

Why does Stevens draw these parallels, change his narrative point of view, and resort to onomatopoetic nonsense? I think he wishes to establish his aesthetic theory on the basis of other realities, such as plant and animal life. So he suggests, for example, that the world awaits spring with the same inevitability that the cock's sexual instinct drives it to court a hen and that men give human, imaginative meaning to independent reality. The nonsense is the actual cry of the animal world making its poetry or song; the direct speech is that of a man expressing his love of the world; the narrative is that of a poet interpreting the action for us.

In this case the poet does not win his beloved. The imaginative vision eludes him, and the failure is reflected in the bizarre simile he employs for the song of courtship: the blonde mistress, he says, dazzles one like "the spittle of cows / Threading the wind." Yet the coarseness and sunny brightness also imply a contact with true reality, not a "romantic" fantasy. Even while complaining of failure, therefore, the poet manages modestly to succeed.

The cock and his nonsense appear again in "Bantams in Pine-Woods" (*CP* 75–76). Here, on the level of human incident, a bantam meets the poet in the woods and, unable to conceive of persons who do not belong to its own species, challenges him as another bird, only bigger. "Fat! Fat!" he says to Stevens, who indeed had a bulky figure.

This poem is a dramatic monologue, and the similes are chosen to suit a bantam's imagination. So the poet becomes a cock, and his poems are "hoos." From the imaginative point of view the audible, moving bird is an aesthetic focus for the wooded scene around it and "points" the tangs of the pine trees: the unique, changing animal establishes an aesthetic order in the motionless world of plants. On the other hand, the poet works by giving general significance to the bird or any other particular, and his imagination strives to illuminate the world as the sun cannot. So he is charged with arrogance: "Damned universal cock, as if the sun / Was blackamoor to bear your blazing tail." Stevens tries to capture the scene in human speech, but employs onomatopoetic nonsense to suggest that the sounds of nature and the words of a poem have a similar function. He would like his own speech to be as true to experience, as spontaneous and expressive, as the call of a bird. He would also like to be tall in a poetic sense, gifted with a large mind, a spacious vision.

The problem of the poet is to dramatize not the behavior of the bantam but the difficulty of grasping and truly rendering the whole situation. The challenge is what the bantam alludes to when it says, "Your world is you. I am my world." It is the man's pretensions as a poet that make the bird ridicule him. As if to shame the human, the bird with its "Fat! Fat!" speaks naturally, effortlessly, and accurately for a world that is always beyond the poet's grasp.

Nonsense syllables seem often to have signified for Stevens the artless power of a natural sound to bring the individual and his world together. "'Ohoyaho, / Ohoo,'" cry Bonnie and Josie as they celebrate "the marriage / Of flesh and air" ("Life Is Motion"; *CP* 83).[2] "Tum-ti-

---

2 Cf. the "shoo-shoo-shoo of secret cymbals," which is rejected when Bawda marries a great captain in "Notes toward a Supreme Fiction" (*CP* 401), because earthly marriage must not be ascetic or fleshless as was that of St. Catherine.

tum, / Ti-tum-tum-tum!" the ploughman sings in "Ploughing on Sunday" (*CP* 20) as he drives into the soil, getting North America ready for spring. His musical rhythm suggests the deep, subrational quality of the pleasure he feels in being at home in the world, ploughing instead of praying. Sadly enough, this expressive ease must be denied to the conscious poet, who has to struggle deliberately with human speech. What "Fat! Fat!" accomplishes for "Bantams in Pine-Woods," the human artist can accomplish only by the careful, yet hardly successful (as Stevens saw it) design of that attractive poem.

In a much later poem, "On an Old Horn" (*CP* 230), Stevens comments on what the bantam was doing.[3] This time we meet a bird with a ruddy belly, evidently a robin welcoming the spring. The poet wishes to suggest that what matters in human nature is the power to respond coherently and imaginatively to the world. Such a power establishes one's individual character and gives shape to a world that would otherwise be chaotic. If a bird had the power, it would possess the special value we attach to humanity. So Stevens conceives of a robin that can make figurative connections between men and birds, just as men make them between birds and men. To signalize its accomplishment, the robin utters its characteristic sounds, or blows a "trumpet." Such a creature would belong in a new place on the scale of being, perhaps as an incipient human with some rodent traits—"A baby with the tail of a rat?"

The poet proceeds to distinguish between odor and color, treating one as objective and the other as subjective. If the bird merely enjoyed the spring smells, he would act mechanically. If he responded to the colors, he would be imaginative (like a human poet celebrating a landscape); that is, he would express the kind of synthesis that alone keeps us from chaos: "a man, or more, against / Calamity."

In a brief second part the poet takes his turn and speaks in a human equivalent of the bird's song. Having reflected in the first part upon imaginative coherence, he will now convey his own spirit by imagining

3   See Frank Doggett's meticulous account of this poem in "The Transition from *Harmonium:* Factors in the Development of Stevens' Later Poetry," *PMLA* 88 (1973):128–29.

chaos. To do so, he conceives of the stars as moving not together but apart, "Flying like insects of fire in a cavern of night." Then, to mark his success, he too blows a horn by uttering some onomatopoetic nonsense syllables: "Pipperoo, pippera, pipperum." Like the bird, he identifies himself by the spontaneous, characteristic notes of his peculiar instrument.

"The rest is rot," says Stevens at the end of the poem; that is, what matters is that one should give voice to one's own view of the world, whether one be man or bird. By imitating a horn, he suggests the spontaneous quality of his sense of things—the natural feeling that underlies his meditations.

"On an Old Horn" is an unpleasantly self-indulgent poem in which Stevens lets theoretical considerations swamp his design. But it shows again how closely music, nonsense, and a feeling of intimacy with reality are joined in his work. Besides expressing a feeling, Stevens's nonsense can also point to some of his doctrines. In "The Ordinary Women" (*CP* 10–12) he deals with his beloved polarity of reality and imagination. To commonplace minds, familiar things are tedious and strange things are interesting. As soon as such minds enter the realm of imagination, they look away at what lies elsewhere. They yearn to abandon the near for the remote, and when they reach that, they yearn for what now looks remote but was at hand a little while ago. The reason for their oscillations is that they lack imagination themselves. Unable to transform their surroundings creatively, they first diminish them and then exchange them capriciously for others. Being conventional, they cannot face the world without reducing it to formulae. Instead of sky and stars, they see old religious symbols: "beta b and gamma g." Erotic thoughts scare them; rather than seek a union between the self and the world, they think of a heavenly union, presumably with Christ. The musicians of their projections are gaunt or ghostly, reflecting the thick sensibilities of the "ordinary women." Having reduced the sights and sounds of the palace to inconsequence, the visitors leave.

Nonsense occurs three times in the poem. The loges of the palace mumble "zay-zay" when the women first arrive. These onomatopoetic syllables imitate the sound of the guitar and suggest the mystery of moonlight, the initial fascination of the new scene. When the women look at the nocturnal sky, they "read of marriage-bed," and the poet comments, "Ti-lill-o!" as if to mock their prudery. The guitarists keep playing, but rumble, "a-day, a-day," as if to suggest that the women have tired of the erotic night of fantasy, and are eager for the release of daytime. At last the music, moonlight, and erotic feelings move them to speech. But instead of making poetry, they merely say goodbye to halls that have grown dim. Leaving dry guitars, they return to catarrhs, that is, coughs rather than eloquence.

The women may be timid impulses of the mind to handle the malady of the quotidian. They may anticipate the sister of Canon Aspirin in "Notes toward a Supreme Fiction" ("It Must Give Pleasure," V; *CP* 401– 2) who is associated with poverty and rejects dreams. It seems signifi- cant that the women do not utter nonsense but shy away from it. If nonsense syllables often express a union of the self with the world, the women have no right to use them. The precious vocabulary of the poem suggests the falseness of the women's "romantic" aspirations, and Stevens's style in the poem ridicules those aspirations, although it is precisely the vocabulary and the patterns of sound that make the whole thing irresistible.

The doctrinal argument comes to a finer point in "A High-Toned Old Christian Woman" (*CP* 59). Like the "ordinary women" and Canon Aspirin's sister, this character has a fearful mind and narrows her imag- ination to correct, religious themes. She is in fact the muse of the religious imagination, widowed because her god is dead. The poet chal- lenges her by pointing out that as a source of consoling ritual and myth the pagan gods served quite as well as the Christian. So he proposes a new source: not a self-denying, ascetic faith directed toward heaven, but self-indulgent joys centered on the earth. The old imagination pro- duced the spiritual music of the spheres; the new may produce some- thing more boisterous, a "jovial hullabaloo." (The epithet points to Jove rather than Christ.)

The poet calls his celebrants of earthly pleasure "disaffected flagel- lants," or lapsed Puritans, and he foresees that they may well be proud of their new forms of art: "Proud of such novelties of the sublime, / Such tink and tank and tunk-a-tunk-tunk." I think that the echo of

Trial by Jury is fortuitous, and that the rhythm of the nonsense suggests banjos, the syncopated jazz and free verse of the early part of the century. It deliberately evokes secular and frivolous pleasures, in opposition to the serious, didactic art of Christian tradition. The poet has adapted the hymn-playing harmonium to worldly entertainments.

So we may give three general meanings to Stevens's nonsense. It can be the joyous sound of the self when directly in touch with reality, or the poet's laughter as he defies the old morality. But most significantly, it can be the voice of reality or of the natural world producing the spontaneous, adequate music that the poet would like to match.

It would be hard to overestimate the importance Stevens attached to this last principle. When *Harmonium* appeared he closed the book with "To the Roaring Wind" (*CP* 113). When a second edition was called for, he added more than a dozen poems, but arranged the new book so that it still ended with that finely tuned coda. He also paired it carefully with the preceding poem, "Tea" (*CP* 112–13). The point of "Tea" is that somebody—an attractive young woman—has arranged the room around her so that it consoles the poet for the advent of autumn. The weather outdoors has disintegrated, but the weather indoors makes up for it: "Your lamp-light fell / On shining pillows, / Of sea-shades and sky-shades." By her imaginative art the girl has given the poet the solace and refreshment—the "palm"—that a focused landscape would have supplied.

In "To the Roaring Wind" the poet suggests that he would like to do what the girl did. "What syllable are you seeking?" he asks the wind. Of course, he would like to find it. He wants to speak for the world as the world might speak for itself. The wind—*pneuma, spiritus,* ghost of religious enthusiasm and creative inspiration—has here become only the wind, voice of reality, independent of human feeling. This is what the poet means to emulate. He calls the wind "Vocalissimus," which sounds like onomatopoetic nonsense but could mean "most expressive." Because the wind speaks in the "distances of sleep," it echoes the opening poem of *Harmonium*, "Earthy Anecdote" (*CP* 3), in which bucks respond aesthetically to the movements of a "firecat" until the spontaneously creative firecat sleeps. In "Earthy Anecdote" nature herself (presumably in the form of a brush fire) acts as an artist, suggesting Stevens's often-quoted words, "I want, as a man of the imagination, to write poetry with all the power of a monster equal in strength to that of the monster about whom I write."[4] So in the last poem of the book Stevens would be about to wake up and start the cycle again, the cycle of trying to play nature's part and of finding that he is only a poet.

If we suspend consideration of nonsense and attend to this important theme, we shall find it exquisitely embodied in "Two Figures in Dense Violet Night" (*CP* 85–86). Here the world takes the form of a young woman who scolds the poet for wooing her ineptly. She wishes him to celebrate her beauty in nocturnal (that is, imaginative) language: "Be the voice of night and Florida in my ear." It is a command that anticipates exhortations to come—"Be thou the voice" in "Mozart, 1935" (*CP* 132), and "Bethou me" in "Notes toward a Supreme Fiction" ("It Must Change" VI; *CP* 393). He is to speak as if she spoke for him:

> As the night conceives the sea-sounds in silence,
> And out of their droning sibilants makes
> A serenade.   (*CP* 86)

Of course, the poet imitates the sibilants of the waves—the self-made poetry of the sea—in these very lines. But then, at last, the proper language emerges, and the girl tells him to describe a moonlit vista composed by the eyes of sleeping buzzards: it will contain stars, sky, palms, and moon, but no men. So the poet gives us, as she speaks, once more a landscape brought into focus not by a human mind but by a bird, standing for reality untouched by human distortion— "simple seeing, without reflection" ("Ordinary Evening in New Haven," IX; *CP* 471), as he put it many years later. The reference to a hotel in the opening line is meaningful because Stevens thought of poetic reality as a place one visited like a hotel.[5]

With such doctrines in mind it becomes easy for one to appreciate

---

4   Letter to Renato Poggioli, 2 July 1953, in *Letters of Wallace Stevens*, ed. Holly Stevens (New York: Knopf, 1970), 790.

5   Cf. "An Ordinary Evening in New Haven" (*CP* 471). For an interpretation of "Two Figures" based on the view that the speaker is a man, see Harold Bloom, "Wallace Stevens: The Poem of Our Climate," *Prose* 8 (1974):8–10.

the poet's preoccupation with musical instruments.[6] The "ordinary women" flit to and from guitars; the ploughman tells Remus to blow a horn. Crispin is a lutanist and a conductor; he plays the banjo, hears horns and trumpets, clarions and tambours, draws comparisons with bassoons and marimbas. In "Anecdote of Men by the Thousand" the poet names the mandoline as being the natural expression of certain places. In "A High-Toned Old Christian Woman" he refers to citherns and saxophones. There are lutes in "Sunday Morning" and gongs in "Cortege for Rosenbloom." Peter Quince plays the clavier; Susanna hears a cymbal, horns, and a noise like tambourines. And along with these instruments go many kinds of singers and singing.

The peculiar feature of music is that it seems both a human and a natural form of pleasing, significant sound. The same rhythms and tones we hear in the compositions of artful men are also produced by birds and the elements. In the latter, moreover, the cause is instinctive, unwilled, perfectly spontaneous. The sea and the robin cannot help making precisely the noises they create, and those sounds convey the essence of their makers. We know the cock by its crowing, the dove by its cooing. Now, as in prehistoric times, the song and the bird are inseparable. Their music has the inevitability that all human art aspires to. As a poet, Stevens wanted to find words that would convey his moods and meanings with such propriety and inevitability. It is in this sense that his poetry aspires to the condition of music, and it is for this reason that he named his first book *Harmonium*.

The connection between music and nonsense is direct enough. Music represents, for Stevens, the effect of adequate poetry, while nonsense is the verbal equivalent of music. In the deeply moving "Mozart, 1935" (*CP* 131–32) the poet is asked to play the music of the present on the piano, "Its shoo-shoo-shoo, its ric-a-nic." The present is ugly and wintry like the rhythms of popular dance tunes. But it is also a challenge to the creative powers of the poet-pianist. As he plays, a "body in rags" is carried downstairs—obviously the body of the noble past, the art that no longer seems appropriate. (This is the same corpse that appears in "The Emperor of Ice-Cream.")

---

6 Cf. Doggett, "Transition from *Harmonium*," 129.

However, the poet is also commanded to become the voice of these years of abysmal wretchedness, the mid-thirties:

> Be thou the voice,
> Not you. Be thou, be thou
> The voice of angry fear,
> The voice of this besieging pain.   (*CP* 132)

These are the words that were to be echoed by the sparrow in "Notes toward a Supreme Fiction," saying to the blade of grass, "Bethou me" ("It Must Change," VI; *CP* 393), which I interpret as, "Give me the voice of your inmost, essential self." Thus, when the poet wishes to speak immediately for his times, he approaches the state of a musician and utters appropriate nonsense—nonsense that stands for appropriate music.

The inmost self is subrational and prelinguistic. It holds the feelings and tastes that move us to speech, not those that issue from speech. Stevens's nonsense syllables bypass the conscious, literary, reflective mind, as music does, to suggest the impulses that determine poetry from within and that link it to the reality enveloping and dominating us from without.

Such a linkage of nonsense syllables with music and the revelation of essence seems natural for Stevens. In "The Man with the Blue Guitar" he calls the truly imaginative, creative mind "man number one" (III; *CP* 166), which may be a political metaphor referring to "premier." Stevens then speaks of getting at the essential nature of such a person and describes the task as performing a biopsy on the brain, or pinning it down the way one might nail a hawk across a barn door. He also compares the process with striking the correct note on a guitar and tuning the instrument perfectly: "To strike his living hi and ho, / To tick it, tock it, turn it true." Music, essence, and nonsense come together here. "Hi and ho" represent not the meaning of number one's words but the timbre of his liveliness, the liveliness that gives rise to his characteristic speech.[7] "To tick it, tock it" suggests picking the

---

7   See *Letters*, 783. Cf. his explanation of "ai-ya-yi" ("The Man with the Blue Guitar," section xxv) in *Letters*, 784.

strings while turning the pegs. The whole series of metaphors suggests fierceness and high spirits, one from the cutting and impaling, the other from the music and nonsense. Finally, these attributes mingle in the playing of the guitar: "To bang it from a savage blue, / Jangling the metal of the strings."

Music too is an immediate expression of feeling, and poems written to be sung often have nonsense syllables for their refrain. It is also conventional for words in songs to be divided so that the separate syllables or vowels receive vocal elaboration while being reduced (apart from the music) to meaninglessness. Therefore, telling a poet to play the "hoo-hoo-hoo" of the present on a piano is the same as asking him to express the quintessential, prelinguistic character of the times in which he lives. So also to entitle a book *Harmonium* is to indicate that one is a modest artist, old-fashioned in sensibility, striving to give immediate expression to the life around one.

The purely musical possibilities of nonsense syllables make themselves heard in "Snow and Stars" (*CP* 133). Again the poet is tired of winter and eager for spring; for he feels oppressed by the wretchedness of the 1930s and longs for an age more propitious to the imagination. Once more, he uses a bird as his spokesman. Generally, birds suggest poetry not only because they sing but also because they fly arbitrarily into view and away, to be seen in glimpses, like glimpses of ultimate reality. A colorful bird, such as a pheasant, brightens the mind with the effects of rich, imaginative poetry. A black bird, such as a grackle, darkens the mind like bleak poetry. In "Snow and Stars" the harsh sound of the grackles is appropriate to the bleak mood of the poet. The lines in which Stevens describes them are heavy with unpleasant sibilants. In contrast, the poem moves at the end to lines ripe with *l* sounds, for the approach of spring. Against this polarity the poet sets the opposition of nonsense syllables, "bing, high bing," and "ding, ding, dong."

The song the grackles sing occupies three of the four stanzas of the poem. It seems to play with the myth of Dis and Persephone. The devil is asked to take and wear earth's robe of winter—snow and winter stars—and in exchange to give the world the clothing of the early-leafing willow, harbinger of spring. The piercing sounds of "bing, high bing" evoke the festiveness of the overheated population of hell when receiving the cold robe. The anticlimactic sounds of "ding, ding, dong" evoke the dullness that will be buried in the "hill" (or hole) of the underworld when wintriness leaves the earth.

Stevens's little game does not yield an attractive poem. The heavy sound patterns and forced imagery coarsen a donnée that required subtle modulation if it was to draw many readers. I suspect that the poet kept this work as a pendant to the superior poem "The Sun This March" (*CP* 133–34), which follows it. But as an experiment with rhymes, alliteration, assonance, and nonsense, it indicates how deliberately Stevens employed such devices.

If I am right, Stevens uses nonsense most effectively when it does not merely stand for the ineffable but also conveys precise suggestions of attitudes or feelings. It should seem casual and unpremeditated, like the subrational moods to which it points. But it should also bear a meaning sufficiently determined by the context. So long as contrasting points of view are associated with the nonsense, we can give it significant direction.

"Anything Is Beautiful If You Say It Is" (*CP* 211) seems a good example of minimal differentiation. Here two similar figures utter similar nonsense syllables; yet the poet distinguishes between them. Both are indecent young women, one a concubine, the other a "demi-monde." They suggest shopworn views of the world, and "demi-monde" may be a pun. One of them is in a garden, the other, on a "mezzanine," suggesting the polarity of outdoors and indoors. Both sound displeased with life. The concubine says, "Phooey! Phoo!" and whispers, "Pfui." The demi-monde says, "Phooey" and "Hey-de-i-do!" These sounds had wide currency in the thirties. "Phooey" of course implies a blasé discontent with the state of the world. "Hey-de-i-do" is typical of the cheerful noises of contentment affected by jazz singers, especially crooners. So we have an outdoor figure and an indoor figure expressing trite moods of discontent, with the latter qualifying her complaint by making the best of the situation.

In the middle section of the poem Stevens continues to balance outdoors against indoors. He abandons the sweetness of spring to the bees, then says that the chandeliers are neat but glaring, and adds some parrots troubled by the cold. People, animals, and things are all inex-pressive, out of touch with the present. It seems therefore that in spite of the presence of spring, the poet's outdated, "beautiful" visions, whether of interiors or of landscapes, leave him dissatisfied.

In the last part of the poem he offers the alternative to such stale images: an intense contemplation of grim reality, uniting things of na-ture with those of man. As if to signal his satisfaction with this choice, he asks an appropriately named servant to bring a suitable wine, a Teutonic, northern one. At last the poem comes to coherent life:

> The Johannisberger, Hans.
> I love the metal grapes,
> The rusty, battered shapes
> Of the pears and of the cheese
>
> And the window's lemon light,
> The very will of the nerves,
> The crack across the pane,
> The dirt along the sill.

The design of the poem is subtly in keeping with the doctrine. The opening and middle sections sound disjointed and trivial, to support the poet's rejection of the two attitudes. Yet these contain the "beau-tiful" things of the title. It is in the last section, when Stevens turns to immediate, ugly reality and transforms it by his language, that the style grows lucid and unified. The role of the tired nonsense is therefore correct: it belongs with the heterogeneous, false half worlds, not with the simple whole.

Among the subtlest uses of nonsense in Stevens's work is the ex-ample of "Page from a Tale" (CP 421–23). This rather hard-worked parable picks up the themes of "Farewell to Florida" (CP 117–18), which is written in the same stanza form and has the same elements of imagery. The peculiar feature of "Page from a Tale" is the way Stevens relates nonsense to meaningful speech. Toward the end of the poem he speaks of the "miff-maff-muff of water," a typical, apparently offhand use of onomatopoetic syllables. Only by a careful response to the whole

poem can one tell how deeply calculated the effect is. At first, the
water makes no sound because the sea is frozen. But Hans does hear
the wind, which speaks in German, presumably his native language. It
says "so blau" and "so lind" and "so lau" (so blue, so gentle, so mild)—
ironically soft cliché rhymes of romantic poetry and ironically soft
epithets for a winter wind.[8] From the thought of water and wind
Stevens goes on to make Hans recall the sounds that the water might
evoke if he could hear it, and these emerge as some words from a
poem in English, a poem in which the speaker keeps hearing the sound
of water. It is Yeats's "Lake Isle of Innisfree." The thought of those
words leads to the image of a steamship caught in the ice; the German
words return, "so blau, so blau." Now big stars come out, bringing
"death" to the ship, which receives a southern name, "Balayne," echoing the German words. The name may mean "whale," perhaps to evoke
Jonah and the theme of resurrection. Certainly it refers to the ship in
"Farewell to Florida," which moved easily through free, southern
waters. So it represents a warm season of the mind, an early Yeatsian
imagination that the poet has discarded.

As Hans thinks of another line from Yeats's poem, lights begin to
move on the ship. He now knows that men will come ashore at dawn,
no doubt abandoning the doomed vessel. Stevens says they will be
afraid of the angels of those skies:

> The finned flutterings and gaspings of the ice,
> As if whatever in water strove to speak
> Broke dialect in a break of memory.   (*CP* 422)

The memory breaking through is, I think, the communal, archetypal
memory of feelings that stay below the level of language. This memory

---

8   In his original note, Professor Ehrenpreis cited poems by Schiller, Heine, and
Stefan George as possible sources for this passage. Toward the end of his life, however,
he struck upon Heine's *Lyrisches Intermezzo*, no. 31, Stevens's true source: "Die Welt
ist so schön und der Himmel so blau, / Und die Lüfte die wehen so lind und so lau"
(ll. 1–2). [Ed.]

takes us back to ancestral impressions, first impressions, the primordial response to the world, without myth, symbolism, human associations.

Such a response produces in turn a new sun, which Stevens describes not as the chariot of Apollo but simply as a wheel. It also produces a new kind of moon, another wheel below the first. These suggest, I think, a new, wintry consciousness and a new, wintry imagination. "Weltering illuminations" appear, and out of them step at last the men from the foundered ship, whom Stevens calls "kin." If we glance at "Large Red Man Reading" (CP 423–24), the poem that immediately follows "Page from a Tale," we shall meet similar figures: "ghosts that return to earth" in order to hear the phrases of the poet. Or if we look back at "A Completely New Set of Objects" (CP 352–53), we shall meet "Shadows of friends" paddling canoes and bearing what seem to be archetypal images for the poet to use.[9]

The men leaving the ship carry electric lamps, or modern imaginations. They act, I think, like souls returning from the underworld in a dangerous, quasi-destructive resurrection. Stevens says they could "melt Arcturus to ingots dropping drops." In other words, these archetypal, ancestral minds underlying our own could, if revived (or modernized and electrified), strip the north star of its familiar associations and melt the ice of the wintry season by enabling men to confront the world directly. Stevens says their gestures could "spill night out" in the "miff-maff-muff" of water. In effect, therefore, they restore the nonsense syllables and remove the language of poems like Yeats's. We are back at the beginning, but with a difference. It is no longer nonsense that sounds like speech but nonsense that sounds like water.

If we want more explicit doctrine concerning nonsense, we may find it in some effortful passages of "Notes toward a Supreme Fiction" (CP 380–408). Frank Doggett has drawn attention to the levels of nonsense in the third poem ("It Must Be Abstract," III; CP 382–83), where Stevens argues that the task of poetry is to restore freshness or "candor" to our perceptions. I take him to mean that a man's imagination enables

9   Cf. Frank Doggett, "Stevens on the Genesis of a Poem," *Contemporary Literature* 16 (1976):463–77, esp. 468–71.

him to throw off stale views of the world and to see things as if for the first time. Working down from conscious thought, the poem ultimately exhilarates our sensations.

To illustrate the theory, Stevens offers three examples, one human, one animal, and one inanimate. First to indicate how men convey their sense of the world, he produces an astonishing metaphor, treating the imaginative self as an Arabian seer who comes into one's room at night chanting "hoobla-hoobla-hoobla-how" and throwing stars around the floor in an act of augury. The owllike sounds are perhaps an audible equivalent for a moonlit night, symbol of imagination. In effect, therefore, the poet has translated a visual experience into sound and identified it with an exotic human being.

The other examples are of a wood dove chanting "hoobla-hoo" and of the ocean, "the grossest iridescence," howling "hoo." Each level of sound thus matches a level of iridescence and of animation: Arabian, bird, water. We associate the personified moon with one kind of nonsense, the iridescence of the dove with a simpler kind, and the grossest iridescence of the ocean with the simplest. Presumably, the reader will for the moment enjoy a fresh idea of these phenomena, thanks to the magical connections the poet has arbitrarily established for them with varieties of "meaningless" syllables. It is significant that the poet associates the Arabian with the future, the dove with the past, and the ocean with the present. Only the human imagination knows of the future; the animal has some memory, but no foresight; the inanimate is ignorant of change. "Life's nonsense," says Stevens, "pierces us with strange relation."

4

POUND

 It is still hard for us to judge Ezra Pound's achievement as a poet. His example has influenced so many successors, he has written so much about the arts and society, that we have trouble fixing our attention on the poems alone. Donald Davie, in a new book on Pound, tries to make the poetry his paramount business. I suppose that is why he hews to the common line of respecting his subject's privacy, and puts careful limits on the use of biographical data.

Those who admire Pound most fiercely write as if his personal history would contribute little to any judgment of his work. But I am not sure a critic's job calls for such discretion. Certainly Pound's choice of themes is illuminated by some features of his private life, especially his waywardness as a husband.

For example, one might ask why Pound, in his late sixties, decided to translate the *Trachiniae* of Sophocles. This is an ill-designed, unpleasant tragedy, much disliked by critics. But it became Pound's favorite among ancient Greek plays.

In the story, Hercules, who has been away for fifteen months, sends home a girl he has seduced, and expects his wife to let her share their bed. The wife, Deianira, feels bitterly shaken but bows to the hero's

This essay was first published 27 May 1976 under the title "Love, Hate, and Ezra Pound" as a review of Donald Davie, *Ezra Pound* (New York: Viking, 1975). Reprinted with permission from *The New York Review of Books*. Copyright © 1976 Nyrev, Inc.

fiat and says (only in Pound's translation), "Let's figure out how we are to manage this cohabitation." She then tries to regain the love of Hercules by sending him a robe anointed with a philter.

But Deianira had been misinformed. The philter turns out to be a fiery poison; and when Hercules wears the robe, it clings to him, burning him with insufferable pains until he arranges to be destroyed on a flaming pyre. Meanwhile, Deianira, discovering what she has blindly done, kills herself.

I suspect that Pound favored the play because it reminded him of the occasion when he asked his own wife to share a home with his mistress. During the Second World War, Dorothy Pound and the poet were living in an apartment on the seafront in Rapallo. The Germans took over the building, and the Pounds moved inland to Sant'Ambrogio and the small house where Olga Rudge, the mistress, was established.

One reason I make the connection is a passage in Pound's *Pisan Cantos,* halfway through Canto 81. The poet here breaks forth into the cry of "AOI" (*Cantos* 519).[1] His daughter has said that the cry is an outburst more personal than any other in the *Cantos,* expressing the strain of "almost two years when he was pent up with two women who loved him, whom he loved, and who coldly hated each other."

That period ended when Pound was arrested by partisans and eventually flown to Washington, to be tried for treason. After half a year, Dorothy Pound managed to join him there. She visited her husband almost daily for twelve years, while he was kept in St. Elizabeth's, a federal hospital for the mentally ill. She took care of his financial affairs, looked after his various wants, and listened to him. When he was released in 1958, the couple returned to Italy. But about three years later, Pound settled down with Olga Rudge. I leave it to specialists to decide how his relations with the two devoted women influenced his treatment of Penelope and Circe in the *Cantos.*

The emotional distance the poet had traveled by the time of the

1   *The Cantos of Ezra Pound* (New York: New Directions, 1972).

cohabitation may be measured from the moods of some early, verse tributes to the woman he was to marry. She was then Dorothy Shakespear, a designer in watercolors. Almost Pound's age, she was the daughter of a London solicitor and his novelist wife. The poet had known her about three years, and had dedicated a book to Dorothy and Mrs. Shakespear.

One of the poems is entitled (in Greek letters) "Doria," and associates the girl with the stern integrity of Doric art expressed as landscape:

> Be in me as the eternal moods
>   of the bleak wind, and not
> As transient things are—
> gaiety of flowers.   (*Personae* 67)[2]

"Doria" is the first of half a dozen poems that Pound finally grouped together, all dealing with the excitement of love, and relating the beloved to the changing aspects of landscape, light, wind, and sea; we hear the carpe diem theme, and the poet's wish to carry the girl out of their present surroundings. The varieties of style, mood, and point of view suggest the energy derived from passion.

When I suggest, in this way, that Pound's published writings bear witness to his most private feelings, I risk the complaints of several devoted critics. When they clarify Pound's numberless obscurities, they rely on his allusions to books, places, and history, to works of art and eminent men; they bring in Pound's own anecdotes about his career; yet they avoid referring to his intimate emotions. How many critics have discussed the gorgeous eroticism of the color modulations in "Phanopoeia"?

 In fact, a good deal of what looks like appreciative criticism of Pound could better be described as exhaustive source hunting.

---

2 *Personae: The Collected Poems of Ezra Pound* (New York: New Directions, 1926).

Hugh Kenner's long essay on a four-word poem by Pound is a miracle of resurrection in which the value of the trifle under scrutiny is never questioned. We are presumed to agree with such an apologist that the poem directs us to the abundant materials he lays out, and is therefore genuinely enriched by them. A friendly critic of Pound naturally makes the assumption because he knows that most of the poet's work is admirably derivative and, in the best sense, imitative. Pound cannibalized other authors as if he were under a divine command to speak only in echoes.

Yet the finished poems often do not call our attention to their sources at all. And if they do, the allusions are often too cryptic to be identified without external aid. Even when they can be so identified, they often take us not to an accessible passage of an accessible work but to a particular text or document that has caught Pound's attention. The text itself is often no help unless one has learned the particular interpretation of it that Pound favors.

Therefore, the docile reader who would like to steer away from Pound's personality finds himself turned back, against his will, in that very direction. If the poet selects a passage from a letter that his schoolgirl daughter once wrote to him, if he then works it into a Canto, and if he frames it in such a way that the implications can hardly be grasped unless one realizes the nature of the source, he does not make it easy for the reader to ignore Pound's domestic life. "Hugh Selwyn Mauberley" is focused so exclusively on the special situation of Pound himself after the First World War that it becomes at points versified autobiography; yet most of it does not repay careful study.

So it seems fair enough for one to ponder the fact that a vast number of Pound's excellent lyrics deal with the experience of sexual passion, which the poet opposes to conventional morality. We know Pound was drawn to women who were artists or musicians; we know he came to believe that sexual potency was a mark of the creative or ordering imagination. In a number of poems he offered what sounds like the usual sneer of literary Bohemianism against normal domestic relations: "Oh how hideous it is / To see three generations of one house gathered together! / It is like an old tree with shoots, / And with some branches rotted and falling" ("Commission"; *Personae* 89).

Surely it is worth observing that although such derision is in a sense commonplace, Pound did live by his principles. When Olga Rudge (a violinist) bore him a daughter, he placed the child with a peasant couple who brought the girl up. A year later, when Dorothy Pound gave birth to a son, the child remained with the parents for a short time but was then deposited with the grandmother, who reared him in England. I think that Pound's whole theory of culture, which sets artists and statesmen apart from the mass of people, is in part a defense of his habit of life.

What makes the amorous themes attractive in the poems themselves is not of course that they give one entrée into Pound's private history. Rather it is that he endowed them with suggestive power—as he did above all in the years between 1912 and 1919. This was the time when he courted and married Dorothy Shakespear (whom he had met in 1909). It was when he lived through the First World War and faced its disillusioning aftermath.

Before this era, the poet was mainly preoccupied with states of attentive rapture or yearning, evoked by sexual passion, the contemplation of landscape, or the enjoyment of works of art. He tried to convey and sustain the states by the use of languorous rhythms, exotic settings, precious language, and solemn tones.

Because a spiritual condition was what the poet longed for, he could regard the various means of reaching it as equivalent to one another. So he could describe poetry as sculpture, women as landscapes, and cities as women: "And svelte Verona first I met at eve; / And in the dark we kissed" ("Guillaume de Lorris Belated"; *Poems* 88).[3]

This sort of correspondence, so pervasive in the Symbolist tradition, is the reason the process of metamorphosis became an important theme in Pound's poems. The act of amorous or imaginative vision, as he conceived it, transformed the poet into something more or less than

3 *The Collected Early Poems of Ezra Pound,* ed. Michael John King (New York: New Directions, 1976).

human. Sexual passion (as in "Piere Vidal Old") could make a wolf out of a man; it changed Daphne into a tree ("A Girl").

Pound generalized the notion and connected all suffering of intense, ideal emotion with transformation. He implied that a good social order would nurture such experiences of love, nature, and art; it would reward creative geniuses for evoking them ("And Thus in Nineveh"). With these values in mind, a poet could raise love songs into celebrations of aesthetic qualities. A woman might become the visible focus of a whole civilization—a divinity integrating a social order; or she might be a bundle of miscellaneities, like a society in decline (*"Portrait d'une Femme"*).

Nearly all of Pound's poetry derives from that of other writers, whether through translation, imitation, allusion, or pastiche. The result, as with Dryden, is paradoxically fresh and original. But in much of his early work Pound affected archaism, as if to signalize his derivative methods and warn us that they were intentional. Implicitly, he lent authority to his aesthetic principles by locating them in the work of poets he admired. So he regularly masked himself and spoke in their person, through monologues supposed to re-create their personalities.

The doctrine that justifies such poetry is one which Pound shared (among others) with Wallace Stevens. It tells us that the definitive property of human nature is not rational morality (as Locke had taught) or emotional morality (as Rousseau had taught), but the creative imagination; and that this in turn is deeply related to the passion of love and to empathy with things loved. Art records and re-creates the process by which the artist blends with what he loves: "And yet my soul sings 'Up!' and we are one" ("In Durance"; *Personae* 21).

This doctrine works well for short lyrics but not for long poems. Being intuitive, it cannot stand up to the rhetoric of evidence and proof. Neither does it flow naturally into the shape of a narrative. To make an exciting story out of the act of creation is notoriously difficult. Although the theme fascinated writers of the late nineteenth century and the early twentieth, only those with a genius for characterization and narrative design (especially James and Mann) invented adequate analogues for the aesthetic drama.

But Pound had no truly dramatic powers, and could act no part but his own. Therefore, the masks he wore differed in name and costume but not in voice. It was a voice of protest against the didactic explicitness of popular verse, the voice of a talent neither patient nor methodical enough to work out its own persuasive rhetoric. Instead, Pound tried to embody his ideals not in lucid reasoning but in suggestive images. But in many poems he also set up a vivifying interchange between his archaic or precious language and a flow of plain or coarse speech that invites us to feel at home in the high culture he evokes.

The early poems are overripe with amorous yearning, songlike praise of mysterious beauty, desire for absent paramours. What saves them from flaccidness is either the subtlety of the versification or the force of the images—often both. Most of the verse we know by more conventional poets follows the simple rhythms to be heard in poems like "The Ancient Mariner" or Frost's "Birches," with a fairly steady beat every two or three syllables. Victorian poets, from Tennyson to Hardy, complicated the familiar rhythms with wonderful variations and experiments but stayed within a regular frame.

Pound went further. In the pentameter he found new and charming rhythms. In his free verse he joined musicality with expressiveness, keeping the lines songlike but also giving the impression of a real speaker, while rhythm and sound changed according to emotion and sense. With the familiar meters he mixed other measures that might spring up, persist, and die down as the mood or theme altered.

If therefore one reads aloud the best of his poems, one feels elusive regularities starting and fading as one pattern interrupts another, gives way to it, and returns with variations. The several kinds of four-beat lines in "Na Audiart" are an example, as they make a counterpoint with two-beat lines and then let an interplay of five- and three-beat lines take hold until the first pattern finally wins out. The poet alternates the drawn-out quality of lines that "fall" away from the beat (ending with unaccented syllables) and lines that "rise" toward the beat (ending with an accent).

To heighten the subtlety of his musical effects, Pound moved the weight of sound echoes away from the line endings. He tried to make his vowel combinations speak against one another between the ends and the middles of a series of verses. Instead of regular rhyme, he used broken and half rhymes. He repeated words and refrains unexpectedly and reechoed the endings of words: "Golden rose the house, in the portal I saw / thee, a marvel, carven in subtle stuff, a / portent" ("Apparuit"; *Personae* 68). Here are Latin, quantitative rhythms, glutted with languorous effects of sound.

Yet all was not languor. Often he spiced the sweetness with savage or cruel emotions: the violence of the artist or ruler imposing his personality on the world ("Sestina Altaforte"). Pound had always kept his verse sentences to the word order of normal speech. He rejected simple figures like similes as pseudopoetic, and preserved the clarity of his images by avoiding merely subjective epithets. In the years before the First World War, he set about eliminating the archaisms except for special effects.

Not yet obsessed with doctrine or with epic ambitions, he was uncommitted to the "ideographic" technique that was to corrupt his poetry. When the total style—rhythm, diction, syntax, and effects of sound—was involved with Pound's peculiarly ironic lyricism, it became his greatest accomplishment.

I suppose the effect of courtship, marriage, and war was to make Pound understand how difficult and fragile his ideal states were, how dependent on circumstance. Besides evoking the rapt experiences of self-transcendence, the poet wrote witty satires on the social order that checked them. In these he centered his imagery on corrupt or inadequate artists and on types of feeble or pathological sexuality, as in the series "*Moeurs Contemporaines.*" But Pound lacked the moral penetration that gives strength to social satire: the poems sound affected and brittle.

The turning point in his positive development as a poet came as

Pound neared the age of thirty. Then he undertook to infuse the irony of satire into his lyric elevations, like a man smiling at his own ardors; and he marked the shifts in tone with his fresh combinations of rhythms and his balance of precious against coarse language. So it was that Pound created his distinctive glides from tenderness or even ecstasy to amused self-consciousness in the same design. The translations of Heine, a master of these effects, show how skillful Pound could be:

> And have you thoroughly kissed my lips?
>   There was no particular haste,
> And are you not ready when evening's come?
>   There's no *particular* haste.
>
> You've got the whole night before you,
>   Heart's-all-belovèd-my-own;
> In an uninterrupted night one can
>   Get a good deal of kissing done.
>
> ("Translations and Adaptations From Heine," VIII; *Personae* 48)

The change of pace in the last two lines reveals the hand of the *miglior fabbro*. In the sustained brilliance of *Homage to Sextus Propertius,* Pound showed how remarkably inventive he could be with this style. But the synthesis did not endure. He felt he must go beyond the mockery of public affairs and the celebration of private raptures. A world that could tolerate the Marne and Verdun needed a prophet more than a minstrel.

Restless and impatient, unable to manage an argument or to organize a narrative, Pound still hankered to write a verse epic that would accomplish for our time what the *Divine Comedy* had done for Dante's. Around 1915 he had begun experimenting with long poems: the theme and variations of "Near Perigord," the sequences *"Moeurs Contemporaines,"* and "Mauberley."

They all come unstuck, to a degree that should have warned Pound away from the fifty years' wilderness of the *Cantos.* Their best parts, like the best parts of the *Cantos,* would gain power if they were isolated. Their direction would be clearer. Their impact would not be dissipated.

"Medallion," for instance, has been misinterpreted largely through its place in "Mauberley."

Even *Homage to Sextus Propertius,* which rests on the firm underpinnings of a Roman poet's matter, has little narrative shape. Its swiftly changing dramatic ironies exhilarate us with a centripetal design because Pound employs his brilliant effects of style to explore a fixed situation from a series of surprising viewpoints.

Meanwhile, his old, aesthetic doctrine did not lend itself to unfolding in a long poem. When, therefore, Pound was seduced by Calliope, he tried to elaborate moral and public doctrines that would support an epic structure: theories of society, government, and economics which no way suited his impulsive leaps of imagination.

At the same time, the requirements of the *Cantos,* as Pound regrettably saw them, dissolved the union of lyric and ironic that he had achieved. He wished his "epic" to act out the process of insight by which (Pound thought) men recognize eternal principles or values at work in the flux of existence. The reader was supposed to identify the shapes and meanings, or—in effect—to accomplish the work of synthesis for himself.

So Pound regressed to the simple style of putting slabs of rapt contemplation beside slabs of document, anecdote, or complaint. As guides to interpretation, he used his would-be "ideographic" images (often repeated) and widely spaced echoes of his own, would-be pregnant phrases. The "ideographs" are charged images, gemlike in themselves but also evoking a source that illustrates the poet's meaning—for example, "the city of Dioce [i.e., Deioces of Media] whose terraces are the colour of the stars" (no. 74; *Cantos* 425). (Clue: try Herodotus.) It is hard to imagine a random set of associations in one man's mind that would not fit into the design the poet proposed.

If his social philosophy had been coherent and rational, it might still have made the *Cantos* viable. But although the poet had visions of love, beauty, and order, although he denounced lust and avarice, yet he established no moral argument that distinguished a megalomaniac from a statesman, or cruelty from justice. The doctrines he bunched together were broad enough to comprehend both Mussolini and John Adams, to feed Pound's hatred of Jews along with his hatred of war.

The confusion darkening the *Cantos* may be traced to a confusion between two concepts of culture. One is the old humanistic ideal, sometimes imagined to be aristocratic, but really available to anyone with the mind and the will: this is intellectual and aesthetic culture, comprehending poetry and the other arts, history, and philosophy. A mark of this culture was that (contrary to some snobbish illusions) it could be passed on from Greek to Roman, from slave to noble, from antiquity to Renaissance. It was in fact essentially democratic, being independent of race or class. It united men over the barriers of social institutions.

The new concept of culture is anthropological. In this sense it becomes the system of beliefs, of social and economic institutions, belonging to a particular society. Rooted in place, time, class, and race, it is independent of intellectual powers. It divides people from people.

Not the least misfortune of our time is that the new sense has invaded the old. For many critics now, any aesthetic culture must be rooted in race, nation, and class. For them, the aesthetic culture of the bourgeois must be different from that of the workers; male culture must be different from female, black from white. We are asked to believe that certain kinds of intellectual freedom and humanistic learning are appropriate for some of us but not for others.

Pound immersed himself in this confusion. He decided early that high, aesthetic culture was not for the mass of people, and that the elementary distinction between the few and the many lay in this postulate. Contempt for uneducated men, for conventional family ties, for bourgeois commerce, provided the emotion that made him feel the elite were threatened by the mob:

> I have met with the "Common Man,"
> I admit that he usually bores me,
> He is usually stupid or smug.
>
> ("Redondillas, or Something of That Sort"; *Poems* 216)

To this elementary distinction Pound gave faint political overtones when he imagined himself condemned as a traitor (in 1913) for preferring true aesthetic culture to American democracy. Addressing the "flatterers" of this country, he declared, "Say that I am a traitor and a cynic. . . . You will not lack your reward" ("Reflection and Advice").

For snobbish Europeans there was nothing odd in the view that democracy was the natural enemy of aesthetic or humanistic culture; and Pound drifted comfortably into the harbor of a pseudoaristocratic ideology. According to his vague program (as I make it out), the peasants, laborers, and bourgeois could provide a harmonious "culture" (in the anthropological sense) for the nourishment of a high, aesthetic culture, but only so long as they had a strong leader to establish order, enforce justice, stamp out usury, and elevate creative genius. Their lives would then be enriched by the ceremonies of the arts.

This infantile ideology is the reason Pound had to meet Mussolini and persuade himself that the Duce understood and admired the *Cantos* (in 1933: see Canto 41): he had to believe the ruler possessed wisdom and taste. This too is why he could so indignantly lament the death of Mussolini and his mistress while ignoring the operations of holocaust and terror. ("Ben and La Clara . . . twice crucified" [no. 74; *Cantos* 425]; "poor old Benito" [no. 80; *Cantos* 495]).

It was a short step downward for Pound to make the class and national barrier into a racial barrier, or to confuse an intellectual elite with a racial elite—like those German classicists who lived through the thirties and forties believing that the *deutsches Volk* were by nature best suited to transmit the heritage of humanism to the rest of Europe. There was nothing eccentric about racism, in this country or in Europe, while Pound was young.

Throughout the empire-building processes and nationalist rivalries of the late nineteenth century, racism served as the apology of Europeans seizing the lands of weaker nations. The theoretical polarity between a naturally ruling race and a subject race was taken for granted. In America, meanwhile, the flood of immigrants from southern and eastern Europe frightened many earlier arrivals into declaring that the true American must be derived from "Anglo-Saxon" ancestors.

In this self-serving melange of ignorance and prejudice, the association of Jews with ill-got gains required no apology. One may speculate that a man whose name meant a kind of money, whose grandfather had invested in silver mines, whose father was an assayer of the U.S. Mint, who had grown up during the campaign for "free silver" ("You shall not crucify mankind upon a cross of gold"), and who then became an expatriate, might well wish to avoid any brush of Shylock's garment.

To support his anti-Semitism, Pound could employ both aspects of his ambiguous notion of culture. Categorized as money-grubbers, the Jews were put down as alien to the tradition of art and humanism. So Pound called upon other poets,

> Let us be done with Jews and Jobbery,
> Let us spit upon those who fawn on JEWS for
> their money.[4]

But if a Jew appeared an integral part of the literary establishment, Pound could accuse him of having no birthright in the culture, and of betraying his own tradition. So in "Mauberley" the poet sneered at Max Beerbohm under the impression that he was a Jew (1919):

> The heavy memories of Horeb, Sinai
>   and the forty years,
> Showed only when the daylight fell
> Level across the face
> Of Brennbaum "The Impeccable."   (*Personae* 193)

The final association was with warmongering. Pound convinced himself that Jewish bankers habitually encouraged gentiles to embroil them-

---

4   "Salutation the Third," *Blast* 1 (1914):45. The version of this poem collected in *Personae* (1926) makes the direction of Pound's derision much more oblique: "Let us be done with pandars and jobbery, / Let us spit on those who pat the big bellies for profit." [Ed.]

selves so the Jews might grow rich on the profits of war. Having reached this level singlehandedly, Pound had little to learn from Moscow, Munich, or Rome. But the deterioration that finally showed in his poetry went further.

Take the speeches he made in 1942 and 1943. He could blame the Jews for wishing to destroy Bach's music, Shakespeare's poetry, "everything that is conducive to civilization."[5] He could describe British Jews as indifferent to the bombing of Canterbury: "The destroyed monuments are not monuments to the glory of Judah. They show nothing that the Jew can be proud of. . . . they were built in open defiance of the Jews' slime."

He could say that the pogrom was merely "an old style killing of small Jews. That system is no good. . . . Of course if some man had a stroke of genius and could start pogrom UP AT THE top, there might be something to say for it. But on the whole legal measures are preferable. The sixty Kikes who started this war might be sent to St. Helena as a measure of world prophylaxis. And some hyper-kike, or non-Jewish kikes along with 'em."[6]

But is the frenzy of those speeches as repellent as the more cryptic utterances floating through the *Pisan Cantos?*—this, for example, from a passage describing the Jews as planning to dislodge "the blond bastards" by luring them into wars: "the yidd is a stimulant, and the goyim are cattle . . . and go to saleable slaughter / with the maximum of docility" (no. 74; *Cantos* 439).

Admirers of Pound have tried to demonstrate the coherence of the *Cantos* by showing how the motifs of any one section are interwoven with those of other sections. I'm not sure how their case would be affected by the weaving of the anti-Semitic lines into the argument of the whole work. But I would suggest that the mentality behind such passages did not possess high powers of intellectual synthesis.

5   *"Ezra Pound Speaking": The Radio Speeches of World War II,* ed. Leonard W. Doob (Westport, Conn.: Greenwood Press, 1978), 120.
6   *"Ezra Pound Speaking,"* 115.

Donald Davie, in his new book on Pound, takes the *Cantos* very seriously, and tries to dispose of the ideological difficulties by separating the "opinions" from the "ideas" of the poem. He pleads, I think, that the appalling doctrines on politics and race belong to mere opinion or prejudice, and are not central to the meaning, but that Pound's ultimate values (justice, beauty, love, order)—not stated but embodied in processes of rapt vision arising from immediate experience—constitute the ideas or real meaning.

I put the analysis in my own words because Davie's account is troubled and obscure; he may well disagree with the paraphrase. But rather than study his terms and quarrel with his logic, I will make a single, literary comment: that if Pound built his poem as Davie indicates, it is a devastating mark of his failure that the poet's ear should have been so deaf to the impact his "opinions" would make on an audience.

Davie is excellently equipped to write an authoritative introduction to Pound's work. He is an accomplished poet and critic, familiar not only with Pound's writings of every sort but also with the scholarship on them. Though deeply responsive to Pound's verse, Davie is acutely aware of his limitations as a poet. He holds a sane, balanced view of Pound's importance in literary history but does not compromise with his evil banalities.

In an earlier book Davie tried to survey the whole of Pound's output, with very uneven results. The new book is as learned as its predecessor but better defined. Davie fixes on the right topics, concentrating upon the poetry itself and not Pound's criticism. He carefully roots Pound's "modernity" in the samples of Victorian forebears and Edwardian contemporaries. He widens an old attack on "Mauberley." He examines Pound's diction at length—if not incisively—and provides a subtle analysis of Pound's metrics. He offers a poet's generous defense of the *Cantos.*

Yet with all his talents Davie has not served us well. Though short, the book is neither orderly, lucid, nor concise. Davie writes carelessly and fills out his text with lengths of unnecessary quotation; he digresses into peripheral topics, like the relation between birth control and the arts. His inaccuracies undermine his learning—e.g., he will give innocent readers the impression that Pound himself translated the hundreds of lines of Dante in the *Spirit of Romance!* Readers who already know a good deal about Pound will find a number of fresh insights in Davie's book. Others will be disappointed.

5

ELIOT

I

 The strength of T. S. Eliot's poetry depends on insights that mediate between morality and psychology. Eliot understood the shifting, paradoxical nature of our deepest emotions and judgments, and tried to embody this quality in his style. "All that concerned my family," he once said, "was 'right and wrong,' what was 'done and not done.'"[1] It became the poet's discovery that what is wrong when acted may be right when remembered, that today's gladness justifies yesterday's grief, and that religious serenity may be the upper side of skepticism.

Most of Eliot's innovations of poetic technique strive to disorientate the reader. They give one a literary experience that follows the contours of reversible emotions. Reading Eliot's lines sympathetically, one enters into a drama (often incomplete) of moral judgment imposing itself on a flux of contradictory moods. His ambitious effects are formal equivalents of the process by which insight interrupts experience.

The reason Eliot assigned such importance to ambiguous or para-

This essay was first published 9 Feb. 1978 under the title "Mr. Eliot's Martyrdom" as a review of Lyndall Gordon, *Eliot's Early Years* (Oxford: Oxford Univ. Press, 1977), James E. Miller, Jr., *T. S. Eliot's Personal Wasteland* (University Park: Pennsylvania State Univ. Press, 1977), and Derek Traversi, *T. S. Eliot: The Longer Poems* (New York: Harcourt, Brace, Jovanovich, 1976). Reprinted with permission from *The New York Review of Books.* Copyright © 1978 Nyrev, Inc.

1   Eliot, as quoted by William Turner Levy and Victor Scherle in *Affectionately, T. S. Eliot* (Philadelphia: Lippincott, 1968), 121.

doxical states is that he required high purpose to live by; and purpose involves choice. The eliciting of true decisions from evasive moods became for him a fundamental occupation. The people he grew up with were addicted to high-minded decisions "between duty and self-indulgence."[2] The affectionate claims of a talented, frustrated, overattentive mother led him to feel at once unworthy of his great opportunities and zealous to make the best use of them. Humble self-doubt and immense aspiration were the obverse and reverse of his character.

Eliot came to make grave decisions secretly, and to disclose them suddenly, as if afraid that opposition might change his mind. His parents had no warning of Eliot's first marriage, which followed his original meeting with the bride by only a couple of months. About the same time, he withdrew abruptly from the Ph.D. course in philosophy at Harvard, though he had completed nearly all the requirements for the degree.

When Eliot determined to be baptized into the Church of England, he told only the priest and the men who were to be his godfathers. The ceremony took place in an isolated country church behind locked doors. When he made up his mind to leave his first wife, he did not advise her beforehand. While visiting America by himself, to deliver a series of lectures, he wrote to his solicitor, telling him to draw up a deed of separation and asking him to deliver to Vivienne a letter from Eliot explaining the decision.

Again, when he was to be married a second time, Eliot did not even warn John Hayward, whose apartment he had been sharing for over a decade. Eliot asked his solicitor to arrange a secret ceremony; and the couple were married by special license in an out-of-the-way London church at half-past six in the morning.

Such cautious impulsiveness points to large stores of diffidence. Evidently the poet could not risk exposure to the painful reactions that

2   "American Literature and Language," in *To Criticize the Critic and Other Writings* (New York: Farrar, Straus, & Giroux, 1965), 44. Hereafter referred to as *CC*.

his choices might produce. He could not be sure of standing up to the anger or grief (or ridicule) of his intimates. This lack of confidence, though derived from humility, was tied up with ambition. For Eliot, no success had much value unless it was hard won.

When a friend gave superlative praise to his book *Poems 1909–1925,* the poet replied with a clipping from *The Midwives' Gazette* in which the following words were underlined: "Blood, mucus, shreds of mucus, purulent discharge." The gesture was more than a rude joke. It conveyed Eliot's poverty of spirit, his honestly diffident view of the poems; and it did so, characteristically, in the words of another person.

We may assume that the attitude sprang from the poet's sense of not deserving (could any deserve?) the measure of love that was bestowed on him. But the feeling persisted throughout his life and darkened his imagination. Ultimately, it blended with religious doctrine, for the creed he clung to (after his fortieth year) rested mysteriously on the gap between God's love and man's unworthiness.

So it was easy for Eliot to conceive of discipline rather than freedom as the first need of humanity. "At the bottom of man's heart," he said when he was twenty-eight—in a phrase that anticipates a line of "Gerontion"—"there is always the beast, resentful of restraints of civilized society, ready to spring out at the instant this restraint relaxes. . . . As a matter of fact, the human soul—*l'anima semplicetta*—is neither good nor bad; but in order to be good, to be human, requires *discipline.*"

The relation between humility and discipline is obvious enough, and Eliot never lost sight of it. Years later, contrasting totalitarian government with his own idea of a Christian society, he said of the latter, "That prospect involves, at least, discipline, inconvenience and discomfort: but here as hereafter the alternative to hell is purgatory."[3]

It was naturally on himself that Eliot enjoined the severest renunciations and discipline. When he surrendered the career of professor of philosophy and accepted the vocation of poetry, he imposed extraor-

3   "The Idea of a Christian Society," in *Christianity and Culture* (New York: Harcourt, Brace, and World, 1949), 19.

dinary demands on his genius. I do not think it farfetched to say that as a poet he submitted to rigors that might be labeled self-punishing, though suiting his idea of the way to wisdom.

In traditional literature (especially plays and novels), it is through education of the affections that the soul achieves moral intelligence: famous examples are Tom Jones and Sophia, Darcy and Elizabeth Bennet. The pursuit of the beloved offers tests and challenges that dissolve impurities and clarify virtue. But Eliot distrusted the easy parallelism between courtship and illumination unless the lover's hopes were unsatisfied. In an early "Song" he yearns for significant passion but anticipates deprivation. This poignancy of revelations missed, of love evaded, was to stay with Eliot to the end of his course:

> The moonflower opens to the moth,
>   The mist crawls in from sea;
> A great white bird, a snowy owl,
>   Slips from the alder tree.
>
> Whiter the flowers, Love, you hold,
>   Than the white mist on the sea;
> Have you no brighter tropic flowers
>   With scarlet life, for me?[4]

The economy, meticulous sound patterns, evocative imagery, and exact versification of this Tennysonian lyric all suggest the eagerness for self-denial that the poem expresses. Not only does one recognize the triple motif of humility, sacrifice, and barely attainable love. One also recognizes the poet's submission to an ascetic conception of art. It is in this spirit that an older Eliot was to say of unrhymed verse, "The rejection of rhyme is not a leap at facility; on the contrary, it imposes a much severer strain upon the language."[5]

4   "Song," in *Poems Written in Early Youth* (New York: Farrar, Straus, & Giroux, 1967), 22.
5   "Reflections on *Vers Libre*," CC, 188.

✦ Humility, I think, contributed to his habit of using other men's words rather than starting afresh with his own. Partly this is an acknowledgment of the older writers' excellence, a hint of the foolishness of making newborn speech do jobs that inherited language can do better. Often Eliot chose expressions that do not sound archaic or identifiable and yet seem to revive recollection like a half-forgotten proverb:

> Inside my brain a dull tom-tom begins
> Absurdly hammering a prelude of its own,
> Capricious monotone.   ("Portrait of a Lady," I)[6]

The touch of regular pentameter underlines the drum beat; the phrasing and rhyme come from J. R. Lowell's "Vision of Sir Launfal"— commonly read at school.

But when the echo sounds strong enough to revive the context of the source, the effect becomes subtler. In discussing Eliot's deliberate allusions, we run the danger of taking them as referring to concrete persons or situations, particularly to conditions of life or heroic figures of the past, supposed to be offered as preferable to those of our own time. But it is always a poet's rendering that Eliot retrieves for us, rather than a fact or deed in its nakedness.

So he produces not the murder of Agamemnon but the tragic resonance of that crime for Aeschylus; not the routines of Italian monasteries under Boniface VIII, but Dante's ideas of the contemplative life. Eliot had an ample supply of historical learning, and did not have to be told how much bleaker the circumstances of most men were in remote centuries than in the present. We are not asked to imitate the domestic manners of old heroes and saints but to discover ideal visions that can haunt us like theirs.

So also in finding our images, Eliot strove to be true to himself without celebrating his personality. He wanted images to be authentic, and therefore drawn from his own experience—if possible, from the

---

6   *The Complete Poems and Plays: 1909–1950* (New York: Harcourt, Brace, Jovanovich, 1958), 9. Hereafter referred to in the text as *CP*.

deepest level of that experience. But they were also to belong to the archetypal sensibility of mankind, or at least be such as evoke strong, lingering associations in most men. He further preferred that they should have appeared in the work of earlier masters. Even for imagery as apparently original as the "Preludes"—

> Sitting along the bed's edge, where
> You curled the papers from your hair,
> Or clasped the yellow soles of feet
> In the palms of both soiled hands   (*CP* 13)

he turned to a passage in a French novel he admired.

Yet again, the images were to suggest the paradoxical nature of moral judgment—that what seems meaningless now may be drenched in meaning later, that what seems like renunciation at dusk may be self-fulfillment at noon. Putting the elements together, one gets highly charged ambiguities in reverberating speech.

So it is that winter may represent both life and death, in words that echo the Victorian James Thomson (*Waste Land*, I). November may be confused with spring, in an image borrowed from Campion (*East Coker*, II). Fire may mean lust or purgation or divine love, in terms used by Buddha, St. Augustine, or Dante.

For the poet himself, the authority of his predecessors validated the images and their meaning. For the listener who picks up the reverberations (whether or not he identifies the source), they enrich the force of suggestion. But at the same time, as an expression of humility, such images diminish the personality of the poet. He hovers over the work without manifestly entering it.

Working within these limits, the poet makes himself something of a martyr. In a sense, he exchanges his identity for his poetry. But he wins a substantial reward; and this is the powerful, tenacious quality of verse that stirs us with its right rhythms, its mysterious overtones, and depth of meaning—verse that belongs to us like our early memories.

Yet on the opposite side, ambition constantly affirmed its claims.

In his critical prose Eliot exhibited from the start a magisterial self-confidence that barely glanced at opposition. His assurance and assertiveness demolished an old orthodoxy and established a new one. They also served, I believe, to fence off Eliot's doubts about his poems.

But the style of the prose is not experimental. It was in verse that Eliot resolved to experiment, innovate, change. He wished to join his name to fundamental transformations of the technique of poetry: hence the variety in the small body of his oeuvre. Having mastered one set of devices, Eliot went restlessly on to another, bolder scheme—*Prufrock,* "Gerontion," *The Waste Land*—till he reached the audacities of *Ash Wednesday.* Then he swerved on himself in a movement of conservation, from "Animula" to the five-part sequence of "Landscapes" (1933–34). These embody the sense of place and the emotional trajectory of the final masterpiece, the *Quartets,* which came soon after.

We may estimate the height of Eliot's ambition from his aspiring to work not only with new metrical patterns but also with fundamental aspects of language itself: disruptions of syntax and meaning that startle the reader into attention while forcing him to reconsider the purpose and value of literary experience: proper names intruding with no reference to identify them, until we question the significance of identity; verb tenses slyly melting into one another, till we ponder the reality of time; third persons becoming second and first, till we stumble in the relativity of perception.

Eliot practiced confusing the literal and figurative sense of the same word; he gave intangible subjects to concrete verbs, and let the verbs themselves look like participles in one clause while serving as predicates in another. It becomes clear to attentive listeners that speech can separate men from each other, as well as join them; and the mystery of a divine Logos begins to seem not so different from the mystery of communication between self-contained persons.

Meanwhile, from *Prufrock* on, the experiments in versification were seducing and startling those who followed them. I think we may distinguish persistent modes related to changing themes. For example, the old poignancy of evasive moments and missed opportunities kept returning on the reader in patterned lines, incantatory and subtly regular: "She has a bowl of lilacs in her room" ("Portrait of a Lady," II; *CP* 9); "Weave, weave the sunlight in your hair" ("La Figlia che Piange"; *CP* 20); "He passed the stages of his age and youth" (*Waste Land,* IV; *CP* 46).

The nostalgic moment recurs in passages of free verse, blank verse, and lyric stanzas: "Brown hair is sweet, brown hair over the mouth blown, / Lilac and brown hair" (*Ash Wednesday,* III; *CP* 63). It triumphs in Eliot's lament over the destruction wrought by the Second World War; and here the echoes of Tennyson are distinct. (The ash is dust settling after an air raid):

> Ash on an old man's sleeve
> Is all the ash the burnt roses leave.
> Dust in the air suspended
> Marks the place where a story ended.
> Dust inbreathed was a house—
> The wall, the wainscot and the mouse.
> The death of hope and despair,
>   This is the death of air.
>
> (*Little Gidding,* II; *CP* 139)

Frail and transient are the things that feed such pathos—too fragile for a man to live by, although they tempt him to make the effort. As Eliot acknowledges and stands back from the temptation, he finds a second mode—irony, or his consciousness of the impotence of momentary yearnings to sustain high purpose. This consciousness may appear in the gentle mingling of pathos and irony, as in "Portrait of a Lady." It may also slip into satire—both self-satire and the ridicule of social types like oneself; or it may sink further, into loathing of oneself and others, as humility becomes a bottomless sense of unworthiness.

Here is the aspect of Eliot touched by Laforgue. We hear the satiric voice restrained, in free verse that tightens at points into blank verse; we also hear it bitter or even raging, in rhymed quatrains. The risk of such satire is that readers can ignore the poet's sense of degraded kinship with the figures he mocks; for his attitude is that of Baudelaire in "*Les sept vieillards.*" If Eliot did not blame himself far more harshly, he would never stoop to injure someone like "Cousin Harriet."

Deeper yet is the risk of the spiteful rants against "Apeneck Sweeney" and "Bleistein—Chicago Semite Viennese." With these one must see that it is the squalor of the poet's own mind, the shallowness of his own culture, the lusts of his own eye, the passivity of his own will that he excoriates in the caricatures. And precisely because he is enlightened as they are not—and still lingers in bestiality—he passes the heaviest judgment on himself.

There are alternative modes to nostalgia and satire. One is the direct confrontation of graceless reality: the view of the world as infernal, or at least as antechamber to hell. This is precisely the view from which one first sought refuge in nostalgia, and the poet flinches as he looks. Sometimes Eliot could wring lyricism from this contemplation, in a sensational mode reminiscent of Baudelaire. Sometimes he could give a more chaste account, in a style one might call Dantesque: "Eructation of unhealthy souls / Into the faded air" (*Burnt Norton,* III; *CP* 120).

He could also leap to the extremes of vision, the very high and very low, both informed by Dante. So we meet the last despair of nightmares like—

> the stair was dark,
> Damp, jaggèd, like an old man's mouth drivelling,
>   beyond repair,
> Or the toothed gullet of an agèd shark
>
>   (*Ash Wednesday,* III; *CP* 63)

and we catch as well the glimpse of salvation—

> And the pool was filled with water out of sunlight,
> And the lotos rose, quietly, quietly,
> The surface glittered out of heart of light.
>
>   (*Burnt Norton,* I; *CP* 118)

I have been suggesting a relation between Eliot's styles and his responses to the human condition. I would also suggest that the satiric impulse died after he wrote *The Waste Land* because to separate himself from any class of humanity, if only in appearance, became in his eyes an immoral act. So also the impulse to embody the various modes in dramatic speakers faded after *Ash Wednesday* as the poet grew less covert about doctrine. The hidden springs of his poetic energy had always been didactic. With age he seemed to accept the fact and to let his unqualified voice be heard. Perhaps the writing of plays absorbed the imagination he had drawn on when assuming roles in verse.

The familiar images and motifs persist amazingly and in many forms, because the poet deliberately built his later work on the earlier. By a cunning irony the motto of *East Coker,* "In my beginning is my end" (*CP* 123), reminds one not only of Mary Stuart but also of the Lady in Eliot's "Portrait" saying, "But our beginnings never know our ends!" (*CP* 11). Thus the close of his career bows to the opening.

Yet the momentum of change continued. In technique the poet kept his instinct for matching form to meaning, but the experimental am- bition dwindled. Instead, Eliot concentrated on refining and transform- ing his habitual modes. By gradations he arrived at the counterpoint of four modes in the *Quartets.*

At least as early as "Animula" (1929) one notices the accents of direct speech; for here, describing the gestures of infancy, the poet seems an unpretentious observer, acting no part:

> Moving between the legs of tables and of chairs,
> Rising or falling, grasping at kisses and toys,
> Advancing boldly, sudden to take alarm,
> Retreating to the corner of arm and knee.   (*CP* 70–71)

As if to compensate for the lack of a mask, Eliot offered expressive variations of regular form. In "Animula" he has pentameter lines rhym- ing with the unpredictability of kittenish movements (like the fog in *Prufrock*), and quiet manipulations to match the shifts from an infant soul's quickness (participles and verbs starting lines, accented nouns ending them) to the uneasy conflicts of an older child (obstructive verbs crowding the lines, and less emphatic endings)—then the cor- ruptions of maturity (initial participles again, but resisting motion); and

to close, the types of meaningless death (irregular lines, feminine endings, no rhyme).

Once more, in the poem "Virginia" (1933) the contrast between the
still heat of the external landscape and the restlessness of a mind agi-
tated by stubborn thoughts implies no mask but is a deeply personal
contrast. Here when Eliot says, "Ever moving / Iron thoughts came
with me / And go with me" (*CP* 94), whatever the source of the words
may be, they do not invite us to think of anyone but the poet. We are
not required to know about the sick wife or the deed of separation;
"iron thoughts" direct us to the anxious speaker as himself; and that is
whom we hear in the *Quartets,* for whose design the series of "Landscapes" including "Virginia" may have been a model.

And it is in the *Quartets* (1935–42) that the great change of direction
after *Ash Wednesday* culminates. Here an unmasked poet gives voice to
his reflections. He uses a fourfold mode of meditation derived from
blank verse but freely expanding and contracting, turning inward and
out on immediate thought and perception; rising to brief visions; in-
terrupted by nostalgic memories; sinking to grim prospects of death in
life.

Against the flow, the poet thrusts intensifications of the extreme
modes: formal lyrics of purgatorial vision and prayer. And now he resolves the strain between humility and ambition by letting the theme
of art emerge, and openly commenting on the labors of creation. In
the brilliantly expressive versification of the last important poem he
wrote (*Little Gidding*), the poet once more triumphs in paradox; for he
reviews the disappointments of the creative imagination in a style of
absolute mastery, and dramatizes his own personality in the voice of
Dante.

To establish an independent point of view, I have tried to examine Eliot's poetry without invoking his own critical principles.
Excellent scholars have surveyed his career with the support of those
principles and without dwelling on his private character. For my own
approach I have leaned heavily on the work of F. O. Matthiessen, Helen
Gardner, and Grover Smith.

Among recent books on the poet, two deal with the relation of his personal life to his published works; another deals with his long poems but excludes the bearing of biography. Certainly the most important of these books is Lyndall Gordon's *Eliot's Early Years,* a biographical study centered on the poet's religious development up to the age of forty.

Miss Gordon was granted access to many unpublished manuscripts, and showed exemplary initiative in tracking down a mass of informative material neglected by her predecessors. She reveals much about Eliot's spiritual development, especially the doubts and hesitations that lay behind his declarations of faith. She also provides a lively account of Eliot's first wife, Vivien, based on her diaries, letters, and other primary sources. Incidentally, Miss Gordon supplies dozens of helpful facts and reproduces fascinating photographs of Eliot himself and of people who were close to him. In two valuable appendices she analyzes the influence of Joyce's *Ulysses* on *The Waste Land* and surveys the stores of documents she drew on for her book.

Miss Gordon's main argument is that religious preoccupations underlay Eliot's poetry during the twelve years preceding the final draft of *The Waste Land.* Several of her strongest pieces of evidence are unpublished manuscripts. For our knowledge of them we are asked to rely on Miss Gordon's descriptions and interpretations; and her case depends on the accuracy and sound insight that she has brought to bear on her sources. Unfortunately, if we are to judge by Miss Gordon's handling of texts already published or easily seen, it would be imprudent for us to accept her accounts of those otherwise unknown.

To detail all the imperfections of a scholar to whom we are much indebted would be ungracious. I shall merely indicate the kinds of errors to be found in the book and cite a couple of examples in each class. Miss Gordon is often unreliable in her facts, quotations, and references. Quoting a four-line passage from "The Death of St. Narcissus"—a poem important for her argument—she chooses the text of an intermediate draft rather than the final copy, and misquotes two of the lines. Quoting a few sentences from the "Appendix" to

Eliot's *Idea of a Christian Society,* she refers to it as the "Postscript" and omits a word.

When Miss Gordon is accurate, she often fails to explain fairly the meaning of her data. Thus she mentions Eliot's inscription on the flyleaf of a book he sent his mother, "with infinite love," but omits the circumstances that make it interesting: the author's name (Gamaliel Bradford), the year of the gift (1919), and the fact that Eliot had reviewed it. Discussing *The Waste Land,* Miss Gordon says that in the earliest sketches Eliot worked with "what he once called 'some rude unknown psychic material.'"[7] Actually, Eliot used the phrase in a lecture delivered thirty-one years after *The Waste Land* was published; and he intended it for the genesis of any piece of meditative poetry.

Miss Gordon's interpretations of Eliot's meaning are often eccentric. She paraphrases the "Song" that I have quoted above, as representing a young man regretfully escorting a "pale white woman" (25). She mentions another early poem, "Humouresque" (misspelled), as revealing Eliot's opinion of "the shoddiness of women's minds," although no woman is mentioned in it (27). Referring to the passage I have quoted from the poet on his family's concern with right and wrong, Miss Gordon says Eliot observed that his parents "did not talk of good and evil but of what was 'done' and 'not done'" (11).

Still worse, Miss Gordon regularly treats the poems as simple autobiography, disregarding the chance that Eliot might have used a mask or spoken ironically, or that he got material from another author. She is likely to take any mention by the poet of a husband and wife as a revelation about the Eliots themselves, any allusion to religion as an expression of Eliot's religious principles, any comment on sexuality as reflecting the domestic life of the poet.

Referring to the scene I have quoted from the third "Prelude"—of a woman sitting on a bed—Miss Gordon describes it as set in a Boston suburb; she does not consider the possibility that the poem was written in Paris and the images derived from the novelist Charles-Louis Philippe. She confidently describes the obscure "Ode" of 1918 as "self-

---

7   Quoted by Gordon, *Eliot's Early Years,* 86. Her source is "The Three Voices of Poetry," in *On Poetry and Poets* (New York: Farrar, Straus, & Giroux, 1969), 110–11.

characterization" (165) and ignores its dependence on Laforgue's version of the myth of Perseus and Andromeda.

Consequently, Miss Gordon tends to simplify and cheapen Eliot's character and talent. When she declares that Eliot "regarded lust as the most corrupting of all sins," she endows him with a grotesquely shallow conception of evil (137).

If Miss Gordon had arranged her findings in an orderly way, supplying an accurate, chronological account of Eliot's life, with brief reports on the literary works, she would have served scholarship well. Unfortunately, though she clusters the material in chronological divisions, she skips about unpredictably within or across the periods, makes disjointed remarks on miscellaneous events, and offers dubious analyses of hidden motives. The sad truth is that after providing herself, through a magnificent effort of research, with immense opportunities, Miss Gordon has used them badly.

❧ James E. Miller's book, *T. S. Eliot's Personal Waste Land,* is narrower and less helpful than Lyndall Gordon's. Miller believes that Eliot enjoyed a homosexual friendship with a Frenchman named Jean Verdenal who was killed in the First World War. According to Miller, the poet expressed his grief over the loss of Verdenal in *The Waste Land,* and the memory of the loss persists in later poems. This line of interpretation goes back to an essay by John Peter first published in 1952.

The evidence for a romance between Eliot and Verdenal is sparse. When Eliot was in Paris during 1910–11, he lived in the same pension as Verdenal, a medical student almost his own age, who wrote poetry. Verdenal died in the Dardanelles campaign, May 1915, and his body may have been lost at sea. In 1917 Eliot dedicated *Prufrock and Other Observations* to Verdenal. Eventually, he added to the dedication an epigraph from Dante expressing deep affection for the dead man.

I'm not sure there is any method of demonstrating that two young friends did not have homosexual relations sixty-five years ago, but Miller hardly demonstrates that they did. It is far from certain that

Verdenal drowned, and it was seven years from the time of his death to the publication of *The Waste Land.*

If Eliot was in love with Verdenal, we must ask why he voluntarily returned to Harvard in 1911 merely (as he said) to study philosophy, or why he did not visit Europe again until 1914, when he planned to continue his study of philosophy not in Paris but in Marburg and Oxford.

We must also wonder why, when he remained in Cambridge, Massachusetts, between 1911 and 1914, Eliot became attached to Emily Hale, in a friendship which lasted until his second marriage, and which is documented by hundreds of letters now deposited in a university library.

Finally, we must wonder why Eliot-watchers have secured no other example of a homosexual liaison during the poet's long life.

Turning to *The Waste Land,* we meet the theory that the poem makes sense if we read it as the grief-stricken reflections of a poet recoiling from a catastrophic marriage to live over the pain of losing his lover years before. To suggest the fragility of Miller's reasoning, I shall examine one fundamental support. A section of the poem which seems crucial for Miller's theory is Part IV, "Death by Water," which in eight lines treats the death of a Phoenician sailor named Phlebas.

Although Miller has read the admirable essay on these lines by Grover Smith, he does not seem to have grasped Smith's implications. Miller supposes that the drowned sailor alludes to Verdenal and he takes the tone of the passage to be affirmative and sympathetic, associated with a key experience of the speaker's, which Miller calls "profoundly spiritual."[8] So he is puzzled by the similarity of "Death by Water" to a distasteful poem "Dirge," only published posthumously, in which Eliot describes the decay of a drowned Jew's corpse.

But in fact, a "Phoenician" for Eliot's generation meant not a hero but a Semitic trader. The opening lines of "Death by Water" echo a passage in William Morris's *Life and Death of Jason* (Book IV), in which the "bright-eyed Phoenician" is described as tempted by greed for pos-

8   Miller, *Eliot's Personal Waste Land,* 112.

sessions to risk his life in commerce until he "rolls beneath [the] waves" (lines 119–34).[9]

Eliot would have been familiar with Frederic Leighton's large painting, in the Royal Exchange, of Phoenicians trading with the early Britons. Here the Phoenicians look like caricatures of Jewish peddlers, and the Britons are depicted as uncorrupted pastoral types. It is with these associations that the poet appeals to both "Gentile [and] Jew" (*CP* 46) to consider the sailor's fate.

As Grover Smith pointed out, not only can "Phlebas" mean penis in Greek, but the phrase "profit and loss" connects the sailor's sexuality with commerce.[10] It would have been a curious tribute for Eliot to celebrate his dead friend through such innuendoes.

Those who seek biographical allusions might reflect that sailing was the one sport which Eliot ever mastered, and that the fortune-teller in *The Waste Land* assigns the drowned sailor's card to the poet himself. In *Prufrock*—written before Verdenal died—the speaker drowns metaphorically.

In general, Miller supports speculations about Eliot's character by forcing interpretations upon the poems, and bolsters interpretations of the poems by invoking speculations about his character. The circularity is not persuasive; and readers who find this path through *The Waste Land* enticing will find a more subtle guide in the old, more tentative essay by John Peter.

Derek Traversi's *T. S. Eliot: The Longer Poems* is a painstaking analysis of *Four Quartets* preceded by shorter but detailed analyses of *The Waste Land* and *Ash Wednesday*, which Traversi regards as leading up to the other poems. He refrains on principle from biographical comment, and similarly avoids didactic interpretations. He warns us not to assume that the speaker in the poems is Eliot himself, and not to raise the issue of the truth of the poet's doctrines. Traversi would like us to

9   *The Life and Death of Jason*, 10th ed. (London: Longman's, Green, 1902), 72.

10   Grover Smith, *The Waste Land* (London: George, Allen and Unwin, 1983), 106–10.

respond to the poems "as poetry," and this tends to mean Eliot's concept of poetry as expounded in his criticism.[11]

The result is a sober, cautious, unexciting series of analytical paraphrases staying close to the poet's text and tending to disclose coherence of design in the verse. Sometimes the summaries are elegantly clear and pointed, as in a paragraph on the setting of the great "terza rima" section of *Little Gidding,* II. Sometimes the comprehensive analyses gather many relevant points into a neat order as in the pages on the general structure of the *Quartets.* Rarely does one feel awakened by quite fresh insights.

The book moves too slowly for the understanding or appreciation it advances. Few new facts are produced; few cruxes of meaning are clarified. To illuminate some not very dark concepts, Traversi brings in long comparisons between Eliot and other writers, expecially Proust and Keats. But these are neither lively nor penetrating, and only seem to delay the unfolding of the argument.

When he turns away from personality, history, and problems of doctrine, Traversi is naturally drawn to imply that internal consistency deserves praise. Yet the search for coherent, purposeful design can also mislead a critic. For example, Traversi assumes that the headland in *The Dry Salvages,* Part I, is the same as the "promontory" in Part IV. But as it happens, the first is on the coast near Gloucester, Massachusetts; the other is at Marseilles. Here as so often, Eliot was seeking diversity. And besides, a coherent design is not necessarily a mark of literary value.

11　*Eliot: The Longer Poems,* 7.

6

ELIOT
II

 At the end of the year 1914, when T. S. Eliot was twenty-six and living in England, he wrote to a friend about the unpleasantness of meeting sexual opportunities in the street and feeling his own refinement rise up to obstruct them. Eliot thought he might be better off if he had lost his virginity some years earlier, and he contemplated disposing of it before marriage. At the same time, he thanked the friend for executing a commission. Writing from England, he had wanted roses delivered to Emily Hale, to celebrate her appearance in a play produced by the Cambridge (Massachusetts) Social Dramatic Club. In his next letter, Eliot wondered whether or not he should get married and sacrifice his independence for the sake of his children. We may conjecture that the poet was meditating marriage and had even begun considering a choice of spouse.

But an unpublished poem which he wrote about this time implies that virginity no longer troubled him. In the first stanza the poet describes himself as standing happily in the corner of a bedroom while a woman lies in bed. In a second and closing stanza, it is morning, the

This essay was first published 7 Dec. 1978 under the title "The Music of Suffering" as a review of Helen Gardner, *The Composition of Four Quartets* (London: Faber and Faber, 1978) and Donald Hall, *Remembering Poets: Reminiscences and Opinions* (New York: Harper and Row, 1978). Reprinted with permission from *The New York Review of Books*. Copyright © 1978 Nyrev, Inc.

woman is asleep, and the poet leaves by the window. The scene may be fantasy, and the date is not certain; but the poet speaks historically in the first person; the joyous mood and the details of the situation imply a quite satisfactory sexual encounter. Since Eliot met Vivien Haigh, his first wife, early in 1915 and married her (with no advance notice to his family) in June, we may speculate that the encounter altered his marital plans. The marriage was of course the disaster of his life.

Dame Helen Gardner, in her new, immensely rewarding book on *Four Quartets,* suggests that when Eliot visited New Hampshire in the spring of 1933, Emily Hale was with him. Dame Helen also reports that when Eliot went to Burnt Norton (Gloucestershire, England) in 1935, his companion was Emily Hale. The language and imagery of the poems "New Hampshire" and *Burnt Norton* make the link: springtime, a bird, children's voices in an orchard. "Twenty years and the spring is over" (*CP* 93), the poet says in "New Hampshire"—taking us back from 1933 to the last academic year he spent as a graduate student in Cambridge, Massachusetts. We know that in February 1913, when Eliot acted in a variety show at the Cambridge home of his cousin Eleanor, one of the other performers was Emily Hale.

The theme of *Burnt Norton* is the difference between the possible and the actual. Speaking in his mind to a nameless listener, the poet says,

> Footfalls echo in the memory
> Down the passage which we did not take
> Towards the door we never opened
> Into the rose-garden.   (I; *CP* 117)

The images evoke courtship, a romance that was unfulfilled.

In Part IV of *Burnt Norton* the poet asks, "Will the sunflower turn to us, will the clematis / Stray down, bend to us?" (*CP* 121). Dame Helen reports that Emily Hale paid long visits to England in 1934, 1935, and 1937, staying with Dr. and Mrs. Perkins, an aunt and uncle who rented a house in Gloucestershire. Eliot enjoyed weekends with them and wrote a poem (unpublished) mentioning the skill with which Mrs.

Perkins, a devoted gardener, "trimmed and trained and sprayed" her clematis. At the end of *Little Gidding*, in the final lines of *Four Quartets*, the "children in the apple-tree" reappear (*CP* 145), tying the whole work to "New Hampshire" and perhaps joining the spring of 1941 to that of 1913.

Such recurrent motifs illustrate a general principle, that Eliot wished his poems to start from deeply meaningful recollection. When he felt unhappy with Part II of *Little Gidding*, he said the defect of that whole poem was "the lack of some acute personal reminiscence"—which he then proceeded to supply with the amazing lines of the "gifts reserved for age" in Part II.[1] It was not that the poet expected a reader to fathom the private allusions; he simply wanted them to start the creative labor.

This need to have a deeply personal impulse nourish one's writing seems linked to the theme of suffering and its significance which rises so often in the *Quartets*. As early as 1914, Eliot was wondering about the emotional sources of creative inspiration. He thought that it required a certain kind of tranquillity but that the tranquillity might derive sometimes from deep or tragic suffering, which takes one away from oneself. When Dostoevsky was writing his masterpieces (Eliot said), he must have known such tranquillity.

Five years later, praising Dostoevsky for connecting his greatest "flights" (such as the final scene of *The Idiot*) with observed reality, Eliot said that Dostoevsky continued "the quotidian experience of the brain into seldom explored extremities of torture."[2] Most people, he remarked, "are too unconscious of their own suffering to suffer much"! For Eliot, I believe, the sympathetic imagination worked best when it extended itself to pain rather than pleasure.

In turn, the theme of suffering leads us to the shape of *Four Quartets*, because it recalls Beethoven's development. In 1931, writing to Stephen Spender about Beethoven's quartets, Eliot said, "There is a sort of heavenly or at least more than human gaiety about some of his later things

---

1   Eliot to John Hayward, quoted by Helen Gardner in *Composition of Four Quartets*, 67.

2   "Beyle and Balzac," *Athenaeum* 4648 (30 May 1919), 392.

which one imagines might come to oneself as the fruit of reconciliation and relief after immense suffering: I should like to get something of that into verse before I die." This principle became explicit in *The Dry Salvages:*

> Now, we come to discover that the moments of agony . . .
> . . . are likewise permanent
> With such permanence as time has. We appreciate this better
> In the agony of others, nearly experienced,
> Involving ourselves, than in our own.
> For our own past is covered by the currents of action,
> But the torment of others remains an experience
> Unqualified, unworn by subsequent attrition.
> People change, and smile: but the agony abides.   (II; *CP* 133)

Soon after he composed that searching passage, Eliot gave a lecture on the music of poetry. He spoke of recurrent themes, of developing a poetic motif as if by different groups of instruments, of transitions in a poem comparable to the movements of a symphony or a quartet, and of arranging subjects contrapuntally. Yet I suspect that these possibilities suggested themselves to him as means of handling dangerous emotions. The shape of *Four Quartets* might be described as musical, therefore, in the sense that it is Eliot's effort to match what he saw as Dostoevsky's or Beethoven's accomplishment. Indeed, we may omit the notion of music from the definition, as well as the name of Beethoven, and say Eliot tried to discover a form suitable for expressing his own sense of reconciliation and relief after immense suffering.

The design of the *Quartets* follows the hovering of the mind when it must deal with painful but ineluctable themes. There is a circling around the subject, avoiding direct confrontation but moving from one related theme to another. Then there is the yielding to acute emotion, absorption in the grief. Finally, there are the life-giving moments of distance or insight, the intermittent power to watch the suffering as if it were external, or to encompass it in a totality that endows it with meaning.

The alternation of meditative and lyric passages, the movement from darkness to illumination, the arbitrary recapitulation of a group of motifs already produced separately—even the way one theme unexpectedly breaks in on another—all suggest a person approaching and withdrawing from the direct experience of grief, pain, guilt, and insight.

This is why, in the poem, so many patterns are both established and defied, why they interrupt each other, why spring appears in midwinter, love in fire, why Krishna (rather than Christ) emerges forty lines after the "one Annunciation" (*Dry Salvages,* II; *CP* 132). Eliot has no rational account of the matter. He merely offers to share the enigmatic experience that in the midst of bewilderment we may receive unaccountable instruction from springs we cannot identify, that inconsolable grief can translate itself into acceptable peace. At the same time, the macrocosm keeps hinting at intention and design, while the patterns of mortal life remain imperfect. "Garlic and sapphires in the mud / Clot the bedded axle-tree" (*Burnt Norton* II; *CP* 118): the gross and subtle desires of humanity obscure the divine semblance of order.

Readers who try to find a consistent, progressive scheme in *Four Quartets* will therefore meet awkward roadblocks. The alternation of the seasons creates much of the imagery, tempting one to assign each set of poems to a particular season. *East Coker,* the second quartet, belongs quite explicitly to summer. Yet the lyric of Part IV of this sequence celebrates Good Friday. Again, if *East Coker* ties in with summer, its predecessor *Burnt Norton* should evoke the spring. Yet the images there are of summer or autumn—except perhaps for the lyric Part IV. *The Dry Salvages* in turn should bring autumn. Yet in Part I, this sequence has spring and winter as well, and the lyric of Part II deals with the Annunciation (March 25). *Little Gidding* begins in winter, but the meeting with the ghost (in Part IV) takes place in autumn, while the theme of Pentecost suggests spring. Thus the quartets as a group touch on the cycle of the year without neatly embodying it. They invite us to look for and to complete designs which draw us on and leave us waiting.

To the four elements, Eliot applies the same mode of welcome irregularity. In Part I of *Burnt Norton* we meet birds and "vibrant air"; Part III is dominated by cold wind, faded air. The most celebrated image of the sequence is, however, water momentarily filling the pool. Earth is certainly the focus of *East Coker,* and water of *The Dry Salvages.* But *Little Gidding* has all four elements openly employed in Part II; the land dominates Part III; and Part V is focused on fire (rather arbitrarily) only in the last three lines.

So also, as Dame Helen showed many years ago, the symbols of the poem are never consistent but keep altering their implications. The river in *The Dry Salvages* is sometimes the Mississippi, sometimes the river of time (as against the ocean of eternity), sometimes the river of human sin and suffering (as in Dante's *Inferno* XIV, 114–20). The fire of the *Quartets* means both purgation and love. The yew tree is both death and immortality.

The most challenging and experimental technique is the arbitrary interruption of one theme by another, one mood by another, the meditative abstract thought by the concrete memory:

> The Sea has many voices,
> Many gods and many voices.
> The salt is on the briar rose,
> The fog is in the fir trees.   (*The Dry Salvages,* I; *CP* 130–31)

If the poem invites us to participate in these modulations, it also suggests a give and take between various aspects of the poet. Just as Beethoven divided himself up among the voices of his instruments, just as we hear his fears and hopes reply to one another, so also in Eliot's quartets the older poet often speaks to the younger, the doubting to the faithful, and the restless poet to the rooted. A friend questioned Eliot's listing of psychoanalysis among "usual" methods of fortune-telling (*Dry Salvages,* V; *CP* 135), but the poet made no response. I think the reason is that a quarter-century earlier, psychoanalysis had attracted Eliot, and he recommended it as a promising advance in individual psychology. The object of the irony in that passage was himself in his late twenties.

Finally, the transmutations and interruptions of the poetic technique suggest the intersections that Eliot keeps before us, of eternity and time, of spirit and place. The arbitrariness of the Incarnation is like the arbitrariness of the movement of the poem. Why now and not sooner, why here and not elsewhere, why this world and not another? Any cosmology must face these questions, and a man may ask them of himself at any moment.

The limits of space and time present the furious imagination with a constant challenge. Our conceptions of the possibilities of life soar tragically beyond the conditions of mere existence. When Eliot (in 1919) spoke of great novelists as driven into art by "the inevitable inadequacy of actual living to the passionate capacity," he revealed his own character. When he spoke of "the awful separation between potential passion and any actualization possible in life," he pointed to the ultimate source of power of *Four Quartets.*

To anybody not fond of historical scholarship, or uncomfortable with the apparatus of textual studies, the fascination of Helen Gardner's splendid book may be less than obvious. It is an account of how Eliot came to write *Four Quartets.* Dame Helen examines the source of the *Quartets* in his experience and memories, in the poems or prose of earlier authors, and in the comments of friends to whom he showed the work in progress. Her material includes transcriptions of the manuscripts and typescripts of the poems at various stages of their development—those drafts which have been preserved; and she records, in meticulous footnotes, the differences between the final text and the earlier stages.

On many of these variant readings, Dame Helen offers illuminating remarks, often showing how they clarify the meaning or form of the poems. In the course of her discussions, she also gives extracts of unpublished letters, of the greatest interest, from Eliot, John Hayward, and others. Because Hayward acted the parts of midwife and nurse to the emerging creations, Dame Helen pays special attention to his contribution and provides some details of his remarkable character and life.

From the book, therefore, one learns about Eliot's personality and his psychology of composition, as well as about the poems. The reason is, as Dame Helen says, that so much of the material came out of his life. We had known of Eliot's visits to Burnt Norton, East Coker, and Little Gidding. We had learned that the Dry Salvages were visible from his family's summer home, and that he used to sail around them. We had found out that the "place of disaffection" in *Burnt Norton* was the London system of underground trains, and especially the Gloucester Road station, also that the "ash on an old man's sleeve" in Part II of *Little Gidding* was the dust settling after an air raid.

Now we gain other controls over our speculations. Dame Helen informs us that Eliot did not know the early history of Burnt Norton, or how its name originated in a hideous act of arson. She warns us that the kingfisher which might seem to appear on the grounds of the estate was in fact seen elsewhere. She shows how much of Yeats belonged to the conception of the ghost in *Little Gidding,* Part II.

A common habit of interpreters has been to trace Eliot's literary allusions back to their original setting and to explain the meaning of obscure lines by referring to those contexts. Even for *The Waste Land,* which invited such treatment, the method has proved as much a curse as a blessing. For the *Quartets,* as Dame Helen argued long ago, the method is generally unwanted. Now she carefully distinguishes the few deliberate allusions, which invite the reader to ponder the context of the source, from the many echoes and imitations that Eliot used unconsciously or because the phrase satisfied his ear—or else because an image seemed evocative without regard to its original function.

She offers abundant instances of echoes and allusions which the poems do not ask us to recognize. At one extreme is a phrase that reverberates for the poet but not for his readers: the injunction, "Not fare well, / But fare forward," in *The Dry Salvages* (III; *CP* 135). Eliot thought he remembered this from the words of a sibyl to Alaric the Visigoth (on his way to Rome); but no scholar has been able to trace it to a literary text.

At the other extreme are words which an ardent reader can over-interpret. One instance is "laceration" in *Little Gidding* (II; *CP* 142), which echoes Swift's epitaph. Since the speaker at this point is a composite of Eliot himself and of poets he admired, one might easily infer that the word discloses an extraordinary interest of Eliot in Swift. But on the one hand, "laceration" was John Hayward's suggestion, accepted by Eliot; and on the other hand, Eliot said the word made him think not of Swift but of Yeats's famous translation of the epitaph.

❋ Unfortunately, Dame Helen herself tries to interpret a crucial passage on the basis of allusions and their context. This is the lyric in Part IV of *East Coker,* "The wounded surgeon plies the steel." In the third stanza, Eliot describes the earth as a hospital endowed by a "ruined millionaire" (*CP* 127–28). Raymond Prestion identified the millionaire as Adam, having got the fact from Eliot himself; and John Hayward made the same identification. But in her book *The Art of T. S. Eliot,* Dame Helen argued that all the figures in the lyric (the surgeon, the nurse, and the millionaire) were types of Christ.

Now she points out that in his notes for the poem, Eliot started with the expression "bankrupt banker" and then changed the word to "millionaire." She declares that the collocation of "banker" and "millionaire" recalls Gide's fable *Le Promethée mal enchaîné,* which we know Eliot read; and from that position she argues that the millionaire, like the banker "Zeus" in the fable, would represent a divine being rather than a mortal creature.

The reasoning does not seem persuasive. The association of a millionaire with banking and philanthropy is natural enough. In Eliot's review of *The Education of Henry Adams,* one finds bankers, millionaires, and philanthropy within the breadth of four paragraphs. The notes for Eliot's lyric do not necessarily recall Gide's story; and if they did so for the poet, he surely discouraged the reader from making the connection. In the lyric itself the changes in point of view from stanza to stanza hardly invite us to treat the three persons as one; and although Dame Helen observes that "ruined" can mean impoverished by generosity, the epithet suits Adam better than his savior.

Among the few oversights in the book is a lack of reference to the first New York edition of the *Quartets.* Since this antedates the London edition by almost a year and a half, it represents a distinct stage in the history of the text. I shall give three examples of what I mean.

A flaw in the text of the poems has been the position of the Greek epigraphs to *Burnt Norton*. The first London edition had them set on the reverse of the table of contents, as if they belonged to all four poems. Dame Helen does not observe that in the New York edition they were correctly placed under the half-title of *Burnt Norton*.

In *Burnt Norton*, line 51, the poet changed his mind between "appeasing" and "reconciles." Dame Helen reviews the changes back and forth, with possible reasons for the final choice of "appeasing" in the London edition. Readers following the analysis might like to know that Eliot preserved "reconciles" so late as the New York text.

In *East Coker*, Dame Helen points out that a meaningful space existed between lines 128 and 129 in all the extant drafts and in the first periodical publication. But the space disappeared in the pamphlet publication and in the first London edition of the *Quartets*, because line 128 then came at the foot of a page. Dame Helen wonders whether or not Eliot accepted the accident of the printing as an improvement. Surely, then, it is worth recording that in the New York edition, the space is kept.

All in all, there are at least nine certain or highly probable errors of spacing, punctuation, spelling, or language in the separate edition of *Four Quartets* now published by Harcourt Brace Jovanovich. By far the most striking is a whole line which the printers apparently dropped from *Little Gidding*, and which Dame Helen has miraculously rescued. It should follow line 19, and it reads, "Summer beyond sense, the inapprehensible."

> Now the hedgerow
> Is blanched for an hour with transitory blossom
> Of snow, a bloom more sudden
> Than that of summer, neither budding nor fading,
> Not in the scheme of generation.
> Where is the summer, the unimaginable
> Summer beyond sense, the inapprehensible
> Zero summer? (*Little Gidding* I; CP 138)

If biography is peripheral to the critical scholarship of Helen Gardner, it is central to Donald Hall's *Remembering Poets*. His book is mainly a gathering of well-told anecdotes about the author's relations with Frost, Pound, Eliot, and Dylan Thomas. Hall deserves praise for the care he has taken to verify his information, to be accurate, to complete stories of which he knew only a part at first hand. The care is visible everywhere but most attractively in the author's frankness about himself. The refusal to cover up his blunders deepens the appeal and the humor of the narrative. His good nature and appreciativeness give it coherence. Readers in general, and young readers in particular, who hesitate to dip into poetry of any sort will find themselves reaching for works of Hall's subjects as they yield to the charm of his voice.

That they will discover much about the poetry itself is less certain. Hall is aware of the limitations of his approach, and insists that one must not confuse the personality of the genius with his work. Yet for all his experience as a poet, Hall rarely shows much penetration or independent judgment when he acts as a critic. Biography is an efficient method of getting into the meaning and shape of works of art so long as the biographer is obsessed with the creative imagination of his subject.

Naturally, the characters of his four poets fascinate Hall and infuse drama into his accounts of them. We hear Dylan Thomas talk about Yeats; we observe the competitiveness of Frost; we see Eliot reluctantly shaking hands with Oscar Williams; and we learn about the obstacles Hall met when he tried to get lecture engagements for Pound in America. Some of the anecdotes move one deeply, like the report of Thomas planning to give up poetry for prose because he could make more money from prose. One also learns much from Hall about the career of a poet in our time—the mechanical, financial, and emotional problems of winning the attention of deafened ears.

But the paragraphs of comment on individual poems, of judgments about the oeuvre of a poet, or of generalization about the art of poetry are not incisive enough. The psychological and moral observations are more often honest than profound. Hall's notions about the relation of culture to society seldom enlighten one—for example, his speculation that if Thomas had lived in a society which "valued life over death," he might not have drunk himself into disaster.

For readers concerned with poetry itself, the most absorbing parts of the book will be the interviews with Eliot and Pound, which have been published before. But scrupulous as they are, these in turn remain less than they might appear to be. They bring us (as the whole book does) the speech of men at the end of their careers. Even the sympathy and intelligence of Mr. Hall cannot transform them into the young, creative innovators whom we yearn to know.

Besides, these men had already put their self-portraits on public display, and consciously or not were preserving them while answering Hall's questions (as he perfectly realized). Finally, they had fallible memories. Eliot told Hall that he had sold the manuscripts of *The Waste Land* to John Quinn. In fact, we know from the correspondence published by Valerie Eliot in her edition that Eliot refused to sell those manuscripts to his benefactor and insisted on making him a present of them. It was other manuscripts that Quinn succeeded in buying from Eliot.

7

ELIOT
III

Among T. S. Eliot's friendships, the longest-lived attachment to a woman was his connection with Emily Hale (daughter of a Bostonian architect who was also a minister), which began when he was a student at Harvard. Miss Hale (1891–1969) became a teacher of speech and drama, and the pair met during the 1930s in America and England. For decades, Eliot wrote to the lady often and regularly, but the correspondence ended in the late 1950s, when he married Valerie Fletcher. Miss Hale gave her friend's letters to Princeton University, stipulating that they remain sealed until the year 2020.

In a new account of Eliot's career as a poet, Ronald Bush offers some piquant reflections on the correspondence:

> [These letters] were undoubtedly full of pointed silences. The letters, however, also must have resonated with that special kind of indulgent tenderness that two people assume when they can be attentive without deception. Yet that kind of tenderness has its dangers. For someone suffering the pains of a marriage like Eliot's, the mannered intimacy of such letters can

This essay was first published 28 June 1984 under the title "Art, Life, and T. S. Eliot" as a review of Ronald Bush, *T. S. Eliot: A Study in Character and Style* (New York: Oxford Univ. Press, 1984). Reprinted with permission from *The New York Review of Books*. Copyright © 1984 Nyrev, Inc.

come to acquire the allure of a fantom that seems to need only a little extra attention to make it come alive. That feeling or something like it seems to have impressed itself on Eliot after he broke with Vivien in America. (185)

Bush says that Emily Hale's meetings with Eliot during the years 1932–35 forced him to "confront one of his most firmly repressed wishes. . . . [She] beckoned him to start over again, and the thought intoxicated him" (185–86). Bush reminds us that the couple visited Burnt Norton together; and he then examines the poem *Burnt Norton* as a meditation on the longings aroused in the poet by the moments in the deserted garden.

Obviously, that garden seemed to Eliot a poignant symbol of the life he had missed; the title asks us to make the bridge. For those who have learned about the presence of Emily Hale in the scene, it is hard to exclude her from the story of the making of the poem. But nowhere in the verses do we meet the least allusion to the lady or the least need to think of her.

Bush's opinions are not a contribution to the biography of the poet and not an illumination of the poem. They excite an interest in Eliot's emotional development like that excited by the play *Tom and Viv,* which has been darkening the London stage. Yet Bush follows his suggestive introduction to *Burnt Norton* with a twenty-page analysis of the poem in which Emily Hale never appears.

The effect is a ubiquitous feature of literary biography. By demonstrating a mastery of the data of an artist's life, by first stimulating and then satisfying our natural curiosity, the scholar seems to validate his authority to interpret and appraise the accomplishment of genius. Nevertheless, it is one mark of genius that the work transcends the circumstances of the life. The most detailed familiarity with a poet as son, husband, and father need not equip one to judge his poems—too many widows' memoirs tell us as much. Data do not speak until they are spoken to; and if one asks the wrong questions, one hears pointless replies.

Biography can indeed eliminate certain mistakes—particularly those which depend on false chronology. It can establish links and make certain influences probable. It can trace the stages of composition of a poem and teach us which texts are authentic. However, it will positively elucidate the works of an artist only to the extent that they invite one to incorporate biographical allusions into their meaning.

The poet himself is simply one more reader when he tries to establish the merits of his work; and any explanations he may offer must be tested by independent study. Eliot has sometimes been proved wrong when he tried to correct the errors of his readers, and the tales he tells of his own development can rarely be accepted without emendation.

In offering this doctrine, I do not underestimate Bush's admirable research. He succeeds a number of careful scholars who have drawn more and more fully on Eliot's unpublished letters and drafts of poems. F. O. Matthiessen, Elizabeth Schneider, Helen Gardner, and A. D. Moody are among those who have commented scrupulously on the poems with the advantage of fresh information about their composition. Nobody has been more energetic than Bush.

Although he sensibly quotes many passages that his predecessors have used, he has mastered a corpus that most critics barely touch. Bush has gone through all the published material, including quantities of early reviews and miscellaneous essays that have never been collected. One example of his thoroughness is an unsigned, brief notice published in *The Criterion* (1936), which bears the marks of Eliot's style and was certainly passed by him as editor. Bush quotes it in relation to the moral claims of the poet in *Little Gidding*.

The writer of the short review deprecates a book that carefully documents the treatment of German Jews by the Nazis. He calls it "an attempt to rouse moral indignation by means of sensationalism." He complains that while the jacket of the book speaks of the "extermination" of the Jews, the title page refers only to their "persecution." He declares that "as the title-page is to the jacket, so are the contents to the title-page, especially in the chapter devoted to the ill-treatment of Jews in German concentration camps" (Bush 226). I agree with Bush's attribution of the review to Eliot, and I agree that it is a frightening sign of what Christian charity meant to the author of *Four Quartets.*

Instead of reviewing familiar judgments and accepting standard biographical matter, Bush has won access to unpublished letters and lectures. He has analyzed drafts of well-known and unknown poems that must be searched out in the special collections of great research libraries. He seems at home in French literature to a degree that lets him examine the influence of authors like Valéry and St.-John Perse upon the style of Eliot.

However, the application of so much learning raises issues that the scholar never resolves. When a poet endures a troubled life, is his talent part of the illness, or is it his spring of health? Reaching, for themes and images, into his most intense and profound experience, does the poet reflect the sufferings that he peculiarly endures, or does he give body to intuitions shared by all suffering men? If a poet is a critic and his doctrine reflects the development of his poems, may we simply use them to illustrate his doctrine? Or shall we say that criticism is a literary genre too; and when a poet speaks as a critic, he does not expose the peculiar features of his own work but deals with those questions which criticism sets before its practitioners?

Many of Bush's pronouncements on Eliot's character are obtrusive, unnecessary, and fashionable. He divides the poet's identity between the life of spontaneous feeling which—we are assured—Eliot yearned for, and the "intellectual and puritanical rationalism" which Eliot allegedly linked to the New England tradition of his upbringing (8–9). Then Bush says that the sarcasm of Eliot's first wife used to strike at "Eliot's New England self and not its emotional antagonists," with the consequence that "her disapproval was soon compounded with his mother's, threatening both parts of Eliot's delicate equilibrium" (54).

This sort of easy Freudian psychology is the language of our time. But to make it precise and demonstrable would call for evidence that Eliot himself could not provide. If the poet does reveal a division between conscience and feeling, we can surely rest in the fact and not justify it with an explanation derived from psychoanalytic commonplaces. Does one gain an insight by attributing to Eliot an Oedipal conflict that one takes to be every man's burden?

Excellent poets have been learned scholars—Milton and Johnson, for example. Some have been great critics as well—Goethe and Schiller (and Johnson again), for example. But the final challenge for such a writer is not to produce a work that glistens with erudition and is, as Gray said, "vocal to the intelligent alone." It is to make something like an "Elegy Written in a Country Churchyard," which seems to rise from the abyss of the human soul and speak to the universal condition of men. Such poetry rests on the words and ideas of earlier authors—is indeed validated by them—but does not luxuriously display its origins.

Eliot, as Bush makes clear, had such ambitions. He was even more aspiring than Housman and Browning; for he hoped to draw on depths of unconscious feelings or intuitions that normally resist the creative imagination. Like Freud, he was willing to experiment on himself. He tried to feel his way back to his most dangerous emotions and to secure from them the energy that, concentrated in language subtly echoing earlier masters, would call up new, profound responses from the reader.

For an acutely self-conscious critic, at home in several national literatures and learned in philosophy, to grope his way below these difficult accomplishments and bring up essences that had hardly been recognized by psychologists, then to embody these in unforgettable speech, is a triumph enjoyed by no more than two or three poets in a century. Bush demonstrates that when Eliot called for impersonal poetry, he meant poetry that should express the common, deepest nature of men rather than the peculiar experiences of the author as a troubled son or lover.

I take seriously Eliot's distinction between the man who suffers and the mind that creates ("Tradition and the Individual Talent," II). I am willing to go a good deal of the way with Nietzschean aesthetics, and to say that when Eliot explores his deepest sensations for the images and sounds of his most powerful verse, he was not examining the self apart—the ego that goes to the dentist or that gives instructions to a secretary. Rather, I think he tried to reach for a self, or a level of self, that shares the definitive experiences of mankind. From this healthy, creative depth he tried to bring up figures, metaphors, that would seem, to responsive readers, to evoke their own inner life. Failure was a chronic danger. But success would be unforgettable.

The theory Eliot worked on may have been unsound. However, if I am correct, it involved a contract with the reader such that the powerful images would not invite an inspection of the poet's domestic or social relations but of the reader's archetypal world. The critic who violates this contract may indeed match the verse motifs to elements of the poet's observable life, but only by reducing Eliot to his noncreative, dental-chair self.

Bush's use of biography is a risky procedure. We know a bit too much and far too little about what went on, hideously, between Eliot and his first wife, Vivien. But I cannot think the guilt-ridden poet simply picked out speeches and gestures from those painful relations and fitted them into measured words. Whoever connects a motif of Eliot's poems with an aspect of Vivien must remember how many aspects he is ignorant of, and must wonder how the connections would look if he had more aspects to choose from.

It is a disaster to encourage readers to search for the specific private histories behind the published works, as if Eliot were Pope or Byron. We are told reliably that in the years 1934–36, Eliot's secretary at Faber and Faber had instructions (from other secretaries) to let her employer know when his wife was in the waiting room. The girl would do so by the office telephone, and Eliot would thank her. She would then go down to Mrs. Eliot and explain that her husband could not see her but that he was well. Meanwhile, the poet would leave the building.

The secretary reports, "She was a slight, pathetic, worried figure, badly dressed and very unhappy, her hands screwing up her handkerchief as she wept. It was a sad contrast from her busy, interested husband. . . . When I thought he had had enough time to get out, depending on what he was doing, I would try to bring the interview with Mrs. Eliot to an end. For the rest of the day Eliot would be on edge, talking even more slowly and hesitantly than usual, and we would keep our mutual contacts to a minimum."[1]

This disheartening glimpse of Vivien Eliot corroborates the account given by Robert Sencourt,[2] and it could be linked to several passages from *Four Quartets,* such as the lines on the permanence of moments of agony:

> We appreciate this better
> In the agony of others, nearly experienced,
> Involving ourselves, than in our own.
> For our own past is covered by the currents of action,
> But the torment of others remains an experience
> Unqualified, unworn by subsequent attrition.
> People change, and smile; but the agony abides.
>
> (*The Dry Salvages,* II; *CP* 133)

If an elderly friend of mine reads the poem and remembers hearing her child shriek under the pain of an illness the mother could not relieve, shall I tell her to think of Mrs. Eliot?

In his continual appeals to literary allusion, Bush follows another risky procedure. Learned critics, during the last fifty years, have shared the regrettable habit of imposing coherent meaning on a writer's work by discovering a common doctrine in various uses of the same image. When Wallace Stevens presents a guitarist in a series of poems, or Jane Austen presents a woman playing a piano in a series of novels, the critic assumes that the guitar or the piano has a stable implication. Yet the author may deliberately or playfully vary the significance of the image. I believe that Eliot strove to make the whole body of his work cohere by drawing on the same images in different poems while altering the implications as Yeats altered those of Byzantium.

---

1   From a memoir by Brigid O'Donovan, published in *Confrontation,* ed. Martin Tucker (Long Island Univ. Press), Fall/Winter 1975; quoted in *TLS,* 30 Mar. 1984, 345.

2   *T. S. Eliot: A Memoir* (New York: Delta, 1973), 173.

Bush takes the standard analytical approach for granted. We meet mysterious presences, "they," in *Burnt Norton;* and we meet others, also "they," in *The Family Reunion.* Yet in the play, "they" are the Eumenides, who frighten Harry; but in the poem, "they" are welcome "guests, accepted and accepting" (*CP* 118). So also there are "footfalls" in *Burnt Norton* as in other works by Eliot; but to give them "ominous associations" because of the use of "footfalls" in "Gerontion" or *The Family Reunion* is to simplify Eliot's genius (Bush 193).

With learned allusions the habit of simplified interpretation is commonplace. Innocent critics keep assuming that when a poet incorporates lines by another author into his own text, he must also invoke the teachings of that author, recommending or (often) ironically opposing them. Readers of *East Coker* meet verses on the midsummer dancing of villagers centuries ago:

> The association of man and woman
> In daunsinge, signifying matrimonie—
> A dignified and commodious sacrament.   (I; *CP* 124)

The spelling reminds us that such ceremonies join our sense of harmonious community with that of our ancestors, for the words are taken from those of an early Tudor writer on education, the humanist Sir Thomas Elyot.

A. D. Moody objected to the ordinary view that the tone of T. S. Eliot's lines is sympathetic.[3] Moody says the dance here is a dance of death, and he observes that the rhythm of the whole passage (over twenty lines) eventually turns leaden:

> The time of the coupling of man and woman
> And that of beasts. Feet rising and falling.
> Eating and drinking. Dung and death.   (*CP* 124)

Moody points out that in Sir Thomas's full exposition of the value of dancing, the Tudor humanist describes the nature of men and women

---

3   *Thomas Stearns Eliot: Poet* (Cambridge Univ. Press, 1979).

in terms that T. S. Eliot must have rejected. Moody quotes from the poet's essay on Dante to show that for the author of *East Coker* the love of man and woman is only made reasonable by a higher love, that of God; or else it is "simply the coupling of animals"[4] (Moody 208–11).

Bush treats Moody's case as valid. He adds to the echoes of Sir Thomas Elyot the echoes of a German story about a town accursed. He also invokes the "mood of Ecclesiastes" (Bush, 212–13).

Alas, the numberless critics who perform in this style are following the practice of numberless mentors. Yet one might challenge the principle that allusions point to meanings. The lines actually employed by Eliot state that the ceremonial dancing of men and women together symbolizes the sacrament of marriage—hardly a dangerous proposition. The poet never calls on us to identify the echoes of Sir Thomas or to trace them to their source—let alone their context—but only to notice that the words are old. The poem nowhere directs us to Gerstarker's tale of Germelshausen; and the Book of Ecclesiastes (echoed earlier in *East Coker,* I; ["Houses live and die . . .]) has many meanings.

Eliot's change in tone from the lines on dancing to the lines on death suggests an enlargement of the rhythms of a human ceremony into those of life in general and then (as the day begins) into those of the whole universe. The change suggests a rueful reflection that harmonious communities must submit to the same earthly doom as other living bodies; and one may infer that under the aspect of eternity, the poet recommends a higher, spiritual order, the order of grace.

I linger over this example because it stands for thousands of exercises by less erudite, less thoughtful scholars than Bush. Eliot characteristically presents first an impression or a sentiment, next stands back from it with a distancing commentary, and then reflects on the commentary. The movement is a seductive imitation of a universal process: immediate sensation (unthinking, transcending selfhood), followed by conscious perception placing the experience in the context

---

4   T. S. Eliot, *Selected Essays* (New York: Harcourt, Brace, & World, 1932), 235.

of individual personality, followed by a response to the perception, a pondering of the response, and so forth. Eliot's poems typically leave us unsure who is speaking to whom and where the poet stands. It is the degrees and shifts of intuition, perception, consciousness, and self-consciousness that fascinate the poet.

Critics who interpret an earlier stage of the process by a later one are reducing the living process to a flat exposition of a stable point of view. If dancers who symbolize the sacrament of marriage must finally turn to earth, are we to make the sacrament itself equivalent to defecation? When Eliot rhymes "mirth" with "earth," are we to ignore Ecclesiastes 8:15, "Then I commended mirth"? Are we to ignore "There is nothing better, than that a man should rejoice in his own works" (Ecclesiastes 3:22)?

No allusion can explain a passage unless the passage urges us to recall it. Even then, when we collect allusions, we still have the job of interpreting them in turn, and at last of reconciling them. A critic who invokes an essay on a Roman Catholic Italian to illuminate verses by a Protestant American expatriate has enough to do without further adducing texts from German fiction and the Hebrew Old Testament.

Unfortunately, when Bush falls back on his independent powers of interpretation, he is often unpersuasive. Sometimes he subscribes to the genetic fallacy and explains a line in terms of a canceled reading. Sometimes he ignores the tone of a passage while searching out parallels with other works. As an example of the difficulties which he repeatedly makes for the reader, I shall take one of the shorter, widely admired poems, "Marina" (*CP* 72–73).

Here Eliot openly alludes to Shakespeare's *Pericles* and recalls the wondering joy of the father on finally recognizing the daughter he had thought was lost forever. The poem opens and closes with images of seas, islands, shores, along with the sound of a woodthrush. The stunned father thinks of a rotting boat that seems to stand for his decaying self, now apparently redeemed by the daughter's grace. In eight parallel lines he produces contrasting images to suggest vices that (I assume) no longer endanger the father.

Bush characteristically attributes to the poem meanings seldom indicated by earlier critics; he supports them with the evidence of allusions and echoes, but then turns his analysis in surprising directions that seem to weaken any coherence his interpretation might have. (One could make similar remarks about his treatment of *The Waste Land, Ash Wednesday,* and other major works.)

For example, Bush disagrees with the view that the poem is "simply" a moment of serenity and transfiguration. Rather, he says, it "presents the feeling of a man in the process of dying to one life and unable to be born in another" (167). The images repeated at the end of the poem—the islands, woodthrush, etc.—suggest, according to Bush, "an ominous premonition of what the submission [i.e., the resignation of the old life for the new] will cost him." Here he agrees with A. D. Moody's impression that the images of the final lines carry "a sense of menace" (Moody 156).

In the poem, the speaker says that certain figures (those for the temptations that his daughter has escaped and that the speaker can at last transcend) are now "unsubstantial . . . / By this grace dissolved in place." Bush has another view. He says that the speaker's recognition of his daughter "corresponds to a sudden assurance of the solidity of the world outside himself." The speaker's "diseased self-consciousness" is dissolved.

Yet Bush also finds that Eliot here "invests the experience of rebirth with poetic authority"; the poet, he says, "finds a way to fuse eros and agape" (168). I suppose these various attitudes to the poem can be reconciled. But I do not easily reconcile them.

The tone of the poem seems less wavering to me. Of itself the particularized boat appears a frail but fortunate vessel. It might suggest the ferry that plies between life and death. Since the speaker says wonderingly, "I made this," and closely mingles references to the daughter (not particularized) and to the boat, his words might suggest creativity as the common feature. One's rescue may come through what one has created or procreated. The child can save the parent who made and lost her. For a poet, the dwindling resources of art, like a decaying boat, may suffice to carry him into a haven: out of the anxieties of a broken life he may build a redeeming poem.

Without pressing such hints, I only worry that the data Bush has so imaginatively assembled may have turned his attention away from matters near at hand. If one wants allusions, one could observe that in "Marina" the eight lines on vices are rich in words from *Pericles*. "Style" is the word that Shakespeare's Marina uses for the brothel from which she escapes unharmed (IV, vi, 90). Eliot's line depreciating those who "sharpen the tooth of the dog" is associated by Bush with "diseased self-consciousness"; yet in Shakespeare's play, "So sharp are hunger's teeth" refers to the famine that followed gluttony in Tharsus, and to parents eating children (I,iv,44–45). There is also of course the tag from *Lear* on filial ingratitude (I,iv,310), here ironically appropriate.

It would be tedious to go any further with analyses that can never be demonstrations. But if biography seems livelier than such an inquiry, one must realize that it too remains controversial. Bush quotes Bertrand Russell's impression of Vivien Eliot shortly after her marriage (54), and does not offer to qualify it. Yet we now know that Russell ended up making love to Vivien; and we also know Lady Ottoline Morrell thought Russell was "obviously interested" in Vivien the first time she saw them together.[5] Since Lady Ottoline had been Russell's mistress, her own judgment was not impartial. Bush too often relies on such witnesses and too seldom questions them. Ultimately, therefore, his whole account of Eliot depends on facts that need a more skeptical examination than he has given them.

5   Robert H. Bell, "Bertrand Russell and the Eliots," *The American Scholar,* Summer 1983, 315–17.

8

WARREN
I

In 1811 a nephew of Thomas Jefferson nearly chopped off the head of a young slave named George. The seventeen-year-old boy had broken a pitcher belonging (we are told) to the deceased mother of his master, Lilburne Lewis. The drunken master, with the help of his own brother Isham, dragged George into the kitchen cabin, tied him down, and assembled the other slaves to witness the punishment that followed. Then Lilburne sank an axe into George's neck, killing and almost decapitating him.

He forced one of the black men to dismember the body with the same axe. The pieces were thrown into the fireplace, where roaring flames had been built up. Lilburne Lewis warned the slaves to tell nobody what had happened.

At two o'clock the next morning a violent earthquake struck the region of western Kentucky where the Lewises lived. The chimney of the kitchen cabin fell down, smothering the fire and halting the process of cremation. Lilburne had the slaves rebuild the chimney and fireplace, hiding the fragments of George's body in the masonry. But the quakes

This essay was first published 11 Feb. 1980 under the title "The Long and Short of It" as a review of Robert Penn Warren, *Brother to Dragons: A Tale in Verse and Voices (A New Version)* (New York: Random House, 1979) and *Now and Then: Poems 1976–78* (New York: Random House, 1978). Reprinted with permission from *The New York Review of Books*. Copyright © 1980 Nyrev, Inc.

continued, exposing the remains; and a dog carried off the head, to gnaw on it until a neighbor noticed and turned the skull over to officers of the law.

Three months after the crime, the grand jury indicted Lilburne and Isham Lewis for murder; but both men were admitted to bail while awaiting trial. Three weeks later, in keeping with a pact they had made, the two brothers went to a graveyard intending to shoot one another. Lilburne showed Isham how to commit suicide if the flintlock misfired, but he accidently shot and killed himself during the lesson. Isham left the graveyard and was jailed two days later as accessory to his brother's self-murder. But he escaped, and we do not know what became of him.

My story of these events is taken from the handsomely documented and well-told account by Boynton Merrill, Jr., in his book *Jefferson's Nephews*. Mr. Merrill asks what Jefferson knew or said about the monstrosities of his sister's children, and he tells us, "No evidence has been discovered . . . that Jefferson ever wrote or spoke a word directly concerning this crime, or that it changed his life or attitudes."[1]

In 1953 Robert Penn Warren published *Brother to Dragons,* a narrative poem based on the crimes I have reviewed. He organized it as a dialogue of disembodied voices conversing long after the event, in an unspecified place. Instead of making the incidents themselves the substance of his poem, Warren treated those as starting a debate on "the human condition," particularly the extent of men's innate virtue or depravity.[2] To suit his plan, he not only altered some of the facts; he not only added some fictitious characters; but he also planted himself and Thomas Jefferson in the poem, giving these outsiders many long speeches. Warren has now carefully revised and shortened *Brother to Dragons* for a new publication, altering many details, reassigning speeches, breaking up long lines, and giving the verse a drier texture.

1   Boynton Merrill, Jr., *Jefferson's Nephews: A Frontier Tragedy* (Princeton: Princeton Univ. Press, 1976), 327.

2   *Brother to Dragons,* xiii.

In Warren's telling, although the sickening episodes emerge gradually from the give and take of the speakers, the element of suspense seems weak; and a reader unfamiliar with the story would not gather it easily from the poet's presentation. Warren diversifies the main line of his narrative with other ingredients: memories of his own research into the historical evidence, fictitious incidents of sexual passion and family tension, monologues in which real and imaginary persons tell us about their feelings of love and guilt. We hear Lilburne's wife recall the stages of her courtship and marriage, and the sexual abuse practiced on her by Lilburne. We hear Meriwether Lewis review his exploration of the northwest territories and supply graphic details of his suicide.

Such secondary narratives, mainly fictitious, illustrate the depravity of human nature. Warren attributes the death wish of Meriwether Lewis, for example, to the failure of the optimistic philosophy which Jefferson supposedly taught him. The other autobiographical speeches lead us in the same direction.

In the choral commentary of the poet's dialogues with Jefferson, Warren suggests that we are all responsible for the mischief done by any one of us; the victim of evil, however weak and vulnerable he may be, participates in the beastly motivations which lead to his destruction, and so does the righteous denouncer of the crime. Jefferson himself, we are told, shared the potentiality for evil which his nephew realized in action. Unfortunately, this doctrine transpires in such a way as to darken Jefferson's character and to brighten Warren's. It is hard for one not to feel that the author takes advantage of his place as inventor of the fiction when he assigns to Jefferson a less perceptive morality than that of the poet who confronts him.

One may ask as well whether a plain historical account, even in my few words, is not more absorbing than Warren's self-indulgent, highly reflexive work. It would take a most dramatic discussion of the problem of original sin to hold us better than a bare chain of startling but true events. Warren composed the poem in flexible, varied free verse, often approximately blank verse. Is the poetic element attractive enough to carry us over the difficulties of Warren's theme?

If we do listen to the verse, we find that the poet's style is more lyrical, descriptive, or reflective than narrative, dramatic, or discursive. When he remembers a landscape or evokes passionate love, Warren's poetic energies seem more deeply engaged than when he rehearses a story or produces moral arguments. His speakers often sound alike, or they talk out of character. They are given to clichés of language or sentiment. Consequently, the ingredients which ought most to please us receive inadequate support from Warren's style. As for the lyrical and descriptive passages themselves, one may judge their freshness and power from a specimen on the coming of spring:

> The red-bud shall order forth its flame at the
>   incitement of sun.
> The maple shall offer its golden wings for the
>   incitement of air.
> Powder of oak-bloom shall prank golden the deerskin
>   shirt
> Of the woodsman, like fable. Gleaming and wind-tossed,
>   the raw
> Conclamation of crows shall exult from the swale-edge.
> The redbird whistles, the flame wing weaves,
> And the fox barks in the thicket with its sneezing
>   excitement.
> The ceremony of joy is validated in the night cry,
> And all earth breathes its idiot and promiscuous
>   promise:
> Joy.   (*Brother to Dragons* 95–96)

If the narrative and the verse are open to censure, the scheme of debate becomes peculiarly important; for it could supply the challenge which an audience seeks from a poem of this length. If the disagreement set forth between the poet and Jefferson—the quarrel over the meaning of the Lewis brothers' crime—were handled forcefully, if the reader found himself drawn into the substance of the controversy (regardless of the data which provoked it and regardless of the poet's limitations of style), *Brother to Dragons* might deserve the attention it invites.

But when an author supports his moral doctrine by a mixture of fact, speculation, and invention, it cannot seem sturdy. The last fifty years of human events have provided abundant evidence of the ugliness of man's inborn character. I suspect that the power of Warren's poem when it first appeared sprang from the precipitate decline of American moral optimism, a decline which followed the full disclosure of the German nation's bestiality, made known in the years after 1945. Since that period, the conduct of other nations, including our own, has not reversed the decline. On this issue, history has overtaken poetry.

Warren dwells on the betrayal of the vision of men like Jefferson by the sins of the republic they conceived. In America—many used to think—history had been granted a fresh opening. Jefferson himself sometimes claimed that for the United States the present was independent of the past. For this people to practice abominations was the last offense to minds that thought of it as a proving ground of human potentiality. Warren lists the disgraces: the destruction of the Indians, the institution of slavery, and so forth; and he declares that all of us—high and low, southern aristocrat and humble slave—are, like the rest of the world, caught in history. The peculiar loathsomeness of Lilburne Lewis was his kinship with the most splendid type of American manhood, Jefferson.

Unfortunately, every aspect of Warren's analysis is now overfamiliar. The failure of our national character is a favorite theme of the American literary imagination. The myth of southern aristocracy has been stripped bare too often for another exposure to move us. Moreover, the appeal to fact, which the poem urges upon us, works against the drift of Warren's argument. Whoever examines the scholarly accounts of Jefferson, the Lewis brothers, or Meriwether Lewis will undermine Warren's case.

So far from being taken in by any optimistic misrepresentation of Jefferson's, Meriwether Lewis himself said, "I hold it an axiom incontrovertible that it is more easy to introduce vice in all states of society than it is to eradicate it, and this is more strictly true when applied to man in his savage than in his civilized state." When Warren says, "We must believe in the notion of virtue," he hardly disagrees with Jefferson, who thought a moral conscience was an integral part of human nature.

Returning from the meaning to the form, I have to wonder whether the enterprise of such a poem as *Brother to Dragons* does not represent one more desire to equip the United States with a verse epic. The ambition to do so goes back to the early years of the republic. But by that date, large-scale narrative had already become the responsibility of the novel. When poets finally accepted this truth, they altered their definition, and spoke of writing a "long poem," which should be neither narrative in the manner of Virgil nor exposition in the manner of Lucretius. One of the monuments of the revised hope is W. C. Williams's *Paterson*. But for all the praise that *Paterson* and efforts like Charles Olson's *Maximus Poems* have received, no one ever wished them longer; and in search of honest pleasure, readers without a vested interest in duration are likely to turn to the shorter pieces in Williams's *Selected Poems*.

American poetry became mature when the novel, the film, and the theater supplied dramatic and narrative works that required hours for their consumption. The genius of our poetry is indeed lyric and reflexive. If we need a verse epic, the want is satisfied by Whitman's *Song of Myself,* which is a cluster of poems kept together by the spirit and theme of the author. The transformations of the self give our poets their best starting point, as they gave Whitman his. Self-conscious, self-dramatizing, self-mocking, self-awed, the poet looks out on a world whose contents are sanctified by his inspection; and it is by identifying himself momentarily with the figures and scenes of that world that he nourishes his identity.

For Whitman, as Richard Chase said, the drama of the self was essentially comic. For poets today, that drama must modulate unforeseeably from pathos to humor, from despair to irony. Poems like Elizabeth Bishop's "Poem" ("About the size of an old-style dollar bill"), Robert Lowell's "Skunk Hour," Richard Wilbur's "Walking to Sleep," and James Merrill's "The Thousand and Second Night" are suitable models, not because they reveal any scandal about the poet but because they involve world and self in the fascinating, funny, terrible work of connecting and disconnecting the immediate sensibility and the experiences that produced it. A group of such poems is the grandest epic we can use.

Warren himself, in his recent and best poems, shows an affinity with this tradition rather than the evasions of Ashbery, the surfaces of Strand, or the monotones of James Wright. His last collection, *Now and Then,* has at least half a dozen good poems. In them the poet looks at himself from the remoteness of old age eyeing death; and he searches for the meaning of experiences embodied in his identity. The strength of remembered emotions, the montage of past and present, the crescendos and diminuendos of sensation provide satisfactions that almost make up for the carelessness of the language. One wishes that Warren's flights were less effortful and that his earthiness were less commonplace, just as one wishes that his metrics were more purposeful. There is also the lushness which troubles one in *Brother to Dragons;* but it is undercut here by the critical perspective of memory.

Although the attitude, in these poems, is highly serious, the intensity of the poet's self-consciousness and the sense one has of extremes in time being pressed quickly together infuse irony into the tone. The themes include earthly and spiritual aspiration, the desire for glory; they include the transformation of the self that will not merely vanish—the possibility of resurrection. As with Whitman, the egoism (for Warren rarely delights in self-effacement) is redeemed by typology, and the poet becomes Everyman.

In this autobiographical verse, the narrative part is easy to manage, because it springs from personal anecdote. Actor and setting partake of each other:

> In the dark kitchen the electric icebox rustles.
> It whispers like the interior monologue of guilt
>   and extenuation.   ("The Mission"; 41–42)

Dramatization is no problem, since the poet speaks of and for himself. Instead of argument and morality, he strives to convey insights and feelings; and we are not troubled with self-conferred rectitude.

Death closes the process of metamorphosis. In "Departure," Warren makes the end of summer into a hint of the end of life. In "Heat Wave Breaks," he turns a summer storm into a foreshadowing of Judgment. In "Heart of Autumn" (74–75) the passage of Canada geese overhead becomes a premonition of the poet's own passage—

> And my heart is impacted with a fierce impulse
> To unwordable utterance—
> Toward sunset, at a great height.

The poems comment on and reply to one another. They cohere naturally and give the reader a beautiful impression of a brave ancient gathering the resources of intellect and spirit against the challenge of finality. For ambitious young poets a sequence of such lyrics could, I think, be more powerfully suggestive than Crane's *The Bridge* or Pound's *Cantos*.

9

WARREN
II

Staying ability is a rare feature of genius. Poets especially tend to fade when they age. But Robert Penn Warren, as his new book testifies, has gained strength with years. The power and freshness of the best poems in *Rumor Verified* will delight a careful reader.

Even the casual turner of pages will be struck by Warren's descriptions of landscape and the effects of light. The imagination of the poet responds on several levels to things seen, heard, or touched. He has the art of bestowing special significance on them without falsifying the simple act of perception. In his work it is rare for a country scene, however minutely observed, to lack symbolic implications.

A favorite motif is dawn. The poet, wakeful and uneasy during the night, watches the dawn "seep in"—"sluggish and gray / As tidewater fingering timbers in a long-abandoned hulk" ("Dawn"; 79). The wateriness of the first trace of light blends with the poet's submergence in fluid half-sleep. The idea of a tide suggests the ebb and flow of light from morning to midnight. "Hulk" suggests the poet's body, cut off from daytime perceptions. The whole poem comes to a focus in the

An earlier version of this essay was published under the title "Continuity and Change" as a review of Robert Penn Warren, *Rumor Verified: Poems 1979–80* (New York: Random House, 1980). © 1981 by Irvin Ehrenpreis as first published in *The Atlantic Monthly*, December 1981.

concept of self-definition, because morning brings a sense of reality to the insubstantial sleeper:

> Are you
> Real when asleep? Or only when,
>
> Feet walking, lips talking, or
> Your member making its penetration, you
> Enact, in a well-designed set, that ectoplasmic
> Drama of laughter and tears, the climax of which always
> Strikes with surprise.

The subtle movement from description to reflection is typical of the poet, but so is the theme of selfhood. If we say the poem brings up the general problem of establishing one's identity, we do not read too much into it. According to Warren, a poem is "a way of knowing what kind of a person you can be, getting your reality shaped a little bit better."[1]

Like most memorable poems composed by Americans, those by Warren kept returning us to the nature of personality, the relation between character and memory, or between immediate experience and analytical consciousness. One feels Warren's power in short lyrics, no more than two or three pages long, in which he confronts the gap between feeling and thought. Again and again the poet yields pleasurably to a moment of strong perceptions or deep emotion. But then he draws back and ponders it, unwilling to let the self dissolve in sensation. Literature, Warren once said, starts from "the attempt to inspect one's own soul."[2]

The persistence of certain images is also a feature of Warren's work. In a new poem, "Minneapolis Story," a gold maple leaf drops from its bough, signifying the autumnal passage from experience to reflection. In another new poem, "Millpond Lost," a leaf "golden, luxurious," falls

1   *Robert Penn Warren Talking: Interviews 1950–1978,* ed. Floyd C. Watkins and John T. Hiers (New York: Random House, 1980), 18.

2   Interview, 1969, in Marshall Walker, *Robert Penn Warren: A Vision Earned* (New York: Harper and Row, 1979), 261.

on a millpond. As it touches the water, the poet stops imagining his own return to a scene from boyhood and confesses that he never went back. The same leaf appeared half a century ago in "The Return," where it fell slowly, "Uncertain as a casual memory," to meet its reflection rising from the depth of the water below.[3] Already it was a emblem of memory trying and failing to recover the past.

Not only themes and images but also the forms of the poems connect the new work with the old. A wholly charming poem, "What Voice at Moth-Hour," is included in *Rumor Verified.* It deals irresistibly with the poet's recollection of a childhood misdemeanor. On a spring evening in Kentucky, young Robert hid after dark among the trees and refused to come home even though he heard his anxious parents calling. The same incident was the subject of a poem published in 1957, "What Was the Promise That Smiled from the Maples at Evening?"

But besides reworking an old theme, the poem has a familiar form, pentameter quatrains with lines rhyming alternately. The five-beat line and regular, four-line stanzas appear several times in the new book and are found as early as "Croesus in Autumn," published when the poet was twenty-two. There they might reflect the example of John Crowe Ransom and Allen Tate. Both these men were Warren's seniors in the remarkable group known as the "Fugitives," who met in Nashville, Tennessee, during the years 1915–28, to read and criticize their own writing.

Tate was six years older than Warren; but with characteristic generosity he quickly recognized the talent of the young man. A description by him of Warren at the age of sixteen has become famous: "He was tall and thin, and when he walked across the room he made a sliding shuffle, as if his bones didn't belong to one another. He had a long quivering nose, large brown eyes, and a long chin—topped by curly red hair. He spoke in a soft whisper."[4] It was the hair that gave Warren his enduring nickname, "Red." Tate's admiration appeared

3 "Kentucky Mountain Farm," in *Selected Poems 1923–1943* (New York: Harcourt, Brace, 1944), 83.

4 Tate, "*The Fugitive, 1922–1925,*" *Princeton University Library Gazette* 3 (Apr. 1942), quoted by Walker, 81–82.

most warmly in a letter four years later: "You know Red is pretty close to being the greatest Fugitive poet. . . . He is the only one of us who has *power*."[5]

Part of young Warren's strength came from his openness to influence. "Ransom was made for Hardy," Warren reported. "So was I as a boy, and still am" (in 1969).[6] Besides Thomas Hardy, there was T. S. Eliot, whose phrases were echoed in Warren's early work. A serious boy who rejected religion and parental authority needs a source of comfort. The bleakness of Hardy's outlook and of Eliot's mood put off the common reader. But they must have seemed sympathetic to an undergraduate who felt suicidal despair over his unprepossessing exterior and a sense of isolation from his family. With such authors as models he could fight against the depression which Tate analyzed in 1924: "It is simply that he has been beaten down so consistently and brutally, that his emotional needs have met frustration so completely, that he was driven into a blind alley."[7]

Some of Warren's feelings at the time were revived, I think, in the poem "Eidolon" (*Selected Poems* 45), published ten years later. Here a boy lies awake through the night on a straw mattress at the top of a farmhouse and hears dogs ranging across the land. His father and grandfather, from whom he feels cut off, are asleep. While the barking continues, the boy imagines the pack as hunting down his inner self, or ghostly "eidolon." The violent emotions that he hides from the older men match the furious noise of the hounds: "I heard the hunt. Who saw, in darkness, how fled / The white eidolon from fanged commotion rude?"

Young Warren recovered from his breakdown. But through it he came to know how close disaster is to glory. His poems deal repeatedly with the mystery of success and failure, the danger of supposing that either is unavoidable or that one cannot become the other. Growing up in a region affected with fatalism, he had to educate himself to

---

5 January 20, 1927, to Donald Davidson, in Davidson Collection, Vanderbilt University, quoted by Walker, 56.

6 Interview, Walker, 245.

7 May 24, 1924, in Davidson Collection, quoted by Walker, 54.

moral action and responsibility. "What poetry most significantly celebrates," he declares in a recent essay, "is the capacity of man to face
the deep, dark inwardness of his nature and his fate."[8]

On the one hand, therefore, his poems assert the value of supreme
achievement. Men long to perform a great deed because the experience
itself is joyful. Once we possess fame, we discover how little it redeems
the terrible disappointments inherent in any life. Yet the experience
remains joyful. This is the implication of a fine poem that Warren
published a few years ago, "Red-Tail Hawk and Pyre of Youth."[9]

On the other hand, the exhilaration wears off, the burden of hope-
lessness descends, and it must be tolerated. One knows the burden will
keep returning, but one also learns that it dissolves in the reality of
love. "Only at the death of ambition," says Warren in a new poem,
"Fear and Trembling,"

> does the deep
> Energy crack crust, spurt forth, and leap
>
> From grottoes, dark—and from the caverned enchainment?
>
> (*Rumor* 97)

While we can trace themes, images, and forms that endure through
all of Warren's long career, change is fundamental to his talent. The
early work is dense in language and deliberate in movement, oblique in
presentation but unified in tone. Poem after poem may originate in
personal crises. The poet, however, separates the finished verse from
the private experience and delivers it as an impersonal statement or a
dramatic monologue.

Even "To a Face in the Crowd" (*Selected Poems* 102), written out of
despair and published when Warren was no more than twenty, reads
as the outburst of an unidentifiable speaker. Here the poet sees a
kindred spirit among a crowd of indifferent people. Calling out, he
warns this man not to repeat his own mistake. For the stranger is going

8   *Democracy and Poetry* (Cambridge: Harvard Univ. Press, 1975), 31.
9   *Now and Then,* 17–21.

on a quest, apparently for a principle of selfhood. And it must be a principle, I think, not derived from religion, yet one that can give meaning and direction to existence.

The poet warns the stranger that he is bound to fail. In the end he will discover nothing but a blank monument set up by an "ancient band" trapped between the mountain and the sea—presumably, religious faith and meaningless chaos. Yet the searcher's forebears are this band. The poem suggests that the rare man of heroic but thoughtless action can establish his selfhood without a guiding principle. However, neither the poet nor the "face in the crowd" is such a man. Better, says the speaker, to abandon the quest at once and join the "lost procession" of indistinguishable, rootless humanity.

The poem is deeply moving even to a reader uncertain of its meaning, because the train of bleak images and the single tone convey the underlying sadness. But the syntax and diction are remote from normal speech. The rhythms are conventional. In the subdued movement of the closing lines we feel the surrender of an exhausted mind:

> Renounce the night as I, and we must meet
> As weary nomads in this desert at last,
> Borne in the lost procession of these feet.

By his mid-twenties, Warren was learning to infuse irony into his tone. Thus he was able to convey bleakness without seeming overwhelmed by it. He could assume an attitude and criticize it at the same time. When Warren in 1939 described T. S. Eliot as probably "the most important influence on American poetry," he did not make style the crucial feature of the poet's work. Rather he singled out "the contemplation of a question which is central in modern life: can man live on the purely naturalistic level?"[10]

The question is of course Warren's own. A desire for life to be meaningful without a submission to divine revelation or to human authority is part of Warren's nature; and the failure of history to supply

10   "The Present State of Poetry: A Symposium, III, in the U.S." *Kenyon Review* 1 (1939):395.

meaning is a major theme of his novels. But irony is a normal tone for those who ask such questions. They feel impatient with easy answers and are honest enough to admit that they have no solution themselves. Their irony expresses self-criticism along with doubt, and it is the mode of Eliot's early poems.

In "Letter from a Coward to a Hero" (1935), Warren sets the thoughtful man (the coward) against the one who ignores doubt and finds himself in action (the hero). Ironically, the hero's confidence is not matched by positive achievement. He fails to accomplish anything significant; yet he also fails to realize the fact, because his only response to failure is further, unthinking action. The speaker smiles at him without denying that his own analytic consciousness leaves him taken up with ineffectual thought:

> Though young, I do not like loud noise:
> The sudden backfire,
> The catcall of boys,
> Drums beating for
> The big war,
> Or clocks that tick all night, and will not stop.
>
> (*Selected Poems* 28)

Irony of this sort is not personality. It is often a means of avoiding self-characterization. Warren's poetic mode was still the impersonal presentation of attitudes or emotions that actually arose from the poet's own experience. In two narrative poems, *The Ballad of Billie Potts* (1944) and *Brother to Dragons* (1953) he explored the problem of evil. The author speaks out in these poems, but only to expound his moral philosophy. The underlying argument of each story is a transposition into secular terms of the doctrine of original sin. Both the narratives and the poet's commentary on them teach us that to be human is to be involved in evil. The mildest, most upright man has, beneath the veneer of his docility, a readiness for the most malicious thoughts and actions.

This judgment was already a theme of Warren's lyrics and novels. He gave it haunting expression in the nine stanzas of the poem "Original Sin: A Short Story" (*Selected Poems* 23–24), which came out during the early months of our involvement in the Second World War. But there, as in the narrative poems, the poet offers his views in a generalized form and did not relate them to particular events of his life. In "Original Sin" the guilt that pursues men of conscience and discloses their participation in evil appears as a patient, speechless, hydrocephalic monster:

> Nodding, its great head rattling like a gourd,
> And locks like seaweed strung on the stinking stone,
> The nightmare stumbles past, and you have heard
> It fumble your door before it whimpers and is gone:
> It acts like the old hound that used to snuffle your door
>   and moan.

What marks "Original Sin" is a relaxation of style. One of Warren's most successful poems, "The Return: An Elegy," moves in strophes that rise and fall with alternations of tight and free verse; and it was composed in 1931.[11] Still earlier, "Pondy Woods" (published in 1928) had long phrases in colloquial language. The narrative poems are of course dominated by easy-flowing speech. But in lyrics Warren still concentrated his energies on careful meters in which formal pattern was more striking than the rhythms or diction of speech. For a series of poems by him in thoroughly colloquial English, we have to wait until the mid-1950s.

During the decade following the Second World War, Warren hardly produced any short poems. But then he gave up writing short stories and altered his conception of a lyric. When he composed such verse again, it was, as he said, "more tied up with an event, an anecdote, an observation."[12] The new poems were closer to the felt life of their author.

Meanwhile, that life was transformed. Warren's first marriage had

---

11   See John L. Stewart, *The Burden of Time* (Princeton: Princeton Univ. Press, 1965), 440.

12   An interview with Richard B. Sale, in *Warren Talking*, 121.

terminated in divorce. He was married again, to Eleanor Clark (in 1952), and the couple soon had a daughter and a son. In 1955 Warren's father died. These large changes inevitably altered the poet's view of his world. He obviously delighted in fatherhood; and I suspect that he responded to the work of authors like W. H. Auden and Robert Lowell, who were widely read at the time. Warren began experimenting with what might be called the poetry of happiness. It strikes one that in his most recent narrative poem, based on the life of Audubon (1969), the act of violence is frustrated. Although Warren dwells, in *Audubon,* on the paradoxes of love and destructiveness, sexuality and death, he also dwells on the interconnectedness of all living things. Audubon shoots the birds he loves (in order to study them), but he also gives them new life in his art.

During the past twelve years, Warren has opened himself up engagingly. *Rumor Verified* continues the development toward a direct use of personal experience. The title of the book refers to the axiom that no man can escape the limitations of the human condition. An opening poem suggests the relation between love and wisdom by presenting an ideal experience of sexual passion. A second poem dramatizes the strength of the human instinct for meaningful existence. The closing poems of the book are centered on the need to accept one's character with all its deficiencies and to work through it—not against it—toward an insight that may never be completely possessed. In the body of the book Warren ponders the mysterious relation between time and history and the self that rises from it and yet persists against it.

Typically, the poems move from a memory or a startling experience to a meditation, sometimes in the shape of a question. Along with large generalizations they exhibit brilliantly concrete detail. Warren once said that what he would hunt for in a poem is "a vital and evaluating image."[13] His descriptive passages indicate that he has retained that attitude.

13 *Warren Talking,* 16.

In form, the poems are surprisingly regular. Only a third are in quite free verse. Another third are in quatrains, usually rhymed. The rest are in various other forms, mainly irregular distichs or tercets. Two poems will show what different sorts of order Warren can impose on sensation. One is the skillful "Sunset Scrupulously Observed," in which the flight of a jet is exquisitely contrasted with that of five swifts. The poet treats the plane as a splendid living creature and the birds as machines. Although in free verse, the poem is a triumph of design, because the main contrast is handsomely framed by the sun going down in the background and a flycatcher perched on a poplar in the foreground, and opening and closing the poem with its presence and absence.

But the surprise of the book is "What Voice at Moth-Hour" (*Rumor* 69), a poem in neat quatrains with expressively soft line endings; gentle, undulating rhythms; and subtle patterns of sound (particularly the use of *i* vowels). All these elements support the nostalgia of the speaker as he remembers how innocence gave way to experience when he made a boyish gesture toward separating himself from his parents; for it was precisely their love that he had to resist if he was ever to grow into a deeply loving selfhood:

> What voice at moth-hour did I hear calling
> As I stood in the orchard while the white
> Petals of apple blossoms were falling,
> Whiter than moth-wing in that twilight?

> What voice did I hear as I stood by the stream,
> Bemused in the murmurous wisdom there uttered,
> While ripples at stone, in their steely gleam,
> Caught last light before it was shuttered?

> What voice did I hear as I wandered alone
> In a premature night of cedar, beech, oak,
> Each foot set soft, then still as stone
> Standing to wait while the first owl spoke?

The voice that I heard once at dew-fall, I now
Can hear by a simple trick. If I close
My eyes, in that dusk I again know
The feel of damp grass between bare toes,

Can see the last zigzag, sky-skittering, high,
Of a bullbat, and even hear, far off, from
Swamp-cover, the whip-o-will, and as I
Once heard, hear the voice: *It's late! Come home.*

10

BISHOP

Has anyone noticed how a poet as deceptively clear as Elizabeth Bishop can reveal the elements of her verse in her prose? Two exemplary prose works by Bishop are a story called "Gwendolyn" and an appreciation of Walter de la Mare's anthology, *Come Hither.*[1] The reason I pick out the story is that it betrays so many of the preoccupations behind Bishop's work. Most of her writing classes itself as obvious fact or obvious fantasy. "Gwendolyn" is a story that demands to be read as autobiography. Bishop sets it in the region where she spent her early years; she populates it with her own relations; and she often refers, in it, to the process of remembering and of correcting her memory.

However, the story is focused not on Bishop herself but on a doll; and the doll is ultimately named after a playmate who had died, while the first-person storyteller never names herself. Let me, for convenience, call this narrator "Elizabeth Bishop." The whole design of "Gwendolyn" should attract any reader by the way it brings together

Portions of this essay were first published 22 Jan. 1971 under the title "Loitering between Dream and Experience." Reprinted with permission of *The Times Literary Supplement.* © Times Newspapers, 1971.

1 "Gwendolyn," in *Elizabeth Bishop: The Collected Prose* (New York: Farrar, Straus, & Giroux, 1984), 213–26; "I Was but Just Awake," *Poetry* 93 (Oct. 1958):50–54.

the themes of pain, dream, and truth. Yet it seems merely a cluster of incident from a provincial childhood.

During a long bout of bronchitis, the storyteller is privileged to play with a beautiful, precious doll belonging to an older cousin who is away. About the same time, she enjoys visits from another little girl, Gwendolyn Appletree, afflicted with diabetes and not expected to live long. Elizabeth sees her friend as fair and pretty in a doll-like way. An inconspicuous feature of the story is that while Gwendolyn has an excessively attentive father and mother, Elizabeth has neither; for she lives with her grandparents. Nowhere are we told that her own father is dead and her mother is mad. But we are told that Gwendolyn's parents killed the pretty child with kindness; for instead of restricting her use of sugar, they sweetened her tea and allowed her extra pieces of cake. There may be a faint, unconscious hint that people without parents are better off—a sentiment that Bishop did express in conversation. One assumes that the hint is a device for coping with the desolation of being an orphan.

Among the episodes of the story is one in which Gwendolyn stays overnight with Elizabeth and does not say her prayers before going to bed. She was allowed to say them in bed, she tells her friend, "because I'm going to die" (220). A couple of days later, she does die; and since the church is across the village green from the grandparents' house, Elizabeth can watch the proceedings. Late in the service, she sees two men in black come out of the church carrying a small white coffin; and she imagines that they leave it leaning against the wall while they return to the congregation. "For a minute, I stared straight through my lace curtains at Gwendolyn's coffin, with Gwendolyn shut invisibly inside it forever" (224). Elizabeth runs howling out her own back door. I suggest that the pain of her isolation (as an orphan) escapes in the fantasy of the lethal, parental figures abandoning the coffined child.

As Bishop tells it, this incident reminds the storyteller of an earlier one. She had gone to look for a little basket full of new marbles of the usual colors, including some handsome large ones and an exceptionally fine pink beauty, probably an inch and a half in diameter. When she finally locates the basket, which had been abandoned in a cluttered cupboard, all the pretty marbles are covered with dirt or dust, mixed with ugly bits of drifted trash. She says, "I put my head down on top of the marbles and cried aloud" (225). Does she feel bereft because the pretty, invulnerable creatures which submit to her whim and keep her company have suddenly proved vulnerable to moth and rust?

A month after Gwendolyn's funeral, the final episode of the story occurs. Playing with her cousin Billy, Elizabeth is so rash as to bring out the exquisite doll that had been entrusted to her when she was ill. The two playmates undress the doll, lay it out in the garden path, and surround the body with wild flowers. Gleefully, they decide the game is Gwendolyn's funeral and that the doll's name is indeed Gwendolyn. But suddenly the grandmother discovers them and is enraged to see the precious doll mistreated. She sends Billy home, and the story ends.

A feature of the narrative style is the enumeration of small, enduring, colored articles arranged in patterns. The doll's clothes received loving attention. Then we meet a button basket, also the scraps of material forming a quilt, a set of small, colored blocks that could be arranged to make designs in a cardboard box, and the varieties of food for a picnic. Even the graveyard is described as a charming collection of colored items (renewable if changeable)—green trees, white stones, wild rosebushes, blueberries: it is "surely one of the prettiest [graveyards] in the world." Bishop describes the lambs carved on headstones for the remains of small children: "Some were almost covered by dry, bright-gold lichen, some with green and gold and gray mixed together, some were almost lost among the long grass and roses and blueberries and teaberries" (223). Later, we have the basket of marble, and finally the renewable flowers outlining the doll.

Bishop discouraged symbolic interpretations of her work, but imaginative play is so important in the narrative, and is so closely connected with the making of designs and the confrontation with pain (grief, loss) that I am tempted to read into the story some observations from the review Bishop wrote of de la Mare's anthology. One of her remarks is that simple repetition of poetry may be a good way of learning to write it: "Isn't the best we can do . . . in the way of originality, but a copying and re-copying, with some slight variations of our own?" ("I Was But Just Awake" 52). To some degree, reality is a work of art to be copied with variations by the artist. It would be easy to account for the story of "Gwendolyn" in those terms.

Bishop also quotes de la Mare's advice to a boy, to "learn the common names of everything you see . . . and especially those that please you most to remember: then give them names of your own making and choosing—if you can." She approves of his fondness for "little articles," or "home-made objects whose value increases with age"—for example, Robinson Crusoe's lists of his "belongings, homely employments, charms and herbs." She approves of de la Mare's wanting poems to be filled with things, and she celebrates the miscellany of curious facts in his notes—"a Luna Park of stray and straying information." The story of Gwendolyn has such features, and so have Bishop's poems (53).

One example in verse is "First Death in Nova Scotia" (written in less than an hour), a poem about the death of an infant cousin named Arthur.[2] Again the poet invites us to read the work as autobiography. Again the little girl (very little) confronts a corpse—this time a tiny infant laid out in a palpably cold parlor and in a coffin like a small frosted cake. Bishop makes an alluring pattern of the red and white objects around the room: a white, stuffed loon with red eyes, the red and ermine robes worn by the royal family (in the "chromographs" on the walls), the white skull of the infant and the touch of red in its hair.

Yet the visual element is not exclusive. Coldness pervades the scene from the opening line to the snow mentioned at the end. Although critics dwell on the abundance of visual imagery that Bishop's work provides, her care for the other senses is exquisite. She has an acute ear and studied the piano. While she was adolescent, she responded to Ezra Pound's opinions on music by getting herself a Dolmetsch harpsichord. The lack of sound in "First Death" suggests the inwardness of young Elizabeth's sense of the occasion.

But the emergence of a design in red and white—a "found" design one might say—indicates how the imagination meets the challenge of death, grief, abandonment. By incorporating Arthur's body into a nat-

---

2   In *Elizabeth Bishop: The Complete Poems 1927–1979* (New York: Farrar, Straus, & Giroux, 1983), 125. All citations from Bishop's poetry refer to this volume.

ural order of seductive vision, the poet balances pathos against beauty. The agony of loss is real; yet it may give rise to an aesthetic process that is equally real but joyous. Instead of stopping at the fact of infant mortality, the poet makes it the germ of a new creation, like the playmates at the mock-funeral in "Gwendolyn."

At the same time, "First Death" strikes one with its profusion of proper names: two Arthurs, Prince Edward, Princess Alexandra, King George, Queen Mary, Jack Frost. Yet the poet names neither her mother (a prominent figure in the recollection) nor herself. The names we hear do not suggest commonplace reality but the remoteness of legend, folktales, and royal courts. The poet and her mother belong to the inconsequential, routine life of illness and pain, death and loss.

Bishop said that she always felt isolated. In many of her poems she appears as a solitary, meticulous observer, not lonely but so voraciously absorbed in what she hears or sees that she never looks around for comrades: these exist in the stable elements of the perceived, patterned world. This purity of selfhood carries over into the clarity and honesty of what she records. One feels that faithfulness to reality inspires every image. The poetry lies not in a play of words and symbols but in the character of the poet, who is herself caught, for example, by the fact that a rusty, barbed wire fence looks like "three dotted lines" ("Twelfth Morning"; *Poems* 110), or that a baby rabbit is "a handful of intangible ash" ("The Armadillo"; 104). (Notice here, by the way, how the reechoed, nasal and sibilant *a* suggests the fragility of the material.)

Bishop once wrote in a letter, "Dreams, works of art (some), glimpses of the always-more-successful surrealism of everyday life, unexpected moments of empathy (is it?) catch a peripheral vision of whatever it is one can never really see full-face but that seems enormously important. . . . What one seems to want in art, in experiencing it, is the same thing that is necessary for its creation, a self-forgetful, perfectly useless concentration."[3] But there is no point in concentrating on something which is not there, independent of the observer. The honesty and the solitude are connected. Bishop strives to be the trans-

---

3   Letter to Anne Stevenson, *TLS,* 7 Mar. 1980, 261 (date of letter not given).

parent *monocle de mon oncle* which adjusts our vision to the actual thing that has always, fascinatingly been right there. She is like Wordsworth, apparently alone, showing us London from Westminster Bridge— when we know from scholarship that his sister was beside him at the time.

An early poem, "The Map" (written in New York in 1934), begins with a comment on the relation between land and water. Bishop says something we thought we knew, that "Land lies in water" (3). But swiftly she challenges one to choose between the two-dimensional abstraction of land represented in a map and the rounded experience of the land we walk on. Both are "shadowed green," one by the mapmaker, the other by nature. So the reader faces the question asked by Wallace Stevens, how the world which, in one's room, is beyond understanding, becomes, when we walk, "three or four hills and a cloud."[4] Memory abstracts, imposes human patterns, creates uncertainty. Experience satisfies the imagination and eliminates doubt. Which is right? Need either be wrong?

Quickly, Bishop's poem escapes from the map to the tangible seashore, where we stand wondering whether the world determines the imagination or the imagination forces itself on the world: "Along the fine tan sandy shelf / is the land tugging at the sea from under?" From this stereoscopic view we slip magically back to the map; but now instead of seeming an abstraction, it takes on the character of a painted landscape itself. The shift in point of view is disguised by the continuity of the verbal texture; for Bishop offers us words (especially "land") subtly repeated in new positions, vowels modulating between consonantal echoes:

> The shadow of Newfoundland lies flat and still.
> Labrador's yellow, where the moony Eskimo
> has oiled it.

"Eskimo" sounds "moony" and belongs in moon-white snow in a re-

---

4   Stevens, "Of the Surface of Things," *Collected Poems,* 57.

gion of white nights. His "oil" echoes the "yellow" of the map color and the "still" shadow of Newfoundland. It suggests the oil paint of an artist who has painted the map or the landscape that rivals reality. The first and last stanzas of the poem are quietly rhymed with an alternation of true rhymes and repeated end words. The middle stanza is free verse: pattern and disorder; land and sea.

The poem continues to flicker back and forth between the immediate sight of a flat map and the idea of a map as a landscape. It continues to look beyond both these views to the world they refer us to. At the very moment when the poet lures us into seeing the outlined bays as homes for plants or fish, she pulls us back and says, "The names of seashore towns run out to sea"—and one is again staring at a map with letters for places. Yet the ambiguity leaps up afresh with "sea," which must be the ocean itself, mysteriously invaded by printed place-names.

Through all these shifting attitudes runs a steady impulse of personification. The elements of the map act like people or animals. Peninsulas take the water between them "like women feeling for the smoothness of yard-goods." Norway is a hare running south, "in agitation." And yet the bold conceits seem unstrained because the tone is low-keyed, the syntax is uncluttered, and the patterns of sound are harmonious. Does the lonely poet make companions out of the parts of the beautiful, abstract pattern fixed on her wall?

In the closing distich, the rivalry between land and sea which dominates the poem resolves itself in the way "favorites" picks up the *t-r-f* of "topography"; "colors" is repeated from an earlier line; "north" fades into "near" and "more"; and the "or" cluster at one end of the last line bobs up in both "colors" at the other end and "historians" in the middle. "Delicacy" is exemplified in the subdued wit of "near" (for "far") West and the softly transformed liquids and *a* sounds: *r* to *l* to *r;* the bright *a* of "displays," "favorites," "makers"; and the sheep's *a* of "than," "historian," and "map"—"Topography displays no favorites; North's as near as West. / More delicate than the historians' are the map-makers' colors." So the quiet designs of the land grow from the quieter conformation of mapped water.

Already in this poem, written in her early twenties, Bishop treats the world as a pattern of colored materials: green land, blue water, tan sand, yellow Labrador. Already she implies that the object examined is one she has actually seen. Already the act of perception loses its simplicity and raises questions about the mind's place in the apparent order or disorder of circumambient reality. Already the poet is content to make us look again, think again, without asking us to see a moral principle in the scene put before us. If there is a doctrine here, it is that the act of losing oneself in the contemplation of seductive patterns can, to a degree, make up to us for the chronic agony of existence.

Bishop strove, I think, to make her work "found poetry." She was of course fastidious about rhythm and the patterns of sound. In a triumph of technique and pathos like "One Art," the closing verses illustrate her genius for getting an exact tone (like a catch in one's voice) into the movement of an apparently unforced line. Here, the words, "*Write* it!" and the repetition of "like" convey the despair with which the poet recalls the death of her friend. (The sudden direct address to "you" is another triumph.)

> —Even losing you (the joking voice, a gesture
> I love) I shan't have lied. It's evident
> the art of losing's not too hard to master
> though it may look like (*Write* it!) like disaster.   (178)

But for all her control over the form of her work, Bishop's meaning regularly emerges from the objects displayed in descriptive passages, objects which come straight into the poetry from the world, with the author's perceptions as the conduit.

One of her great works is called "Poem," and begins, "About the size of an old-style dollar bill" (176). Much of it is an enumeration of the details in a painting: brown houses, white houses, elm trees, "a wild iris," "white and yellow," and so forth. The poem turns as Bishop goes over these details, for she suddenly recognizes the scene to be a familiar one and then relives her childhood experience of it. The original perceptions push their way into the brush strokes, and the poet thinks how surprising it is that she and the painter—a great-uncle—both had the same view of the place:

> our looks, two looks:
> art "copying from life," and life itself,
> life and the memory of it so compressed
> they've turned into each other. Which is which?
> Life and the memory of it cramped,
> dim, on a piece of Bristol board,
> dim, but how live, how touching in detail
> —the little that we get for free,
> the little of our earthly trust. Not much.
> About the size of our abidance
> along with theirs: the munching cows,
> the iris, crisp and shivering, the water
> still standing from spring freshets,
> the yet-to-be-dismantled elms, the geese.

The charming art of the painter has supplied a frame for the profound art of the poet, which puts us in touch with life itself.

When I say that Bishop would like her work to seem like "found poetry," I mean that she wishes not to impose designs but to discover them, the way a photographer notices an evocative composition as he looks around the place he stands in. The simplest example is the poet's description of an assemblage or scene that has significant form through the natural juxtaposition of objects that just happen to be there. A sandpiper looking for food ignores the bits of patterned color under its feet: "The millions of grains are black, white, tan, and gray, / mixed with quartz grains, rose and amethyst" ("Sandpiper"; 131). Bishop reminds us that such things exist, and that if we look, they will refresh, compensate us (a little) for the routine bleakness of our days.

But another element deepens the satisfaction. This is the choice of names. Bishop balances the simple colors and their familiar vowels with the more seductive sounds of "quartz grains, rose and amethyst," in which the lingering vowels, the liquids and sibilants, offer something rich but accurate. The act of naming—"rose" rather than "pink," and "amethyst" rather than "purple"—endows the particles of quartz with their rarer beauty, and suggests the operation of imagination transforming the world. The effect is all the stronger because "amethyst" rhymes with a word above, and echoes "mixed" at the beginning of its own line. The colored blocks in the story of Gwendolyn lack this attraction.

The kind of composition that Bishop searches for is trance-like, a moment that rescues us from the humdrum and abrasive, a moment when reality imitates dream. In "Twelfth Morning: Or What You Will," a fog screens the seashore from clear sight, and bizarre objects rear themselves pleasingly out of it: a boy, a fence, a horse, a ruined house. The poet connects these with her patterns of rhythm and sound till they seem to have a meaningful, mysterious relation. She illuminates them with her wit, and she encloses them with the sounds (rising in volume) of the ocean, the sandpipers, water in a can, and the voice of the boy, Balthazar, whose words bring the melange into an ambiguous focus: "'Today's my Anniversary,' he sings, / 'the Day of Kings'" (111). Bishop joins her words to his: it is her day too, for she has re-created it. The scene presented itself to the poet, exciting her to find the language that would make it strange and coherent at the same time.

When Bishop wished to explain her fondness for George Herbert, she praised his "absolute naturalness of tone" but said some of his poems were "almost surrealistic."[5] She might have been describing her own effect. "Naturalness" implies honesty, lack of artifice. Surrealism suggests fantasy, mystery, witty illusions, the moment when the little girl thought the men had left the coffin leaning against the church wall. The combination of natural manner and exotic matter is a feature of Bishop's work.

The form her mixture takes is not the traditional representation of wonders as truths or of the commonplace as wonderful but rather an absorbed loitering in the marches between dream and experience. One could make a book of Bishop's poems about sleeping, dreaming, and early-morning waking. As pendants to those she provides descriptions of landscapes or objects that become dreamlike as the poet watches them. Finally, there are portraits of people who seem to live in a dream.

5 Ashley Brown, "An Interview with Elizabeth Bishop," *Shenandoah* 17 (Winter 1966):10.

Few of Bishop's poems fall outside these classes. The poems also reveal more humor than satire, more sympathy than fear. The poet does not resist the inexplicable but enjoys it, like the little girl studying and arranging the colored marbles.

One method she employs to establish her subtle voice is witty anthropomorphism. Here is a sample from "At the Fishhouses," a poem set in Nova Scotia. Speaking of the seawater, Bishop writes,

> Cold dark deep and absolutely clear,
> element bearable to no mortal,
> to fish and to seals. . . . One seal particularly
> I have seen here evening after evening.
> He was curious about me. He was interested in music;
> like me a believer in total immersion,
> so I used to sing him Baptist hymns.
> I also sang "A Mighty Fortress Is Our God."
> He stood up in the water and regarded me
> steadily, moving his head a little.
> Then he would disappear, then suddenly emerge
> almost in the same spot, with a sort of shrug
> as if it were against his better judgment.
> Cold dark deep and absolutely clear,
> the clear gray icy water.   (65)

The seal is puzzled and intrigued by the poet as the poet is by people who attract her. The water, suitable only for fish and seals, becomes at the end of the poem a symbol of knowledge, "dark, salt, clear, moving, utterly free" (66). That is to say, on the one hand, closed off to us as the souls of fish and the essence of clouds are closed off, and on the other hand, delivered too late; for the experience from which we learn about the world is the experience for which we need that very knowledge. Bishop's fantasy and wit are devices for stopping the rift between passion and wisdom, hope and truth.

In "Cirque d'Hiver" it is a little toy horse, carrying an unresponsive ballerina, that watches the poet:

> Facing each other rather desperately—
> his eye is like a star—
> we stare and say, "Well, we have come this far."
>
> (31)

They have both learned what they cannot act upon. The humorous resignation (veiling bitter disappointment) is a means of extracting some profit from the impasse, like using a friend's death as the start of a poem. It is a way of saying that one knew it all along, or smiling at oneself for expecting anything different.

To this sort of wit Bishop joins her ear for subtle rhythms, incongruous rhymes, well-placed repetitions. These signalize the control of the artist over the experience of suffering. The formal patterns allow the reader to grasp the difficult emotions. So in "Questions of Travel," Bishop asks herself why she has to visit a place like Brazil:

> To stare at some inexplicable old stonework,
> inexplicable and impenetrable,
> at any view,
> instantly seen and always, always delightful?
> Oh, must we dream our dreams
> and have them, too?
> And have we room
> for one more folded sunset, still quite warm?   (93)

The witty synesthesia of "folded sunset," like the witty anthropomorphism of the encounter with a seal, and the personifications in "The Map," bridges the gap between sense and sensibility. The rhymes and half-rhymes, appearing where one would never look for them, elegantly convey the theme of uncertainty. The varieties of repetition suggest an economy of language suited to the plain, unaffected manner of a poet faithful to the inscrutabilities she records. It is life that seems dark, not Bishop.

The difference between Bishop and the surrealists is that she takes the real and not the fictive as the point of departure for her contemplations. It is wrong to suppose that a search for truth leads one away from intuition and imagination. In the most confined of arts, like that of the map-maker, one is most profoundly liberated from the quotidian: "More delicate than the historians' are the map-makers' colors" ("The Map"; 3). Honesty becomes her peculiar resource. She once said it was almost impossible not to tell the truth in poetry. Wherever one can verify the facts, one discovers that Bishop has not made them up. Even the ballad "The Burglar of Babylon" is taken from newspaper accounts; and the poet herself saw the soldiers hunting for the wretched outlaw:

> Rich people in apartments
> Watched through binoculars
> As long as the daylight lasted.   (115)

Sensing that the external facts are reliable, one naturally assumes that the poet does not misrepresent her response to them. One also assumes that the dreams she writes about, like the map, are her own (the map certainly was), and that she takes the dreams to be not private phenomena but examples of the proximity of fantasy to fact. On these principles depends the sympathetic comedy of many poems. In "Sunday, 4 A.M." the poet wakes up to find her cat jumping to the window with a moth in his mouth; and she writes,

> Dream dream confronting,
> now the cupboard's bare.
> The cat's gone a-hunting.
> The brook feels for the stair.
>
> The world seldom changes,
> but the wet foot dangles
> until the bird arranges
> two notes at right angles.   (129–30)

We have no way of verifying the existence of the brook, apart from the poet's word. Yet if we did not believe in it, the wit of the line would be duller. One is not charmed by a non-existent stream manufactured for the sake of a detached conceit. Somewhere is a brook that rustles through the night like a man looking for the stair in the dark. Near it is a poet wondering whether it belongs to sleep or waking; and she listens with what Bishop calls "self-forgetful, perfectly useless concentration," or with her foot dangling in its water. We believe in the poet and feel reassured to know that she who sees so much and listens so hard shares our uncertainty. So also we feel able to enjoy not only the poem but the mysterious uncertainty itself.

11

BERRYMAN
I

Under a cryptic style, this sonnet sequence delivers a familiar story, told as usual in the first person. During the spring of 1946 a thirty-two-year-old lecturer at Princeton University falls in love. His Danish mistress is younger and tougher, bound far more lightly to him than he to her. Both lovers are married; the couples are acquainted; and "Lise," for all her recklessness and alcoholism, is a mother. So the affair becomes a chain of deceits, separations, furtive meetings, and—for the poet—lacerating guilt. Before autumn Lise decides she can live without him; he is left at the end, therefore, with these poems and his "helpless and devoted wife."

If the obvious parallel is *Modern Love,* this is not to say Mr. Berryman had it in mind. But without suggesting that he stands on Meredith's shoulders, we may ask how much farther he sees. In this kind of narrative the direct expression of strenuous emotion rarely succeeds by itself; most readers want freshness of style, dramatic turns of action. Meredith starts with what seem advantages. Adopting an unconventional sixteen-line form, he shifts his point of view novelistically, speaking either as the husband or as a brooding observer. Meredith's plot is peculiarly dramatic because the husband takes a mistress only after the

This essay was first published 4 July 1968 under the title "A Tortured Tryst" as a review of *Berryman's Sonnets* (New York: Farrar, Straus, & Giroux, 1967). Reprinted with permission of *The Times Literary Supplement.* © Times Newspapers, 1968.

wife has betrayed him; unlike Berryman's passive sufferer, he dominates the action.

But Berryman's modern attitude of demanding sympathy for a weak, vicious protagonist has more power than Meredith's symmetrical development. Our lingering pity for the wife, our disgust with the poet's submissiveness, give this collection a brilliantly sustained energy. By appealing to self-destructive impulses like masochism and incontinence, Berryman provokes in the reader a fascinated wavering between critical and sentimental responses. In form only a few of Berryman's sonnets are not conventionally Italian. Between the octave and the sestet there is generally the tonal contrast that skillful sonneteers like to create. But over the expected patterns rushes a staccato fury of language and syntax, making a structure beside which Meredith's innovations sound timid.

Admirers of *Homage to Mistress Bradstreet* will know what these exercises led to, because phrases and situations from the sonnet sequence reappear, movingly transformed, in Berryman's best-known poem. What reappears with them but becomes the ruin of the earlier work is its verbal extravagance. Puns and imitations alternate with archaisms and allusions. The texture of sound often grates on one's ear; the conceits make broken hops from image to disparate image. Berryman's syntax, para-Miltonic, is so densely crowded with inversions that one studies many lines like a schoolboy construing Horace. Such mannerisms reflect the near-hysteria of the poet and suggest the division in his nature; for even while squirming deliciously with guilt and anxiety, he cannot help foreseeing the inevitable moment when those pains will appear properly trivial. In praise of the style, one may describe it as suitable for chaotic emotions conveyed through an obsession with will and order.

But if Mr. Berryman overworks his words, he badly underpays them. Neither Lise nor his passion seems deep enough for the care he devotes to each. Her character receives little analysis; his lust hardly escapes from the familiar walls of desire, shame, pleasure, and loneliness. And what should be virtue increases the damage. For the subtle particularity that one welcomed in Mr. Berryman's earliest work pervades the sonnet sequence. Here again time, place, and public event belong to the design. The Princeton bicentenary occurs in the one poem, a class reunion in another. We even discover the names of Lise's favorite composers. To a situation so narrowly defined the application of post-Symbolist devices is unfortunate. Wallace Stevens treated his Sunday morning as a chance to meditate on art and religion. Mr. Berryman moves the scene out of doors and merely lets nature approve of a tryst in New Jersey. At several points the lover's yearning does become the poet's desire for fame, and the mistress blends with the muse. But these metamorphoses are too weak to carry the stylistic effort; and the whole affair remains a shop window for a display of Mr. Berryman's technique.

12

BERRYMAN
II

John Berryman's poetry ripened from dignified impersonality to comic egoism, and declined from that into sober self-exploitation. It is the work of the middle period that holds and rewards its reader best. But to create that union of mask and exposé, the poet had to come to terms with the dismal facts of his early life.

Berryman's parents were devout Roman Catholics living in a small town in Oklahoma. From the age of five John used to serve at mass for a priest he adored, and he went to a Catholic school. But his father, a prosperous banker named John Allyn Smith, often and baselessly accused his wife of wishing to leave him. The couple had two sons, John and a younger child, Jefferson. It looks as if the father preferred John; he went fishing and shooting with the boy, and sometimes took him along on military maneuvers—for Mr. Smith was an officer in the National Guard. The mother, a schoolteacher, seems to have preferred the younger, less volatile son.

When John was ten years old, the family moved to Tampa, Florida, on the Gulf of Mexico. Here the piety survived while the matrimonial

This essay was first published 23 Feb. 1973 under the title "The Life of the Modern Poet." Reprinted with permission of *The Times Literary Supplement.* © Times Newspapers, 1973.

agitation grew. Mr. Smith now began threatening to take one of his sons, swim out to sea, and drown himself with the boy. Finally, the father shot himself outside the window of John's room.

Mrs. Smith then moved her family to New York, where she was courted by another banker, John Angus McAlpin Berryman, whom her elder son feared and disliked. She married Mr. Berryman and he adopted the boys, who took his name. Meanwhile, John gave up Catholicism and began writing. When he was fourteen, he left home to go to an Episcopal school in Connecticut. Here he came to like the chaplain and Episcopalianism, but spent four unhappy years at odds with the other boys and thinking constantly of suicide. Once he lay down on the tracks before a train and had to be pulled off.

Only when he reached Columbia University did Berryman meet a fatherly mentor who suited him as a lifetime model. This was Mark Van Doren, the distinguished scholar and teacher who also had a reputation as a poet. At Columbia, Berryman lost his religious faith, attended all Van Doren's classes; and evidently decided to follow his master's example; for poetry, teaching, and scholarship became the lines of his own career. He now wrote poems about death and learned to admire first Auden, then Yeats. On taking his degree, he won a fellowship that sent him to Clare, Cambridge. In England, Berryman launched himself as a man of letters. He met Dylan Thomas and had tea with Yeats. He wrote more poetry and projected a critical life of Shakespeare. Returning to the United States in 1938, he found his way into the literary circles of the *Partisan Review,* the *Kenyon Review,* and the liberal weeklies. Delmore Schwartz, even more dazzling in conversation than in print, became the closest of his friends.

For the next sixteen years Berryman showed much ambition but did not distinguish himself in a memorable way from other poets of his generation. He taught at various universities and published poems in visible places. He composed a powerful sonnet sequence but kept it in his desk. He wrote good criticism and a few short stories. He also produced a superb biographical study of Stephen Crane.

Only in the work on Crane, glowing with psychological insight and deeply sympathetic with its subject, do Berryman's real preoccupations obtrude themselves. His sense of guilt over his father's death had encased him in a melancholy that turned him to alcohol. It was probably disillusionment with his mother that made him into a frantic Don Juan, inclined to humiliate every woman he might seduce. His feelings toward his brother were transformed into a rivalry with other young poets, screened by quasi-fraternal affection. His rootlessness—abrupt changes in his home, his religion, his name—brought out a troubled awareness of the gap between the social person and the private self.

Excluded from the early poems was the hesitant inarticulateness of the worried beginner trying to find his feet on strange and challenging ground. As a talker Berryman held listeners with irreverent anecdotes and comic outbursts; as a poet he strove to sound dignified and meditative. Over his disorderly cycle of melancholy, alcohol, and sex he maintained a literary facade that grew thinner and thinner. "The Lovers," a story he published in 1945, suggests the uneasiness Berryman felt at the fraudulence of his act.

Yet the early poems disclose some qualities that mark all his verse. Bewitched by Auden, Berryman preferred rhymed, stanzaic forms to free verse. To frame or start many of the poems, he used public facts—international crises, social disorders, the miscellaneous news of the day; and there are subtle particularities of time and place in the designs. For all his impersonality, the disembodied poet intervenes constantly between his subject and the reader. Often, a deliberately ruptured syntax quarrels with the unbroken surface of style, suggesting an inarticulate self behind the literary character. To see the more transitory features of the poems Berryman wrote before 1946, one need not look far, because he summarized them, half-deliberately, in a sketch of Auden's early work: "ominous, flat, and social; elliptical and indistinctly allusive; casual in tone and form, frightening in import."[1]

Berryman married in 1942 (on Dylan Thomas's birthday, the day before his own) a bright, patient woman. But the melancholy, heavy drinking, and sexual gamesmanship went on. At Princeton in the spring of 1946 he fell in love with a bibulous younger woman who beat him at his own sport. She had a husband and child; so the affair turned into

1 "Poetry Chronicle, 1948: Waiting for the End, Boys," in *The Freedom of the Poet* (New York: Farrar, Straus, & Giroux, 1976), 297.

a chain of deceits, separations, furtive meetings, and—for the poet—scorching guilt. Berryman's chronic need to suffer pain became acute in sexual passion; the woman who lured him and hurt him would hold him. Before autumn his mistress decided she could live without the poet, and abandoned Berryman to his "helpless and devoted wife."

The hysterical sonnets in which he recorded this affair exhibit the chaos of his hidden personality. Their energy, furiously breaking over the pattern of the Italian rhyme scheme, almost justifies the rupture of syntax which the poet indulges in. But the hodgepodge language and jumble of images reduce the total effect to grotesquerie. What Berryman gained from the experiment was the discovery that his inner character made a stronger center for a poem that the ones he cultivated as an author. He also began to appreciate the grace of inarticulateness as a disarming style for conveying the nature of his protagonist: weak, corrupt, and self-absorbed.

Suppressing the sonnets (which were not published for twenty years), Berryman continued to write impersonal poems, with the influence of Robert Lowell added to that of Auden and Yeats. One group called "Nervous Songs" made use of his panics and introspective gloom. In them the poet tried to re-create the consciousness of several neurotic types. All of them are obscure, morbid self-examinations by anxious persons. Since Berryman could only imagine other people as aspects of himself, the element of dramatic monologue fails. Yet these poems fix some of his old virtues and establish new ones. He keeps the exhilarating dialectic of the sonnets, in which the poet speaks from sharply contrasted points of view, replies to himself or his mistress, and suddenly drops one tone for its opposition. Each poem has three stanzas of six pentameter lines rhymed unpredictably. The form is looser than the sonnet but rigid enough to make significant barriers to the waves of feeling. Dedicated to his brother, the "Nervous Songs" suggest Berryman's feeling that he had now produced something not matched by his rivals.

The outcome of his Princeton love affair darkened the poet's suicidal gloom, and he turned to psychoanalysis. For the rest of his life he had to spend long periods in private or group therapy, or in a hospital; and finally he joined Alcoholics Anonymous. But with all this care he still deteriorated, and during his last months the Minneapolis police used to pick him up and take him to a "detoxification center." If the knowledge he wrung from so much sorrow could not at last preserve him, Berryman was able to apply it to scholarship in a profoundly rewarding way; and his Freudian study of Stephen Crane appeared in 1950. Meanwhile, it seems, he had conferred on Robert Lowell the part of the younger brother whom he wished to excel. After Lowell brought out *The Mills of the Kavanaughs,* Berryman completed a poem matching its design. The two works are stanzaic and of comparable lengths. Both of them are humorless meditations in which a wife considers her relation to her husband while the poet's voice moves in and out of the frame. American history and problems of religious faith supply the intellectual substance of both.

Berryman's *Homage to Mistress Bradstreet* includes two peculiarly strenuous passages. In one, ending the first third of the poem, the young Puritan bride tries to express the pain she feels in giving birth to a child. In the other, much longer passage, filling the middle third, the poet imagines himself communing with her spirit and in effect seducing her.

It is entirely in Berryman's character that he should have Anne Bradstreet speak of the miseries and isolation of colonial life, dwell on the agony of an accouchement, and undergo a seduction of her spirit by that of the poet. His imagination of women tends always to the idea of a lonely girl who desires him and whom he may love and leave because otherwise she will leave him. His idea of love tends to voluptuousness, not tenderness, and not a passion for an irreplaceable person. Because he liked to compare writing to parturition and poems to children, Berryman could easily supply the voice of a wife who writes didactic verse while producing eight children. Because he believed the creator of high art must serve an apprenticeship to pain, there is hardly any limit to the suffering he can inflict on Anne Bradstreet. Infatuated with his own creation, he cries, "I miss you Anne." Absent from other joys, she says, "I *want* to take you for my lover." [2]

2   *Homage to Mistress Bradstreet* (New York: Farrar, Straus, and Giroux, 1956), numbers 25 and 32.

The stanza form is difficult, involving four different line lengths and an intricate rhyme scheme. To fit his words in, Berryman disrupts his syntax even more arbitrarily here than in his sonnets. His conceits and language are again frantic with incongruity. If the poem received unusual attention, the reason is that a shocking mixture of religiosity with sexuality will attract intelligent readers if it is served in exalted language. The rapt solemnity of the poet's posture discouraged a frivolous response to his vagaries. The obscurity of the poem, its air of historical learning, its quasi sublimity of tone, all protected it from the judgment it might have drawn.

With the bizarre design of *Homage to Mistress Bradstreet* one finds valuable devices. If Berryman chose a difficult stanza, he employed it flexibly, varying rhyme scheme and line length. One sees the possibility of a form complex in itself and so handled as to offer interesting variations. The give and take between author and protagonist, the quick changes of voice and viewpoint—especially in the middle section of the poem—recapture the life-giving dialectic of the sonnets. The blurring of identities, sometimes leaving us unsure of the speaker, reminds us of Berryman's brooding over selfhood. A thoughtful reader cannot escape the impression that the poet is often talking to and indeed consoling himself: "I am a man of griefs and fits / trying to be my friend" (no. 35).

About the time the poem was published as a book, Berryman's first marriage ended in divorce; and though he married again in 1956, he was divorced once more, only to marry a third time in 1961. Meanwhile, he worked on another long poem, or collection of poems, ultimately known as *Dream Songs*.

The speaker of these poems is called Henry, a name given Berryman by his second wife in a routine domestic joke. In his book on Crane, he had examined the novelist's addiction to this name and observed that it belongs, among other characters, to the main figure of a long story called "The Monster," which Berryman analyzed and praised at length. Crane deals in that story with the relation between a doctor and his Negro hostler, Henry Johnson. The doctor's little boy is fond of Henry, turning to him for comfort when he is in disgrace. Henry prides himself on his good looks, stylish clothes, and effectiveness with ladies. When the doctor's house catches fire, Henry in effect rescues the little boy. But while doing so, he collapses, his face is destroyed by acid, and his mind is unhinged. Though he survives, he becomes a crazy, if harmless, monster with no face. He terrifies everyone who sees him and must live finally wearing a veil, cut off from almost all companionship, singing incoherently to himself. The doctor alone can and will look after him. In a savage irony, the doctor's faithfulness to his son's rescuer ruins his medical practice and brings down social ostracism.

Crane pays attention to the hostler's speech. Henry Johnson is fluent and elaborately polite; but he talks in the deepest southern accent, with no regard for grammar. Outside the doctor's home he makes two speaking appearances, both scenes of courtship. In the first, the young lady is thrilled by his elegance and conversation; she keeps him for hours. In the second, when he is the escaped monster, she flees, leaving him to mumble repetitiously into the void, sentences like, "I jes' drap in ter ax you 'bout er daince."

As an undergraduate, Berryman had told a fellow student named Brooks Johnson, who hated Negroes, that he himself had "some coon blood." One assumes that Crane's story excited Berryman's fears about the division of his own life between the eloquent public figure and the inarticulate, hidden self, the fear that alcohol and skirt-craziness might turn him into a monster, the fear that his love would destroy those who hoped to rescue him. Berryman's Henry is a white man in black-face who speaks at times the dialect of Crane's monster; and the poet presents Henry with the same blend of farce and pathos that Crane uses for Henry Johnson.

But Henry is only one of the poet's masks in *Dream Songs*. The drama of Berryman's work is often taken from that of the old minstrel show. In this there were two end men, Mr. Bones and Mr. Tambo, who responded to questions put by the middleman, or interlocutor. Just as Mr. Tambo played the tambourine, so his opposite number played the bones, or flat sticks used as rhythmical clappers. It is as impulsive Mr. Bones that Henry bandies questions with a shrewder self. The sound of "bones" is almost a condensation of "Berryman"; and two Shakespearean allusions probably enrich the name. In *A Midsummer Night's*

Dream, Titania, bewitched, asks Bottom, wearing the ass's head, whether he will hear music; and Bottom calls for "the tongs and the bones" (IV,i,29). In *2 Henry IV* Doll Tearsheet curses the skinny beadle who is dragging her to punishment, and calls him "Goodman death, goodman bones" (V,iv,28). Berryman knew Shakespeare too well to miss these references. But even without them it is clear that the death-loving music maker Bones wants answers from the poet's more reflective faculty, the voice of chastened wisdom. "Come away, Mr. Bones," says the middleman. Among these forces hovers the poet who sings to himself of love and despair, whose veil conceals his ugly void, and whose ugliness hides his nobility.

As the *Dream Songs* proceed, the machinery of the minstrel show often rusts in idleness. But the motifs connected with Henry dominate the work. When Berryman analyzed Crane's story, he lingered on the theme of rescue; and it is obvious that he found great power in the doctrine that whoever preserves another man from ruin is likely to be destroyed for his zeal. In *Dream Songs* Henry appeals for rescue to a number of figures, male and female; but he also fears they will harm themselves if they help him. "Cling to me," he says, "& I promise you'll drown too" (no. 355, p. 377).[3] He yearns to succor those who need him; he feels guilty for failing allies like Delmore Schwartz. He writes a string of elegies for poets who were not preserved. He wishes he had rescued his own father, and that his father had rescued him. Above all, he disarms the reader, who must pity, love, forgive, and save this martyred poet.

Lowell published *Life Studies* while Berryman was writing the *Dream Songs;* and Lowell's habit of undercutting his own despair with a humorous, ironic commentary probably influenced his friend's work. But long before he read *Life Studies,* Berryman admired Pound's *Cantos.* He had been struck by Pound's use of masks and once described the subject of the *Cantos* as "the life of the modern poet," which is nearly the

---

3   *The Dream Songs* (New York: Farrar, Straus, & Giroux, 1969). All quotations from *The Dream Songs* will be followed in the text by poem number and page number from this edition.

description he gave of his own subject.[4] An older model still was *Song of Myself*. Whitman frames his cheerful egoism in disarming humor. He makes a drama out of self-observation; for he is "both in and out of the game and watching and wondering at it"; and in *Calamus* he warns any followers, "I am not what you supposed. . . . The way is suspicious, the result uncertain, perhaps destructive."[5]

There are signs that Berryman hoped to impose order on his work not only by a web of recurrent motifs and the drama of self-consciousness but also more mechanically. The number seven finds its way into the scheme. *Dream Songs* is 7,000 lines long, divided into seven books, of which 1–3 were published separately as 77 *Dream Songs*. The number of poems in book 4, books 5–7, and the entire collection is also divisible by seven; and these sections are not insignificant. The middle book, 4, is a descent into hell; here the poet speaks as a buried, decaying corpse but surfaces at the end of the book. One thinks of book 6 of the *Aeneid*, also marking a halfway point. Berryman's father's suicide is dealt with in the first poem of book 1, the penultimate poem of book 3, the last poem of book 5, and the penultimate poem of book 7, in which the poet imagines himself returning to Oklahoma, digging his father up, and destroying with an ax the "start" of his own tragedy (no. 384, p. 406).

If one looks for coherence in *Dream Songs*, the metrical form may satisfy the need best. It is derived from the form Berryman had used in his "Nervous Songs." Each poem has three stanzas of six iambic lines. The pattern they approach is that the third and last lines of the stanza should have three beats, the other five. Rhyme is normal. The tendency is for the third line to rhyme with the last and for the rest to pair off either in couplets, or alternately: *a b c a b c*, or *a a b c c b*. But the pattern is handled freely. Often the lines are an odd length or do not rhyme. When the form is most regular, the poem is likely to be weak.

The charm of this form is that the short lines both enclose and

---

4   "The Poetry of Ezra Pound," in *The Freedom of the Poet*, 260.

5   *Song of Myself*, sect. 4, l. 79; and "Whoever You Are Holding Me Now in Hand," in *Calamus*, l. 7.

connect. They define and link the tercets and stanzas within each poem; they also tie the poems to one another. Sometimes the poet seizes the opportunity for a dialectic of strophe, antistrophe, epode. Berryman has no skill as a rhymester. Yet the unpredictable absence and appearance of rhyme works; for it gives an ironic bounce to bleak passages.

None of these elements will account for the appeal of the best *Dream Songs*. It is true that as one advances through 7,000 lines, one gathers information and learns habits that make the shape or meaning of the separate poems clearer. But the unity of the work is no greater than that of a sonnet sequence. In fact, the design of *Dream Songs* involves a return to that of Berryman's sonnets, with the focus shifted from the figure of the mistress to the sensibility of the poet.

Here, of course, the imagined dialogues are not between different persons. Neither are they, as in "Nervous Songs" and *Homage to Mistress Bradstreet,* embedded in a dramatic monologue. What had been the frame in those poems moves to the center of *Dream Songs:* the dialectic is internalized. At the same time, by the device of naming the protagonist Henry or Bones, and speaking of him in the third person, Berryman transcends his egocentricity; not the poet's self but his attitudes toward himself become the theme. The mask replaces the speaker. This fact opens the way for the splendid virtue of the *Dream Songs,* their irony, sometimes comic, sometimes grim:

> You couldn't bear to grow old, but we grow old.
> Our differences accumulate. Our skin
> tightens or droops: it alters.
> Take courage, things are not what they have been
> and they will never again. Hot hearts grow cold,
> the rush to the surface falters,
>
> secretive grows the disappearing soul
> learned & uncertain, young again
> but not in the same way:
> Heraclitus had a wise word here to say,
> which I forget.   (no. 263, p. 282)

By assigning his despair to Henry and Mr. Bones, Berryman puts it outside himself; it is now tame and approachable, something to play with and ridicule. Even when the despair is explicitly suicidal, one feels (wrongly, alas) that the poet can control it and put it to work:

> My eyes with which I see so easily
> will become closed. My friendly heart will stop.
> I won't sit up.
> Nose me, soon you won't like it—ee—
> worse than a pesthouse; and my thought all gone
> & the vanish of the sun.
>
> The vanish of the moon, which Henry loved
> on charming nights when Henry young was moved
> by delicate ladies
> with ripped-off panties, mouths open to kiss.
> They say the coffin closes without a sound
> & is lowered underground!   (no. 373, p. 395)

As Henry, the poet can drop his civilized speech along with the anxiety that civilization breeds. He develops an expressive style out of the inarticulateness that fascinated him and that belongs to our time; and through it he not only disarms us but shares the wordlessness of readers who distrust elegance and fluency. The inarticulateness of the misnamed monster talks for those who see monsters taking over the world, and who have found no coherent language to express their horror.

> A rainy Sunday morning, on vacation
> as well as Fellowship, he could not rest:
> bitterly he shook his head.
> —Mr. Bones, the Lord will bring us to a nation
> where everybody only rest.—I confess
> that notion bores me dead,
>
> for there's no occupation there, save God,
> if that, and long experience of His works
> has not taught me his love.   (no. 256, p. 275)

There was nothing to keep Berryman from going on with the *Dream Songs*. Two appeared in his posthumous volume; and a thousand more might have come out in his lifetime. Henry might have grown into a public figure like Mr. Dooley, airing his moods and opinions from day to day before an audience that had learned what to expect. In the way of general ideas and moral insights Berryman has little that is fresh to offer. Neither is he a phrase maker, nor a magician with words. It is emblematic that a childhood disease should have weakened his hearing, because his ear for rhythm is undistinguished. For all his talent and learning, Berryman could not come near the intellectual style of Auden or the middle-aged Lowell. Once he had circulated the most sensational facts of his private life, his richest treasure was the ironic drama of Henry's diary.

So it strikes one as a hero's mistake that Berryman should have turned his back on this invention and chosen a simpler exploitation of autoanalysis for his last two books. Both these collections are carefully organized. In *Love & Fame* one moves from part to part in a visible direction. Sexual passion gives way to literary ambition, which is overtaken by spiritual darkness; and at last the poet turns to God with a set of prayers. In *Delusions, Etc.* (published posthumously), Berryman hugs his faith revived. From his new belvedere his old rationalism seems hard to tell from delusion; and he knows his faith must seem foolish to his old readers. After prayers of doubt about his right to mercy, the poet celebrates artists who suffered ordeals like his own and met difficult deaths. Imminent mortality then makes him eager to use death, to bring the remainder of his life into harmony with faith. In a further group of poems he defiantly accepts his uniqueness and perhaps the need for a death of his own. And so a closing set of prayers shows him ready, disbelieving in hell and accepting death as salvation or nothing. The book amounts on some pages to a suicide note: "I've *had it*. I can't wait" ("The Facts and Issues").[6] Yet the final poem remains affirmative: "Aware to the dry throat of the wide hell in the world . . . / mockt in abysm by one shallow wife, / with the ponder both in

6   *Delusions, Etc.,* (New York: Farrar, Straus, & Giroux, 1972), 69.

priesthood & of State / heavy upon me, yea / all the black same I dance my blue head off!" ("King David Dances"; 70).

The coherence of the last books cannot replace the pleasures of the *Dream Songs:* their deliberate humor and indirection; viewpoints that never stand still; a tone that hops from aspiration to bathos. In the last poems, the strongest humor seems unintentional; it would be cruel to deal seriously with their serious argument; their inarticulateness is painfully artless. Having discovered that his sensibility could bewitch us, Berryman made the error of growing solemn about it; and the reader's attention must move back from the poet's attitude to his mind. Speaking in the first person, without Henry to screen him, Berryman challenges comparison with the most brilliant poets alive. But his thoughts, as bare thoughts, neither please nor fascinate. The last books have an intense but narrowly documentary appeal. Those who are attached to the poet will read them for the scandalous information they supply about his life, for the pathetic account of his journey homeward to religious faith, for the brave valediction of a man who chose his own way to die.

13

LOWELL

I

For an age of world wars and prison states, when the Faustian myth of science produces the grotesquerie of fallout shelters, the decorous emotion seems a fascinated disgust. After outrage has exhausted itself in contempt, after the mind has got the habit of Dallas and South Africa, the shudder of curiosity remains. Every morning we think something new and insufferable is about to happen: what is it? Among living poets writing in English nobody has expressed this emotion with the force and subtlety of Robert Lowell. In an undergraduate poem Lowell described himself as longing for the life of straightforward beliefs and deeds, of simple lust, conventional faith and boyish sports. But "sirens sucked me in," he said; and painful, feverish contemplation was his fate: "On me harsh birches, nursing dew, / Showered their warm humidity" ("The Dandelion Girls"). Like Baudelaire, he saw things so disturbing that they almost kept him from making them into poetry.

Yet the confident life of public action might have seemed young Lowell's certain destiny. For his family line ran about as high as an American genealogy could go. His mother was descended from Edward Winslow, a Pilgrim Father who came to America on the *Mayflower*. Edward's son was a mighty Indian killer and a governor of Plymouth

This essay was originally published under the title "The Age of Lowell," in Irvin Ehrenpreis, ed. *American Poetry* (New York: St. Martin's, 1965). Reprinted by permission. © Edward Arnold (publishers) 1965.

Colony. Lowell's mother also traced herself to the New Hampshire frontiersman John Stark, who was made a colonel at Bunker Hill and a general in the Revolutionary War. Lowell's father, though trained as a naval officer, belonged to the intellectual family that produced teachers and clergymen as well as fighters. The original R. T. S. Lowell, five generations ago, was also a naval officer. Another namesake, Lowell's great-grandfather, "delicate, sensitive, strangely rarefied," was a poet best known for a ballad on the relief of Lucknow, and spent four years as headmaster of St. Mark's, one of the most fashionable boys' schools in the United States. Lowell's great-great-uncle, James Russell Lowell, a Harvard professor and one of the famous poets of his era, became ambassador to the court of St. James's. For most of the memories on which Lowell was bred, Puritan New England, especially Boston, provided the setting; and in the history of the Massachusetts Bay Colony he could find his Tree of Jesse.

It was on these very elements that he was to turn his first great storm of poetic disgust. They supplied the object of a clamorous repudiation. The shape the outburst took, however, depended less on ancestry than on a set of experiences that seem to have determined Lowell's original literary color: his meeting with the circle of John Crowe Ransom and Allen Tate, his conversion to Roman Catholicism, and his dramatic response to the Second World War.

At St. Mark's School, Lowell found his interest in poetry encouraged by the poet Richard Eberhart, one of the teachers. He began experimenting with free verse but soon switched to stanzaic forms. As an undergraduate at Harvard he went to see Robert Frost, bearing a "huge epic" on the First Crusade. The great man perused a page, told the visitor that he lacked "compression," and read him Collins's "How Sleep the Brave" as an example of something "not too long."[1] For a period Lowell tried to write simple, imagistic poems like those of W. C. Williams; but the university around him seemed less than a nest of singing birds, and he heeded a recommendation that he should study under John Crowe Ransom. In the middle of his undergraduate career,

---

1   See Frederick Seidel, "Robert Lowell," *Paris Review* 25 (Winter-Spring, 1961).

after a summer spent with Allen Tate, he left Harvard altogether and went to Kenyon College, in rural Ohio, where Ransom was teaching.

For a while now, Lowell even lived in Ransom's house, and later shared lodgings with two other young writers, one of whom, Peter Taylor, has published a short story based on their college friendship ("1939"). During these years, the critic Randall Jarrell taught English at Kenyon, and he too lived a while with the Ransoms. It seems obvious that the network of literary affiliations gave the young student, who had been growing "morose and solitary" at home, a welcome substitute for blood relations who felt small sympathy with this talent. Lowell often describes himself as belonging to the second generation of the Fugitives; he spent long periods in a quasi-filial or fraternal connection with three or four of the authors he met in the years before the war, and he speaks of them with the sort of loyalty one extends to kin. The conservative politics, strong but orthodox religious faith, and high literary standards to which these southerners were attached must have seemed to him seductive alternatives to the commonplace republicanism, mechanical churchgoing, and materialist aspirations that characterized a "Boston" formed (as he saw it) by successive lines of Puritans, Unitarians and low-church Episcopalians. To Lowell the home of his forebears stood for a rootless but immobile sterility.

In 1940, when he took a step toward establishing a family of his own, Lowell not surprisingly married another writer, the novelist Jean Stafford, whose "flaming insight" he commemorates in a recent poem. He was also converted to Roman Catholicism, the church peculiarly associated in Boston with the large populations descended from humble Irish immigrants, natural enemies, in politics and culture, of his own class. But the poet already felt committed to a kind of moral vitality that could for only limited time be expressed in Roman terms. During the period when his newfound church was something defiant of the Boston he had repudiated, and so long as the language, symbols, and ritual represented materials to be conquered and employed for explosive purposes, he could use Catholicism as an ingredient of poetry. But when it was only the faith he had to accept, the church came to seem as oppressive and self-contradictory as the code of his native class.

It was during the years of his first marriage and his adherence to the church that Lowell's earliest books of poetry appeared. Apart from what had come out in an undergraduate magazine, the first poems he published were a pair in the *Kenyon Review* 1939. But years went by before any successors could be seen in print, partly because the few he wrote were rejected when he sent them out. Then in 1943 about a dozen of his poems turned up in the literary quarterlies, to be followed the next year by a collection, *Land of Unlikeness*. This gathering, withholding, and sudden releasing of his work is typical of the poet's method; for he labors over his poems continually and plans each collection as a sequence, the opening and closing poems in each making a distinct introduction and conclusion and the movement between them tending from past to present, from questions to resolution, from ambiguous negation to hesitant affirmative.

Above the influence of Ransom and Tate, or the steady use of Catholic religious imagery, or the many motifs drawn from Boston and New England, the most glaring feature of Lowell's two earliest volumes was a preoccupation with the Second World War. Not long after the United States joined that war, he committed the most dramatic public act of his life. Characteristically, this act seemed at once violent and passive, and was calculated to make his parents very uncomfortable. In what turned out to be no more than preliminary steps, he twice tried to enlist in the navy but was rejected. Soon, however, the mass bombing of noncombatants shocked his moral principles; and when he was called up under the Selective Service Act, he declared himself a conscientious objector. Rather than simply appear before the responsible board and declare his convictions, he refused to report at all, and thus compelled the authorities to prosecute him.

In order to give his deed the widest possible significance, he released to the press a thousand-word open letter to President Roosevelt. Here Lowell drew repeated attention to the historic eminence of his ancestors. He described himself as belonging to a family that had "served in all our wars, since the Declaration of Independence"; he told the president that the Lowell family traditions, "like your own, have always found their fulfillment in maintaining, through responsible participation in both civil and military services, our country's freedom and honor." He said that he had tried to enlist when the country was in danger of invasion but that this danger was past, and the intention of bombing Japan and Germany into submission went against the nation's established ideals. He could not participate in a war, Lowell said, that might leave Europe and China "to the mercy of the U.S.S.R. a totalitarian tyranny committed to world revolution."[2]

Twenty years later he was still signing open letters of protest to newspapers; and although his opinions had altered, their direction had not shifted. "No nation should possess, use, or retaliate with its bombs," he wrote in a 1962 symposium. "I believe we should rather die than drop our own bombs."[3] It is suggestive of the poet's sensibility that he should link suicide with mass murder, as though the way to prevent the second might be to commit the first. The themes of self-destruction and assassination are often joined in his work, the one apparently redeeming or proving the altruism of the other. Yet parricide becomes a mythical, guilt-ridden route to justice and liberty; for by throwing over the traditional family pieties, the young Lowell seems to have felt he was destroying his begetters and oppressors.

The poems that appeared in *Land of Unlikeness* (1944) were mostly written during a year Lowell spent with the Tates after leaving Kenyon College. In them he devoted himself mainly to a pair of themes reflecting recent history. One was the unchristian character of the Allies' role in the Second World War; the other was the causal connection between the doctrines of America's founders and the desolate condition, spiritual and material, of the country in the thirties. Looking back, Lowell saw in the ideals and motives of his ancestors the same contradictions, the same denial of a Christ they professed to worship, that made his own world a land of unlikeness, i.e., a place obliterating the image of divinity, a culture where the old metaphors that made created beings recall their creator no longer operated. Those who had flown

---

2   Information on Lowell's dealings with his draft board comes mainly from the *Boston Post* of 9 Sept. and 2 Oct. and the *Boston Globe* of 9 Sept. (morning), 1943.

3   "The Cold War and the West," *Partisan Review* 29 (Winter 1962):47.

from persecution came here to persecute the red men; those who hated war made war on nature, plundering whales and neighbors for unspiritual profit.

In order to dramatize and generalize this view, he drew parallels between divine and human history: between the war and Doomsday, between the dust bowl sharecroppers and Cain. And he set up antitheses: between profits and mercy, between political slogans and charity. To the Second World War he opposed Christ. In the social and political theories of the Fugitives, Lowell found support for his tendency to identify degeneracy with the city, the machine, and Roosevelt's centralized democracy, even as he associated true civilization with rural, aristocratic society. And since the South itself was yielding to the rapid movement from one set of conditions to the other, Lowell could apply his argument to humanity in general, through parallels drawn from Genesis and Revelation, from the myth of Troy, and from history. Thus the advent of cosmopolitan industrialism becomes a sign that we are all descended from Cain; the first Eden becomes a symbol of that antebellum, ostensibly Augustan society which the North supposedly destroyed; the fall of Troy becomes the analogue of the defeat of the South. Since the new war had the effect of speeding the hated process, it was easily drawn into this aspect of Lowell's rhetoric.

By the time he composed these poems, Lowell had given up free verse and was writing obscure poems in meter in a style of his own. Most of those in *Land of Unlikeness* are savagely ironical. Besides employing puns or conceits repeatedly and with great earnestness, he brought in hackneyed phrases and common tags of quotations, giving sarcastic new directions to their meaning. He invented grotesque metaphors, such as "Christ kicks in the womb's hearse" ("Satan's Confession").[4] Although the stanzas of most of the poems are elaborate, the rhythms are heavy, the sounds are cluttered, alliteration occurs often and unsubtly.

Into such verse he pressed enough violence of feeling to stun a sensitive ear. Certain dramatic monologues and visionary pieces on

---

4   *The Land of Unlikeness* (N.p.: Cummington Press, 1944). Pages are not numbered in this limited edition. All citations will be made by poem title only.

religious themes make the greatest uproar. The tighter the stanza forms, the wilder the bitterness: erratic rhythms, blasphemous images, deliberately hollow rhetoric erupt over the objects of his onslaught. But instead of the tight form providing an ironic contrast or intensifying counterpoint to the violent tone, it seems arbitrary. The mind that follows the form seems cut off from the mouth that screams the sacrilege:

> In Greenwich Village, Christ the Drunkard brews
> Gall, or spiked bone-vat, siphons His bilged blood
> Into weak brain-pans and unseasons wood.

> ("Christ for Sale")

In another poem the speaker is a slum mother apostrophizing the corpse of her baby, who has died on Christmas Day, 1942 (soon after the sinking of the British aircraft carrier *Ark Royal*):

> So, child, unclasp your fists,
> And clap for Freedom and Democracy;
> No matter, child, if Ark Royal lists
> Into the sea;
> Soon the Leviathan
> Will spout American.

> ("The Boston Nativity")

In this kind of satire the irony sounds so wild that most readers ignore the poet's meaning while observing his frenzy. The caricature of the nativity scene does not succeed in mocking America's moral pretensions during the war. It only forces upon one's perceptions the distorted religiosity of the writer. After all, by Lowell's own argument, there could be no real heroes in history apart from Christ. As in Tate's "Aeneas at Washington," the southern gentlemen comes finally to seem less like Hotspur than like Richard II, standing for ideals he did not die to defend.

Yet not every speech is a tantrum. In a few of the poems Lowell's detachment suggests that his churnings, in the others, are an effort to produce a heat wave in a naturally cold climate. Observation, dry and wry commentary, fascinated disgust—these are the marks of his subtler self, and these are what appear, for example, in "The Park Street Cemetery." This poem, a survey of the tombstones in a Boston graveyard, has less violence than distaste in its tone. Lowell treats the site as a repository of those Puritan colonists who bequeathed to the America they founded their own confusion of grace with fortune. The form is appropriately relaxed: three stanzas, each of seven unrhymed, irregular lines; and the poet ends not with a scream but a dead note: "The graveyard's face is painted with facts / And filigreed swaths of forget-me-nots" ("Park Street Cemetery").

The positive doctrines of *Land of Unlikeness* seem less significant than the negative directions. Whether Lowell espouses southern agrarianism or Roman Catholicism, his principles attract him less as ideals of aspiration than as possibilities disdained by his ancestors. Against early New England the real charge he makes is that it failed to meet its own ultimate standards; for Lowell is after all another sober moralist with a Puritan's severity. He scolds Boston as Blake scolded London: for the death of vision and the death of conscience. Nowhere does he imply that dogma bestows serenity, or that, as some southerners would argue, the integrity of a ceremonious traditionalism outweighs the human misery on which it may rest.

For the poet, finally, the real problem remained unsolved. In most of this volume his best-integrated poems were his understatements; those that showed the highest technical ambition were bathetic. He had to find a style that would reconcile his interest in technique with his interest in justice, that would identify private with public disturbances. For such a style the elements lay not in the regularity of his stanzas, not in the depth of his piety, and not in his political judgments. It lay in Lowell's preoccupation with tone, in his humanitarian conscience, and in his sense of history. When he employed these to enlarge the meaning of an immediate personal experience, he produced the best poems in *Land of Unlikeness*: "The Park Street Cemetery," "In Memory of Arthur Winslow," "Concord," and "Salem."

Not only the older writers belonging to the circle of Ransom and Tate but also several other critics gave unusual attention to *Land of Unlikeness*. It was praised briefly but intensely by F. W. Dupee and Arthur Mizener. There was a careful review by Blackmur and a eulogy by J. F. Nims. But when Lowell's next book, *Lord Weary's Castle* appeared (1946), the critical reception became a thunder of welcome.

As usual, there is a link between the old work and the new. In the last poem of *Land of Unlikeness* ("Leviathan") the poet had mentioned the curse of "exile" as the alternative to the blessing of Canaan: God offered Israel the choice, says the poet; and when Israel chose to turn away from God's "wise fellowship," the outcome was Exile. The opening poem of *Lord Weary's Castle* is called "The Exile's Return," suggesting a common theme for both books. But the theme has broadened. In the new collection the poet implies that nothing was or could be settled by the war. In rejecting divine leadership, it is moral justice, the creative principle bringing order out of chaos, that we have banished from its self-made home. Thus if the expatriate is taken to mean Christ, the lord still waits for the world he built to pay him his due homage. He still menaces us with the judgment that the war prefigured. As a creator, however, the Exile is also the poet or artist; and in this sense he wants to be paid for the truthful visions with which he has blessed an ungrateful world. For he holds out the threat of a poet's curse, and his isolation remains the mark of society's misdirection. In a private extension of this sense the Exile is Lowell himself, released from jail after serving about five months of the year and a day to which he had been sentenced. Coming back to ordinary routines, he meets in new forms the same moral issues he had wrestled with before his imprisonment.

All these implications are in "The Exile's Return." Here, an emigré comes back to his German home after the war, under the protection of American garrisons. But the shattered place looks the opposite of Eden; and if the first springtime brings lilies, it brings as well the agony of responsibility. To suggest the aspect of the neglected artist, Lowell crowds the poem with allusions to Mann's Tonio Kröger, who stood "between two worlds" without feeling at home among either the bourgeoisie or the artists. To suggest the themes of heaven and hell, he has seasonal references to an infernal winter, a spring of rebirth, the "fall" of autumn, and the entrance to Dante's hell. For the motifs of imprisonment and release he uses a jaillike hotel-de-ville, a Yankee "commandant," and a parcel of "liberators" who are as yet innocent or "unseasoned."[5]

In direct contrast, the closing poem of the book, "Where the Rainbow Ends," deals with an American city, Boston, that has never been bombed but that faces the dissolution caused by decay of conscience. Not war but winter devastates this city. Not as a refugee but as a voluntary exile from worldliness, the poet-prophet offers his people the alternative to the Judgment prefigured by the cold season:

> What can the dove of Jesus give
> You now but wisdom, exile? Stand and live,
> The dove has brought an olive branch to eat.
>
> ("Where the Rainbow Ends"; 69)

Repeatedly in this book, Lowell shows an understanding of how his elemental powers might be fused, how his unnatural calmness of tone in dealing with horrifying material might be supported by an apparent casualness of style screening a meticulous exactness of underlying structure. His sense of the past justifies ironically the calmness of tone. For to the degree that one considers human misery and cruelty as the reflection of permanent instinct—rather than transient ignorance— one will view one's own corruption and one's neighbor's not with scandalized outbursts but with comprehending calm. Furthermore, through the distancing effect of history, as through the shaping effect of complex form, one can even achieve a coherent grasp of one's own deepest, most secret anguish. With these several powers Lowell also made good use of a set of influences that he had earlier felt only at some remove, as they were present in the work of Tate, Eliot, and Ransom. These influences emanate from the great line of French Symbolists and post-Symbolists, to whom the "modern" experimental movement in poetry owes its origin. When Lowell turned to Rimbaud, Valéry, and Rilke for

5   "The Exile's Return," in *Lord Weary's Castle* (New York: Harcourt, Brace, 1946), 3.

models, he was accepting the cosmopolitan conception of literature that American poets as diverse as Whitman and Pound have worked with.

The defect of *Lord Weary's Castle* is the same as that of *Land of Unlikeness*. In Whitman, Tate, and Hart Crane, one cannot help noticing a habit of substituting rhetoric, in the form of self-conscious sublimity, for poetry. If Lowell, their heir, yields to this habit, it is because, like them, he has the highest conception of the poet's task. But the mere posture of soaring, the air of prophecy, does not make a speech either noble or prophetic. In Lowell's most commonly overpraised work, "The Quaker Graveyard" (8–14), the use of rhetoric joins with a denseness of symbolism to make a poem that seems more impressive for aspiration than for accomplishment.

Throughout this poem he contrasts two views of saving grace: the ideal of a special gift to the elect, and the idea of something that infuses not merely all men but all creatures. The in-group's complacency Lowell attaches to the Protestant sects of colonial New England and to his patriotic cousin, who died at sea for a cause Lowell rejected. As a measure of the limitations of this ethic, which he associates with war-loving capitalism, Lowell invokes the great evolutionary chain of created beings. The world, he keeps saying, exists as a moral order in which separate men are not masters but participants: both the sea slime from which we rose and the whale that we plunder lie beneath the same law that subsumes humanity. To sectarian arrogance he opposes the innocence of the humbler orders of creation, for whom cruelty is an accident of their nature. As the solvent of arrogance he offers the Catholic compassion of Christ embodied in Mary his mother.

In Lowell's usual manner, the end of the poem recalls the beginning. We move back to the Quaker graveyard on Nantucket Island off the coast of Massachusetts. But where the initial scene was of violent death in a great war, the closing gives us the lifeless cemetery of wind and stone and tree. Now the poet glances back to the very start of the evolutionary process and contrasts that moment, when life and death were born together, with the present outlook of a corpse-littered sea. And suddenly the capacious cemetery of the Atlantic becomes a symbolic contrast to the filled graveyard of the Quakers: God has more room than this; the old covenant has given way to the new gospel.

In this fascinating work the failure of the rhetoric grows obvious if we notice the weakness of the poem's penultimate section. Here Lowell puts the snug, familiar salvation that his cousin might aspire to beside the Catholic vision of the universal but quite unknowable God reflected in the image of Our Lady of Walsingham. Though this passage is a deliberate understatement, the effect is not powerful by implication; rather, it sounds bathetic. Beyond human griefs or joys, says the poet, the Virgin

> knows what God knows,
> Not Calvary's Cross nor crib at Bethlehem
> Now, and the world shall come to Walsingham.   (13)

If we compare Lowell's two stanzas, in their attempt to express the inexpressible, with similar passages in Eliot's *Dry Salvages* (which is, with *Lycidas,* one of the models for this poem), we must admit that there is a posed air, a willed simplicity, in Lowell's lines that never appears in, say, "Lady, whose shrine stands on the promontory" (Eliot, *CP* 135). This forced tone seems the more regrettable because Lowell's passage is meant to deliver the positive alternative to the errors he denounces with such thoroughness. It is in the overcharged stretches of churning sounds, eruptive rhythm, and violent imagery that we seem to hear the authentic voice of the poet:

> In the great ash-pit of Jehosaphat
> The bones cry for the blood of the white whale,
> The fat flukes arch and whack about its ears.   (12)

We cannot help feeling that he enjoys his destructive vision in a way not compatible with his role as prophet, moralist, or recipient of wisdom.

In another long poem, "At the Indian Killer's Grave" (*Lord Weary's Castle* 54–55), Lowell gives a more appropriate display of his powers.

The history of its composition reminds us of his habitual alteration of his own work; for much of the poem comes out of the "Park Street Cemetery," and the closing lines are a magnificent adaptation of verses from another early poem. Moreover, as he transforms these materials, the poet enlarges their meaning. Like the speaker in Tate's "Ode to the Confederate Dead," the poet here contemplates a graveyard where his direct or spiritual ancestors are buried among their peers. Unlike Tate's speaker, however, he searches for the meaning of their sins, not their virtues. Staring about at the figures carved on the gravestones among the vegetation, he contrasts the Puritan dead with the living Irish who now hold political power in Boston. The sound of a train stopping underground makes him think of time stopping and of the Judgment to come; and he wonders about the fate of the Pilgrims' souls. He imagines the spirit of the Red Indian chief King Philip, addressing the Puritan Indian killers and reminding them that all their pretensions to being the chosen of God have left them only the corrupted bodies that now serve as carrion for sea gulls. He looks at the toothed railing, thinks of dragon's teeth, and ponders the double source, natural (i.e., Cadmean) and spiritual (i.e., Adamic), of our instinct for evil. Then in a sudden, astonishing close, the poet turns from the old law to the new, from Adam to Christ; and he calls on the four evangelists to guide him toward the inclusive faith of the Roman Catholic church, to a vision of salvation that more than admits the Indian chief; for it promises Philip that the blessed Virgin herself will deck out his head with flowers:

> John, Matthew, Luke and Mark,
> Gospel me to the Garden, let me come
> Where Mary twists the warlock with her flowers—
> Her soul a bridal chamber fresh with flowers
> And her whole body an ecstatic womb,
> As through the trellis peers the sudden Bridegroom.   (57)

And there, in a fine identification of his private conversion with both the history of Massachusetts and the religious or mythical account of all human history, Lowell brings his poem to a close.

Generally, the poet sounds a tone of self-restraint, of calm but engrossed repugnance, that reminds one of Ransom's poems "Necrological" and "Armageddon." This tone he drops appropriately in two counterbalanced passages: the outburst of Philip, who speaks with a savage violence of sound and image, and the lyric close and climax, when calm is replaced by rapture. The apparently loose-knit free associations rest on a carefully adjusted underpinning. Even the setting of the poet's meditation belongs to his subject, because the Puritan colonists brooded hourly upon death and the grave. They dressed in black and regarded the beauties of animate nature as bad diversions from the proper study of man, namely, death and judgment, heaven and hell. Nevertheless, they proudly gave themselves the title of the elect of God, promoting themselves to Paradise. It is a tremendous historical irony that their haughty Calvinism should have given way, in Boston, to the avowedly humble, Catholic faith of the Irish—to the church that in colonial times proselytized among the Indians instead of beheading them. In effect, the Whore of Rome waltzes over the Puritan graves: "the trollop dances on your skulls" (56).

A shimmering elaboration of imagery in the Symbolist manner connects the past and the present, the beginning of the poem with the end, the surface and the meaning. As the poet questions the spectacle before him, he wonders whether the fate of the dead is knowable or whether the pagan ideas of vengeance may not be carried out, so that Philip may eternally scalp the self-styled righteous men (Blake's "just man") who killed his people. This scalp-head-skull image appears again and again in the poem, reaching its most brilliant transformation at the end, when the Virgin is pictured as twisting Philip's "warlock," or pigtail, with flowers. Between these points the head becomes the English crown, responsible for building King's Chapel—a motif that opposes King Charles to King Philip. It then turns into the "dome" of the Statehouse that replaced the royal authority. Next, Philip's head reappears on a "platter" or gravestone. The phrasing recalls St. John and therefore the apostle or evangelist Philip. As a prophet now, the Indian can address his damned enemies and point out that the Catholics are raised over their heads. The dome becomes a globe that is the natural world, rejected (so says the poet) by the Puritans as they "hurled /

Anathemas at nature" (56). The head reappears in the headstones of the graves and finally in Mary's handling of Philip's head.

Parallel to these metamorphoses move the images of the garden. We start in the desolate garden of the cemetery, which the Puritans have reached in place of Paradise. Shrubs and sculpture remind one of similar scenes. So the view expands into both the Public Garden, where the Beacon Hill brahmins walked, and the Boston Common, which was more likely the playground of the Irish. Lowell toys with the ironies implicit in "garden" and "common," and with the further irony that though fashionable Beacon Hill is where his own class lives, it is topped by the Statehouse that in effect belongs to the Irish. Under the Common, meanwhile, runs the subway, analogue of hell, with its serpentine green trains, symbolic of time. Easily enough, the Garden and the Common expand in the whole "land" that the Puritans denounced and despoiled. This contracts at once into the mud that buries them now. The buildings around the Common are like palisades around the early settlements, intended, however, not to keep the wilderness from swallowing the villages but to keep, as it were, the remnant of natural ground from spreading. Finally, the motif reminds the poet of the ground in which Cadmus sowed the dragon's teeth, emblematic of original sin.

It seems remarkable that while some of the best poems in *Lord Weary's Castle* were imitations, or free English versions, of works in other languages, some of the least effective were dramatic monologues. In a poem like "The Ghost," based on Sextus Propertius, Lowell performed a superb job of giving his own voice to another poet. But in the double monologue "The Death of the Sheriff," the structure of which depends upon changes of voice and shifts in point of view, the speaker's smothered, crowded, dull murmur hardly alters from beginning to end. It's as though Lowell had too much to say to be able to submerge himself in an imaginary personality, and for that very reason found it easy to submerge a sympathetic author's character in his own.

His next book, *Mills of the Kavanaughs* (1951), brought these complementary tendencies to a crisis. The unqualified successes in it are a dazzling pastiche of Virgil and an adaptation of Werfel. But the longest and most ambitious works are five attempts at narrative dramatized through monologue. In four of these one feels that the poet has contrived situations offering the greatest opportunities for allusiveness and symbolism, and has sacrificed to such opportunities the absolutely essential narrative line upon which any dramatic monologue depends. He had obviously worked with immense pains over the title poem, running to more than five hundred lines, many of them beautiful evocations of the Maine landscape that gives the piece its setting. Nevertheless, although the plot would sound irresistibly sensational in summary—dealing with the madness and suicide of a patrician Catholic who married his sister by adoption—the poem is so hemmed in by cross-references and correspondences as to be wholly static. At one point Lowell goes so far as to match the number of a figure on a bird guide, once memorized by the protagonist, to the number of the stanza in which the man tries to recall the bird's name. The same substitution of arbitrary parallelism for narrative drama almost makes an impasse out of the last poem in the book, "Thanksgiving's Over." Here Lowell sends his main characters to a church on Thirty-first Street in New York, and situates their home next to the Third Avenue elevated train ("El"), in order to supply allusions to the Trinity.

Yet "Thanksgiving's Over" is one of the most revealing of Lowell's poems. Published two years after his divorce from Jean Stafford and the year after his marriage to the essayist Elizabeth Hardwick, it comes from a time when he no longer felt buoyed up by the church. Louise Bogan called the book *Mills of the Kavanaughs* a "dark midpoint" in his development, "which must in some way be transcended."[6] In this closing poem Lowell shows that he was passing the midpoint and going on. All the ingredients of his false rhetorical style are here: the monologue, the nightmare, madness, murder, suicide, and blasphemy. But the implications are not the old ones.

To the speaker of the poem Lowell gives the voice of a man who has lost the struggle to maintain his Christian faith and now ponders the

6 Review of *The Mills of the Kavanaughs*, New Yorker, 9 June 1951.

events that culminated in his failure. He is a Roman Catholic, a New
Yorker, and a widower, whose young, demented wife had believed herself impregnated by the Holy Ghost. After she tried to kill herself by
jumping from a window, he sent her to a sanatorium in the mountains
of Vermont, where she died. It is now Thanksgiving Day 1942, and
Michael the widower half remembers, half dreams of his dead wife. As
he tries to make sense out of the monstrous experiences, he thinks he
hears her talking.

The themes of the wife's increasingly disconnected chatter are love
and peace, her assumption being that these are united in the church.
But as her incoherence deepens, it becomes clear that the serenity she
offers is available only to those who are as credulous as children.
Within the wife's character, therefore, the themes are split so as to
suggest the opposition between religious doctrines and human nature.
She would like to feel love as spiritual charity, and therefore denies her
passionate impulses. She would like morality to issue from the passive
acceptance of authority, and so she denies the need for a struggle between the good and evil in our constitution. Through suppression, her
hidden passions become adulterous lusts projected on other persons.
Toward Michael her affection turns to jealousy, and she feels like killing
him. When this wish is thwarted, the hate turns inward, and she tries
to kill herself.

The poet implies that by giving up religion one might resolve some
of these conflicts, but one would then have to face the pain of a life
without ultimate meaning. Michael must choose between abandoning
God and abandoning his rational conscience. As the peculiarly shocking
symbol of his dilemma the poet focuses on the doctrine of the Trinity.
Thus the action of the poem is set at the very end of the Trinity season,
the week before Advent Sunday. Since the third person of the Trinity
appears iconographically as a dove, there is a profusion of sacrilegious
bird imagery. In order to involve other aspects of doctrine or ritual,
the poet complicates the central theme with allusions to the Eucharist
(etymologically "thanksgiving"), the Incarnation (as enacted in the Annunciation), and so forth. As a kind of parody of each, he produces
natural analogues. Within the fantasy of the girl's unconscious the Trinity takes the form of a love triangle. She confuses the Dove with a

celluloid parrot and imagines herself pregnant with birds. Since the conventional dish at an American Thanksgiving dinner is a turkey, the poet introduces grotesque ambiguities signifying the sterility of the Holy Ghost or the end of Michael's belief: "My fowl was soupbones."[7]

In flying from adultery to death, the girl was impelled by a guilt due to religion. So against the ideal of sexless conception displayed in paintings of the Annunciation, the poet sets the pagan fertility of "St. Venus" in Botticelli's *Primavera.* Against the child's sexless world of faith (evoked by allusions to Mother Goose rhymes, nursery tales, and Peter Pan) he sets the world of parenthood. In a distortion of phrases from the *Messiah* we hear the solution that Michael cannot yet accept: birds singing, "Come unto us, our burden's light" (55)—not the Dove but the birds of nature, of light and Lucifer and reason.

Over such themes the poet builds his characteristic sort of towering edifice; for the poem stands on an amazing reticulation of allusions. *Paradise Lost,* for obvious reasons, is continually evoked. The wretched couple are identified with Faust and Gretchen or with Hamlet and Ophelia. From her asylum window the wife sees the harpies of Baudelaire's "Cythère." Yet the essential image and meaning of the poem do not hinge on such clues. Michael sits and listens at the end of the poem, but he does not pray or receive a sign. It seems certain that when he boards a train, it will take him away from "this deaf and dumb / Breadline for children" (55)—as the wife unintentionally describes Roman Catholicism for the poet.

In Michael we confront again those linked themes of passive observation and wild impulse to travel that underlie so much of the nightmare violence in Lowell's poems. The wife's confinement in a cell reflects Michael's emotional seclusion. For the faithful Christian, life is a cage from which he escapes to Life; for the fallen Christian the limits of mere life make another kind of cage. Afraid to stir, for fear of wrecking the object of his stirring, the poet repeatedly speaks as a walled-off voyeur frantically watching the lives of others. Like a traveler in a sealed railway car, he passes over the earth, looking but never

7 *The Mills of the Kavanaughs* (New York: Harcourt, Brace, & World, 1951), 51.

doing, always on the move and never in motion: he has replaced action by vision.

✿ Lowell has said it was hard for him to find a subject and a language of his own. He can describe himself as writing a rather formal style coming out of Tate, Hart Crane, Ransom, and Eliot. But when he composed the brilliant, influential poems that were collected in *Life Studies* (1959), he took a line less reminiscent of those masters than of Pound. At last he had discovered his language and subject.

By the time this book appeared, Lowell had received enough prizes and awards to ease most men's desire for public recognition. He was the father of an infant daughter (born January 1957); he was a member of the Boston University Department of English; and he held the honorary degree of Doctor of Letters. Yet he had suffered a deeply disturbing experience when his mother died (February 1954); and the emotional pressures evident in his poetry had undermined his health until he was forced to turn for aid to hospital treatments.

The continuance of the emotional strains, tempered by domestic amenities and balanced by extraordinary marks of success in his career, seems to have enabled Lowell to discover the best uses for his talent. Superficially the transformation appeared in the lightening of his style. Lowell has said that soon after the *Mills of the Kavanaughs* came out, the pace of his writing slowed almost to a halt, and his allusive, rhetorical manner came to seem "distant, symbol-ridden, and willfully difficult." He felt that his old poems too often hid what they were about, presenting a "stiff, humorless, and even impenetrable surface."[8] So he began paraphrasing Latin quotations when he used them, and adding extra syllables to lines in order to make them clearer or more colloquial. With such a poem as the short, perfect "In the Cage" (1946)— a tetrameter sonnet recapturing the grimness of the months he spent

8   Here and there the author has ventured to paraphrase a few remarks made by Mr. Lowell in the course of informal discussions in a small class at Harvard University in the spring of 1963. [From Professor Ehrenpreis's headnote to this essay in *American Poetry*. (Ed.)]

in jail—he had already shown the strength of a comparatively un-adorned language, free from obscurities but suffused with irony. This manner now became not the exception but the rule. Line after line, in poem after poem, reads like a well-turned but easily spoken remark made by a fastidious, self-critical speaker who is at home with slang.

But the ease of language was only the outer sign of Lowell's new attitude toward his own nature. Without losing the tone of fascinated disgust, he now found it possible not only to treat himself as part of history but to treat history as part of himself. The course of his life became the analogue of the life of his era; the sufferings of the poet became a mirror of the sufferings of whole classes and nations. It was not as judge that he now claimed his authority: it was as the heroic artist, the man capable of turning vision into act. Through the title of his book Lowell gave himself the status of a craftsman who reveals life in general by the rendering of his own life.

Appropriately enough, *Life Studies* opens with a train journey from the city of priests to the city of artists, Rome to Paris. But the speaker is neither a character in a dramatic monologue nor an impersonal com-mentator. He is the poet talking about his own experiences. Here as generally in the book, Lowell has of course invented facts and altered truths. Yet the reader feels himself in touch with the real author and not with a mask. Similarly, the entrance into the poem is deliberately casual, with what look like random associations suggesting the real flow of a unique consciousness.

If the formal frame is thus a common earthly journey, the object presented is a miraculous one: the bodily assumption of the Virgin, proclaimed as a dogma in the jubilee year 1950. So the title "Beyond the Alps" means not only a trip toward France but also its opposite, "ultramontane," or the old epithet for supporters of papal infallibility. Lowell is using that doctrine, which the proclamation of the new dogma pressed to a record-breaking extreme, as the emblem of vulgar human credulity—the decay of imagination into superstition—a prin-ciple embodied in the pope. To escape from such tempting corruptions, the poet struggles within himself, during the night of his train journey, emerging at dawn into a sense of rebirth, a commitment to the creative imagination. Turning toward the intellect and the arts—toward Athene and Apollo—he rejects Mary and Pius. The pope is depicted, with grotesque irony, between a purring electric razor in one hand (the cat of rational science) and a canary in the other (the dove of faith).

In keeping with the opposition between religion and art, Lowell treats the mountains that appear in his poem as versions of Parnassus. So the journey recalls the celebrated simile, in Pope's *Essay on Criticism,* comparing the Alps to the challenge that art sets before the ambition of genius: "Hills peep o'er hills, and Alps on Alps arise." It is thus appropriate that at the time the poem opens, the inartistic Swiss should just have failed to climb Everest.

Violence, as usual in Lowell's work, accompanies the polarity of still-ness and movement. By mentioning the Swiss (historic mercenary sol-diers), the poet hints at the third principle of human nature which the poem deals with, i.e., destructive violence, personified by the warrior-king. The success of Caesarean terror in chaining the mind differs only in mode from the success of the magician-priest: Mussolini is as Roman as Pius. For an ideal culture, that could make violence, magic, and reason work together, Lowell offers not Rome but inimitable Hellas; and while the morning sun, like the imagination, transforms the bleak moonlit peaks into dazzling Parthenons, the reborn poet thinks of an-other traveler, Odysseus, escaping symbolically from the dark cave of Polyphemus by blinding the Cyclops with a dazzling firebrand. Athene, the guide of Odysseus, easily united in herself all the roles to which popes and dictators aspire; the reader recalls that she was also *parthenos,* or virgin, born miraculously without a mother, inspirer of a temple outshining St. Peter's; and Lowell reminds us that she sprang not from the flesh but from the intellect of Jove. To this white height the poet dare not attempt to climb. Only Paris is left, the "black classic" city of our own disintegrating culture; for our age seems unable to give direction and purpose to the primeval, irrational violence of human nature.

The intellectual design of this exhilarating poem has little system about it. Yet the texture, phrasing, and versification offer immediate pleasures to the ear. It consists of three sonnets with slightly irregular rhyme schemes, the last of the three ending in a couplet that also serves as epigrammatic close to the whole work.[9] This pattern is enriched by a fullness of alliteration, assonance, and internal rhyme that, so far from obtruding upon the offhand casualness of phrasing, only seems to deliver an ironical counterthrust to it. Puns and other witticisms supply an elegant distance from which the poet can regard his own discomfort:

> I envy the conspicuous
> waste of our grandparents on their grand tours—
> long-haired Victorian sages accepted the universe,
> while breezing on their trust funds through the world.
>
> (*Life Studies* 3)[10]

The imagery has the same sort of forceful inconsequences: mountains and birds, tyrants and feet, reappear in startling transformations as the wonderfully managed tone deepens from humor to bitterness to sublimity. The elaborate manipulations of height and depth, white and black, the four elements, are old habits of the poet. But the similar treatment of tiny details turns accidents into beauties. Thus the train stewards' tiptoe walk (while they ritually bang on their dinner gongs in a startling allusion to the Mass) becomes, in the second stanza, the toe of St. Peter, superstitiously kissed by pilgrims; and then, in the third, the splendor of the dawn of our culture as the poet sees "Apollo plant his heels / on terra firma through the morning's thigh" (4).

It is not easy to overpraise *Life Studies*. I suppose the most startling ingredient in the book was the new direction taken by the poet's conscience. In place of either direct protest or the fusion of his own morality with that of a Christian community, Lowell attached himself to several classes of heroic victims: children, artists, imprisoned criminals, and the mentally ill. Though these have always been linked in the romantic tradition, most poets dealing with them risk the dangers of

9   When Lowell revised this poem for *For the Union Dead,* he also restored a fourth stanza which was judiciously omitted from the text in *Life Studies.*

10   *Life Studies* (New York: Farrar, Straus, & Cudahy, 1959).

posturing and sentimentality. Precisely through making his own case
the central case, Lowell avoids either fault. Instead of merely seeing
him, we see his view of his peers.

Thus by reviewing his early memories not as they point inward but
as they revolve about this or that pathetic adult, he gives a toughening
perspective to the sufferings of the child; for these are balanced by the
sufferings the child either causes or ironically ignores in the adult.
Dealing with poets, he secures a similar distance by balancing the ig-
nominies of the external life against the victories of the imagination.
When he handles his most recalcitrant material, the humiliating lives
of psychotics, he can allow himself a comical irony that would sound
intolerable coming from anyone but the inmate of an institution:
"There are no Mayflower / screwballs in the Catholic Church" ("Waking in the Blue"; 82). Of course, each of these figures also stands as a
measure of the disorder in society: the unrewarded artist, the corrupted child, the madhouse that mirrors the world. Each further becomes an extension of the past: thanks in part to the mere movement
of decades, Lowell can bestow on personal recollections the dignity of
history: "These are the tranquillized *Fifties,* / and I am forty" ("Memories of West Street and Lepke"; 85). Not through the public aspect of
his ancestry but through the independent private experiences of the
struggling poet, he can serve as the record of his age, and connect that
age with the sweep of earlier epochs.

In all these accomplishments the controlling factor is a matter of
tone. If Lowell had not managed to infuse the despair of his disgust
with the humor of his irony, he could not have established the frame-
work that screens the reader from the simple pathos of most confessional verse. In the production of this tone, the use of slang, reshar-
pened clichés, and witticisms is crucial: instead of straining, as in Lowell's earlier work, to give the banalities of life a moral urgency (often
without succeeding), they now suggest the speaker's mastery of his
experience. It is this saving irony, energized by disgust, that carries him
across his most difficult, self-destructive nights. When he emerges from
the darkness of "Skunk Hour," the penultimate (originally the last) and
almost the finest poem in this almost uniformly splendid book, what

supports him and us is surely the power of his tolerance and humor, shoved smack up against a hideous crisis.

In tracing Lowell's career up to 1960, one may describe it as following two successive motions. When he wrote his earlier works, the poet tried to give them importance by starting from the great moral issues or crises of history and then matching those with themes derived from his private ordeals. After *Mills of the Kavanaughs,* however, he was willing to start from his private experiences and project these upon history and public life. Since the effect of the change was a fresh and distinctive kind of poetry, Lowell seems to have felt impelled to push his explorations further. Preoccupied as he was with the continuity of his own work, and educated as he was in Eliot's idea of literature as a body of classics that the innovator alters and enlarges, Lowell naturally looked around among established masters to find either foreshadowings of his discoveries or parallels to his themes and tone.

From the very beginning he had in a sense been doing this. When he incorporated other men's lines into his own verses, when he made a Latin, French, or German author's words the basis for a new poem in American English, he was suggesting that at least in certain corners of their oeuvre the strangers shared his moods. As if to show there were no limits to his ambition, Lowell now set about discovering his own qualities in the whole range of European literature. Having projected his experiences as a human being upon the history of the twentieth century, he now projected his identity as an artist upon the meaning of "poetry"; for he began producing free adaptations, or "imitations," of the work of a dozen and a half poets from Homer to Montale. Even before they were reprinted in the collection entitled *Imitations* (1961), these poems were received with a surprising degree of incomprehension, which was aggravated rather than lightened when the whole book came out. Only the rare reader either observed that the arrangement of the book was not chronological, or accepted the author's statement that the contents were a sequence rather than a miscellaneous collection.

In fact, of course, *Imitations* is Lowell's attempt to find his voice in the high places of literature, to fashion retrospectively a tradition for his accomplishment. He is legitimizing his progeny, replacing the Lowells and Winslows by Baudelaire, Rimbaud, and Rilke. In drawing up such a genealogical tree, Lowell again implies that he has found his essential identity not in a social class or in a religious communion but in his character as a writer. So it seems appropriate that the bulk of the models belong to the Symbolist tradition. For Symbolism is the movement that defined the creative mind as the supreme object of poetic contemplation.

Once again, the opening and closing poems have special significance. Lowell begins with a startling extract from the *Iliad*, which picks up the motif of his "For the Union Dead"—the last poem (under a different title) in the revised edition of *Life Studies*. "For the Union Dead" had dealt with the mystery of heroism, in which a human life reaches nobility by the manner of death: "man's lovely, / peculiar power to choose life and die." To open *Imitations*, Lowell gives us "The Killing of Lykaon."[11] Suddenly Homer is not the Olympian whose view shifts with dignified ease from Greek side to Trojan, or from man to God; but he is the singer of the "mania" of Achilles. "Mania" rather than the conventional "wrath," says Lowell in his version of the epic invocation. No doubt he is punning on *menin*, the first word in the first of all our poems. However, he is also, and quite fairly, discovering in the ancient poet his own tendency to regard any irresistible passion as a sort of madness. The extract that follows the bit from the invocation comes from book 21 of the *Iliad*, and contrasts heroic murder with ignominious death: Achilles insists on dispatching the vanquished Lykaon and spurns his victim with a tirade on the killing of Trojans. The hero, foreseeing the dissolution of his enemies' corpses, suggests that the reduction to nothingness eliminates their value as persons. Lowell makes the speech his own by infusing it with a love-hate hysteria that

11   *For the Union Dead* (New York: Farrar, Straus, & Giroux, 1964), 71; *Imitations* (New York: Farrar, Straus, & Cudahy, 1961).

sounds feverish and self-conscious but possesses a marvelously nervous vitality:

> You too must die, my dear. Why do you care?
>
> . . . . .
>
>   the dark shadows of the fish will shiver,
> lunging to snap Lykaon's silver fat.   (1-2)

The answer to Achilles' debasement of the human spirit is the final work in *Imitations,* "The Pigeons," from Rilke. In the middle of this poem we meet a band of Greek warriors about to die. But here they personify the poet's army of creative impulses, destroyed through being realized. The word "mania" appears too, in the last line of the poem and the book (149). Yet it is no longer Achilles' rage to annihilate; it is now the resistance of reality to the artist's drive toward perfection; for the imagination of course opposes itself to nothingness and aspires to eternity. So the metaphor changes, and a poem becomes a ball flung from "all-being" toward eternity, "almost out of bounds," but gaining a tragic intensity, or "body and gravity," from the pull that draws it back toward nonexistence. In the exquisitely phrased first half of this fine work, Lowell-Rilke employs not a ball or any army but the flight and return of pigeons as a metaphor for the artist's impulses. Each bird is like a creative vision seeking independent life. So the most beautiful pigeon is always the one that has never left the coop, the pure conception not yet embodied; for to be fixed is to be finished. Nevertheless, says Lowell, "only by suffering the rat-race in the arena / can the heart learn to beat." The soaring unity, in such lines, of slang, passion, and insight reveals the strength of Lowell's talent.

The progress from the death-bounded battles of Achilles to the tragic campaigns of the artist reaches its peripety in the poems from Baudelaire, placed ironically after Hugo's tributes to the defeated warrior Napoleon and the dead artist Gautier. In Baudelaire the great themes of *Imitations* surge together: death, love, and art. Lowell has selected poems that carry us from the revulsion of the artist against passion to the welcome the artist gives death. If his style sounds drier than Baudelaire's and less felicitous in rhythm than Pound's, it has a decorous violence of language and imagery that no other American poet can produce. Yet not intensity of expression alone but strength of intellect, the consciousness enveloping the intensity, draws the disruptive forces together. Lowell's confident meters, the bold, catchy phrases, express not simply what Baudelaire felt but what we still want: a power to transcend lust and decay by the imagination that digests them:

> reptilian Circe with her junk and wand
>
> .   .   .   .   .
>
> Desire, that great elm fertilized by lust
>
> .   .   .   .   .
>
> It's time. Old Captain, Death, lift anchor, sink!
>
> ("The Voyage"; 66, 69, 72)

If in artistic sensibility Lowell seems peculiarly at home with Baudelaire, he seems as a person still more at ease with Rimbaud, whose work is placed at the exact center of the book. With both poets he finds continual opportunities for employing his own tone and his imagery of passivity eager for motion. But Rimbaud brings out attitudes toward childhood and corrupted innocence that remind us at once of *Life Studies*. Mme Rimbaud as "Mother" inexorably recalls Mrs. Lowell: "she thought they were losing caste. This was good— / she had the true blue look that lied" ("The Poet at Seven"; 78). So also the isolated "poète de sept ans" brings back the "last afternoon with Uncle Devereux Winslow." Yet in revealing what he shares with Rimbaud, Lowell also reveals what the rest of us share with them both. The double image here has the distancing but clarifying effect that irony produces in *Life Studies*. When he gives us his amazingly fresh, rich version of "The Lice-Hunters"—with its symmetry of disgusting perceptions, its complexity of assonance or rhyme, and its steadiness of rhythm— Lowell evokes the whole tendency of our nagging generation to inspect, regret, and enjoy emotional crisis:

> He heard their eyebrows beating in the dark
> whenever an electric finger struck to crush

a bloated louse, and blood would pop and mark
the indolence of their disdainful touch.   (91)

From a glance at Lowell's most recent work, coming out in period-
icals, one can prophesy that his next book will establish his name as
that normally thought of for "the" American poet. It will be a wide
shift from the fame of Robert Frost, whom so many nonreaders of
poetry were able to admire along with the literary audience. Frost did
many things that Lowell does not. Though unsuccessful as a farmer, he
could celebrate aspects of rural life that Lowell never touches. He knew
how to tell a story. He was the last important American poet to use
the old forms and the old language convincingly. If Frost endured, in
the fate of his family, more frightful disasters than Lowell, he was
blessed with the power of maintaining his ego against them. Yet he
stood for few extraordinary or wayward ideas. His connection with
literature outside the conventional English and American models was
slight. It is remarkable how often his early poems are indistinguishable
from the early poems of Graves or Ransom. He opened few roads that
other writers could travel. No one could call Frost a poet's poet.

Lowell, on the contrary, seems determined to maintain his intellectual distinction, his subtlety, his rigorous complexity of form. What
appears most astonishing about the recent work is the way old motifs
persist in new transformations with deepening significance. There are
the city garden, the parallels of beast with man, the bitter pathos of
memory working on the fixed character. But in the new poems of
private recollection Lowell inclines to emphasize the hold that history
has on the present, the powerlessness of the self to resist the determination of open or hidden memories. The insatiable consciousness of
the poet comments sardonically on the very self-censuring autoanalysis
that produced *Life Studies*.

At the opposite extreme from the private self the poet can now
draw human as well as Symbolist analogies between the terrible numbers of suffering people and his own unique experiences. "Buenos
Aires," one of his finest new "public" poems, has the wit and clever
phrasing that make lines attractive on a first reading: "old men denied
apotheosis" (i.e., equestrian statues of defunct dictators); "Peron, / the

nymphets' Don Giovanni."[12] The poet's games with expressive sound have unusual vigor—for example, a crescendo of echoes of "air" toward the end, preparing for the name of the city that is the subject of the poem. This "air" becomes a sarcastic pun; for foul air, miasma, "hot air," cold fog, emptiness, seem what the place betokens. In the final line the last word, "crowds," echoes the last word of the first stanza, "herds," and reminds one of the likeness drawn throughout the poem between cattle and people; for it is the suffering and passivity of the humblest class that connect them with the author.

As usual, the images are what make the poem work. This time they depend on the old partners, love and war, Venus and Mars, united here by means of Peron's name *Juan,* which suggests the Don Juan legend. Lowell, disgusted by the official facade of the city, treats it as a depopulated, overfurnished opera set, which he contrasts with the offstage crowds of the real Argentina. The opera is of course *Don Giovanni:* and the center of the poem recapitulates history with dead generals in white marble recalling Mozart's Commendatore. Instead of the file of Don Juan's abandoned mistresses, we meet marble goddesses mourning deceased heroes; of sex and death joined in a skull-like obelisk. Instead of the great lover in hell, we hear Peron bellowing from exile, the seducer of his people.

Among these scenes the poet moves on foot in a circular path, as spectator or sufferer. He starts from and returns to his hotel, caressing inanimate statues (his muses) en route but speaking to nobody. Instead of virile love, he encounters homosexuals in a park; but like Donna Anna, though unlike Argentina, he fights off seduction. Fascinated as so often by what repels him, he sees the truth behind the scrim and delivers it to us by way of his conscience.

A similar solidity of structure and depth of implication pervade the best of the new poems of introspection, "Eye and Tooth" and the superb tribute to his wife, "Night Sweat." "Eye and Tooth," a skillful extraction of humor from despair, illustrates a truism about middle

---

12   "Buenos Aires" was collected in *For the Union Dead,* 60–61, after this essay was published. Professor Ehrenpreis analyzes an earlier version of this poem as it appeared in the *New York Review of Books,* Feb. 1963, 3. [Ed.]

age: namely, that so far from bringing us serenity, the years leave us naked; only we learn, not without some disgust, that the self can survive even the shabbiest humiliation. The poem depends on a brilliant use of the *eye-I* pun. Treating vision as memory or id, Lowell presents the voyeur poet's eye as an unwreckable showcase of displeasing memories that both shape and torment the person. The dominating metaphor is, so to speak, "I've got something in my I and can't get it out." Toward the end Lowell neatly ties the public to the domestic by implying that just as his readers observe his gestures with the unease provoked by their own recollections, so his familiars must in the routines of living find his condition hardly more bearable than he does:

> Nothing! No oil
> for the eye, nothing to pour
> on those waters or flames.
> I am tired. Everyone's tired of my turmoil.
>
> (*For the Union Dead* 19)

Ransom once played with the idea of Lowell's becoming the Ovid or Virgil of America. But if Lowell feels drawn to themes of epic scope, his mode is neither narrative nor celebratory. For a closer parallel we must look at another epoch in another nation, at the difficult life and disquieting art of Baudelaire. Besides the fundamental similarities of their childhoods, Baudelaire during adolescence inclined like Lowell to a lonely, morose disposition; and it was in the community of artists that he found a lasting family. He was attracted to painting but not to music. As an adult he responded more intensely to city scenes than to country landscapes. In his personality he combined deep passivity with an eagerness to keep working and moving. Though he had begun writing poetry while at school, he always procrastinated about publication, working over his poems with perfectionist ardor. When he produced a book, it was no miscellaneous gathering but an organization of separate poems into a general scheme reflecting his peculiar outlook.

Still more persuasive are the similarities in the works. Both men have the posture of a fallen Christian. Both deal rather with the horrors of passion than the pleasures of love, and treat death as more seductive than frightening. For both of them, art emerges from profound intellection, from labor, suffering, self-disgust. They build their best poems around complex images linked by connotation, and not around arguments or events. They introduce coarse, distasteful words into a style that is rich and serious. Their poems follow circular movements, with the end touching the beginning.

Their differences are obvious. Lowell's use of history is deliberate; Baudelaire clings to immediate reality. The development of Lowell's characteristic successes depends on an impression of haphazardness at the start turning into a highly wrought climax, whereas Baudelaire's surface has elegance of workmanship throughout. Lowell relies overwhelmingly on visual imagery, whereas Baudelaire appeals elaborately to sounds, and is remarkable for a synesthetic use of smells. Rhythmically, Lowell sounds less interesting than Baudelaire.

Yet if we search still further, if we place "Le Cygne" beside "For the Union Dead," the two sensibilities reveal still more intimate kinship. There is the same sympathy with the wretched, the same disgust with the life that imposes wretchedness upon them, the same transformation of the city-pent poet into an emblem of the human spirit exiled from its original home. Finally it seems important that Lowell and Baudelaire take so much of the matter of their poems from the most secret rooms of their private lives; for the true biography of them both emerges not from a tale of their friendships or families or external careers but from their works alone. The real Lowell, like the real Baudelaire, is met with in the poetry to which he has given himself altogether.

14

LOWELL
II

 Going through Robert Lowell's *Selected Poems,* one realizes again how funny and witty his work can be—"With seamanlike celerity, / Father left the Navy, / and deeded Mother his property" ("Commander Lowell"; 77). Lowell's comic power was manifest in *Life Studies.* But as the poet moved into middle age, humor became a subtler element of his work, displacing the vindictive sarcasm of his early books.

The effect of Lowell's comedy is reductive: Clytemnestra becomes a figure not unlike the poet's mother but with a simpler sexuality—"our Queen at sixty worked in bed like Balzac."[1] Lowell takes persons or situations that threaten one with anxiety. But rather than immerse himself in the primitive response, he stands outside like an independent observer, and sees the danger as (after all) finite: it shrinks into the commonplace, fades into the trivial, or vanishes into the unreal. Napoleon enters in the small bathtub he used on campaign ("1930's: My legs"; *History* 107); death turns into a family trait: "our family cancer— Grandmother's amnesia, Grandfather's cancered face . . . with us no husband can survive his wife" ("Gods of the Family"; 204).

This essay was first published 28 Oct. 1976 under the title "Lowell's Comedy" as a review of Robert Lowell, *Selected Poems* (New York: Farrar, Straus, & Giroux, 1976). Reprinted with permission from *The New York Review of Books.* Copyright © 1976 Nyrev, Inc.

1   "Clytemnestra 3," in *History* (New York: Farrar, Straus, & Giroux, 1973), 35.

In general, the threat of the dangers is to confine the poet, to deprive him of dignity, power, life—above all, of freedom. But the comic element releases him and gives him a feeling of magical transcendence. Often the danger springs from his own unmanageable emotions, the frightening impulses drilled into him during childhood, impulses that now seem predetermined and external, beyond control. But the source may also be perfectly natural, like the coming of death.

So, as the poet starts many poems, he sounds hemmed in by psychic traumas, the deteriorations of age, or the resistance of language to art. He should be too old for love, too tired to write. Yet the turn of the poem is repeatedly comic: he remains productive, and he is loved. The fate that seemed ineluctable is softened or avoided, because life defies theory.

One way of framing and therefore controlling the peculiarly human dangers is to set them off against the condition of animals. Guilt-free, untroubled by our conflicting emotions, the beasts and birds of Lowell's poems attract the smiling sympathy we extend to very young children. At the end of "Skunk Hour," the mother skunk feeding her young is absurd as well as admirable when she "jabs her wedge-head in a cup / of sour cream" (96). So is the seal swimming "like a poodle" in "The Flaw" (133).

But Lowell builds his most elaborate comedies around the personality of the poet, especially as the inner man confronts the outer. "Near the Ocean" is a remarkably involved, essentially comic meditation on the ego's fight to deliver itself from lust and guilt. Here the poet seems to smile at the antitheses connecting his public and private characters.

In the poem he pictures himself first as a theatrical Perseus, heroically freeing mankind from the tyranny of the Medusa. But then he quickly revises the scene and appears as an indecisive Orestes, about to kill his own mother. The two deeds become absurdly equivalent: liberation of oppressed victims and betrayal of a parent; or else, love for Andromeda and hatred of Clytemnestra.

It was Aeschylus who linked tyrannicide with both Perseus and Orestes (in the choruses of his *Libation Bearers*—which Lowell once translated). But in "Near the Ocean"—especially in stanza three, which he has now deleted—the poet finds the link ironical. He draws a witty contrast between the Mediterranean world and our own Atlantic seaboard. The one possessed myths and institutions to absorb the more wasteful passions of humanity: there were Greek furies to punish matricide, Christian crusades to wear down battering rams. In that world, sin and saintliness produced known consequences.

But in our own, troubled nation, the causal ties between character and action, past and present, are fading. Psychological determinism obscures the guilt or shame we might feel for our moral excesses; God has lost the right to blame us for the sins our parents inculcated. In "Near the Ocean," therefore, the poet treats the Atlantic as an emblem of moral chaos, and seesaws his way to its edge in contrasting episodes of restraint and abandon, innocence and exhaustion, night and day. Scene follows scene: Maine, Greenwich Village, Central Park, Fire Island; there is no stopping place before the water's edge.

Pondering the fact that every involvement with a lover means a betrayal of an earlier love, the poet can only forgive himself for his trespasses after shriving and the penance of self-ridicule. Then in the privacy of his bed, flanking his wife, he stops fussing with judgment and analysis. Oceanic passions have worn away his attachment to ritual and tradition. Ambiguous love remains. So he turns mentally to his wife and wonders whether he must transform her too into a gorgon, so as to find an excuse for betraying her. "Monster loved for what you are" (155), he says tenderly, not sure how serious or comic the epithet will be.

Behind the ambivalent attitudes one detects a friendly ribbing of Matthew Arnold's "Dover Beach," which supplied the epigraph for an old poem of Lowell's. "Ah love, let us be true / To one another!" said Arnold in the face of a world meaningless and chaotic. Lowell suspects that the recipe is too simple, that love cannot be true either, and that perhaps the chaos within us requires betrayals even as the chaos without deceives our hopes and dreams.

"Near the Ocean" is a difficult poem. One of the simplest poems Lowell ever wrote suggests the ideal that floats, like Eden or Atlantis, above the humor. This poem is "Will Not Come Back." Here the poet recalls and apostrophizes a girl he met in Mexico, during a literary institute (I suppose) held at a deconsecrated monastery in Cuernavaca!

Unforeseeable, narrowly limited in time and space, the experience took on a unique intensity. It was like a free, spontaneous circumvention of the doom of middle age; and because it seemed unique, the poet could yield to it again in memory.

He celebrates his love in his common way of transferring emotion from the principals to their surroundings: the swallows, the honey-suckle, the season. And in the manner of Ronsard's similar sonnet, "*Quand vous serez bien vieille,*" he also moves the sense of loss from the lover to the beloved. Yet even in such earnest, conventional circumstances, the poet cannot resist a dash of ridicule. Knowing birds rather better than most poets, he observes that the insectivorous swallows who looked in on the couple were not simply to-ing and fro-ing: they were feeding in flight (as usual), and snapping up the romantic night-flies, even as reality must devour the illusions of the middle-aged seducer:

> Dark swallows will doubtless come back killing
> the injudicious nightflies with a clack of the beak;
> but these that stopped full flight to see your beauty
> and my good fortune . . . as if they knew our names—
> they'll not come back. The thick lemony honeysuckle,
> climbing from the earthroot to your window,
> will open more beautiful blossoms to the evening;
> but these . . . like dewdrops, trembling, shining, falling,
> the tears of day—they'll not come back. . . .
> Some other love will sound his fireword for you
> and wake your heart, perhaps, from its cool sleep;
> but silent, absorbed, and on his knees,
> as men adore God at the altar, as I love you—
> don't blind yourself, you'll not be loved like that.   (198)

The swallows of "Will Not Come Back" reappear in Lowell's best play, *Benito Cereno,* which mingles the bitter ridicule that marks his early poems with the reflective humor of his later. When Delano, the naive American captain, examines the Spanish slaveship through his telescope, he sees gray birds close above it, "like swallows sabering flies before a storm."² Delano's own vessel is a sealing ship, token of the human army mobilized to destroy humbler creatures. The same aggressive impulses that move Yankees to enslave Africans also direct them to butcher seals.

In the play, therefore, an ironical relation exists between the bleak natural setting and the grim human drama. Ordinarily good omens, the swallows here join the prophets of evil. The storm ahead is the rebellion of colonial peoples against their oppressors, a rebellion sure to produce savage repression. As the hideously unpleasant action of the play begins, the sun comes out, misleading Delano to expect happy events.

The play (based on Melville's story "Benito Cereno") deals with the failure of the young American republic to break the lockstep of imperialism that undermined the Spanish and French empires. Lowell sardonically contrasts the laughable illusions of the American captain with the suicidal gloom of the Spaniard, who has learned, through atrocious suffering, how flimsy his own claims were to heroic or even honorable character; for the rebellious slaves made him connive at the humiliation, torture, and murder of his best friend, and then forced him to work hand in hand with the murderers.

Like a comic butt, the American fails to understand that the threat to his own safety comes not from this agent of a decayed monarchy but from the vengeful blacks. When he at last identifies the real enemy, Delano has the slaves mown down with gunfire; and in a final gesture of bizarre vindictiveness, he shoots bullet after bullet into the corpse of their leader.

Lowell distinguishes carefully between the cosmopolitan, liberal captain and his narrow, puritanical bosun Perkins. With all the intolerance of provincial New England, the bosun does grasp the universality of evil. He can therefore be merciful as the captain cannot. It is he who tries to rescue the last and chief rebel: "Let him surrender. / We want to save someone." But Christian salvation means little to the captain.

2   *Benito Cereno*, in *The Old Glory*, rev. ed. (New York: Farrar, Straus, & Giroux, 1968), 143.

In a denial of *caritas* he says to the surrendering leader, "This is your future," and murders him (*Benito Cereno* 214).

The whole line of action is conceived in harshly ironical terms; ambiguities and puns reveal the complex absurdities that line the conscience of Captain Delano; and if the visible form is a melodrama, the inner design is a bitter farce. The playwright's own sympathies seem divided between the melancholy Spaniard and the rebellious black: disillusioned age and New Left youth. For the question is whether one is determined by the other.

Among the matters that most deeply underlie Lowell's poetry is the dilemma of free will and determinism. Must adolescent revolt lead to senile reaction? Must America follow the route of violence and expansion laid out by older empires? Determinism (whether Christian, Marxist, Freudian, or metaphysical) fascinates Lowell as joining men to the rest of nature and offering us relief from guilt. Free will fascinates him because he knows life loses its point when men take no responsibility for their actions.

So in his excellent poem "The Flaw" he treats human existence as a picnic in a graveyard, and sees our peculiar nature as the flaw in a universe where every other creature feels at home—as much at home as a seal in the sea. Here he compares free will to a fault in one's vision, a lopsided way of seeing reality: "if there's free will, it's something like this hair, / inside my eye, outside my eye, yet free" (*SP* 133). By imposing moral choice, it spoils our simple response to instinctive desires.

Such attitudes deeply influence the form of Lowell's work. He loves to give a theatrical setting to his meditations on the human condition. The reason is not so much the ordinary contrast between appearance and reality as Lowell's peculiar sense of playing an assigned part. Reading over a book like *Imitations,* or *History,* one is struck by the poet's habit of casting himself and his intimates as historical figures: King David suffering from the poet's own night sweat; Solomon asking, "Can I go on keeping a hundred wives at fifty?" (*History* 28). The effect is often hilariously reductive: "for Judith, knowing / Holofernes was like knocking out a lightweight——/ smack! her sword divorces his codshead from the codpiece" (*History* 29).

Yet the deeper, ironical comedy lies in the contrast between a "great" man's feeling of power or freedom, and history's judgment that he only conformed to a prepared script. Lowell does allow a few exceptions like Thomas More and Colonel Robert Shaw——men who consciously chose their fate. But that choice was self-sacrifice; and the poet seems to intimate that one realizes freedom best when one dies for a noble ideal.

For Lowell, even nations fit the deterministic scheme. So in "Near the Ocean," ancient Greek myths are reenacted on our side of the Atlantic, and a Greenwich Village Orestes succumbs to his own mother's depravity. Or in *Benito Cereno* the founding fathers of the United States seem to enjoy the vices of the tyrants they had denounced, while their young republic willingly inherits the criminal character of the Spanish and French monarchies.

In the making of his verse, Lowell shows his humor by incongruities that run parallel to his sympathies. Like many innovators, he has the admirable custom of adapting the material of other authors to his own purposes. When the old source shows unsuspected affinities with the new subject, we hear reverberations that are not only comic but instructive. For example, Lowell gives Caligula the voice of Baudelaire: taking the sonnet "Je suis comme le roi d'un pays pluvieux" (with a hand up from Anthony Hartley's translation), he adapts it to the spleen of the Roman tyrant; and we realize that the same gloomy boredom that sends a dictator to his sadistic pleasures can also propel the creative imagination of a genius. The final joke of course is that Lowell, elsewhere, not only describes himself as subject to fits of spleen but also uses "Caligula" for his nickname, and that he has been compared with Baudelaire.

A subtler aspect of comic technique is Lowell's use of the rough sonnet form. He has written hundreds of these poems, playing with their structures and arranging them in ways that show the variety of his wit. So *History* closes with a poem called "End of the Year," and the book contains almost exactly one rough sonnet for each of the 365 days.

By fixing on a much-used form, Lowell puts himself in the same position as the persons who inhabit his works; for the innovator and iconoclast must now accept the technical assignment bequeathed him by his predecessors. He must work with their rules, submit to their discipline, act the predestined part of a sonneteer, along with Petrarch, Ronsard, and Shakespeare. It would be fair to say that when Lowell wrote these poems, he was creating all the roles in a comic theater of the sonnet.

So in the poem on Cleopatra ("*Nunc est bibendum,* Cleopatra's Death"; *SP* 162), reduced from his translation of Horace's ode, Lowell wittily preserved the Latin opening but magically transformed it from the original Alcaic meter into the pentameter normal to a sonnet, even fitting the line into a rhyme (bought at some sacrifice of grammar). He turned the poem neatly in the traditional way, between the first eight lines and the last six. But as if to draw a mustache on the familiar face, he also insisted on reversing Horace's admiring picture of Cleopatra, and made her finally not "unhumbled" as in the Latin, but "much humbled," with an epithet that draws more sympathy from the modern reader.

Even wittier is the way Lowell miniaturized his old translation of Villon's "*Dames du temps jadis.*" He got the three and a half octaves down to fourteen very short, irregular lines; but he rhymed all except the last, with only three rhyme sounds, thus producing the ghost of a sonnet for the ghosts of dead ladies.

These games with form and technique become poignant as well as comic when the poems touch on Lowell's career as a father or poet. "No Hearing (Discovering)" deals with a runaway child. There is something preordained about the episode; one feels caught up in a recurrent myth of "the runaway." This father takes his turn and conducts the usual helter-skelter search through the side streets and corners of the town, a seaport; but as the myth requires, he discovers the girl in his own back yard.

The form of the poem combines the appearance of freedom with the reality of inherited shape. Under the spontaneous syntax, Lowell makes ingenious use of the traditional strain between lines one to eight and nine to fourteen: in the two divisions he balances opposing actions, sights, and sounds. So the octave shows the poet as restless hunter, scouring the town with his car's headlights and coming moodily to rest in view of the ominous waterfront and its hint of drowning. It is, as Marjorie Perloff says, crowded with busy participles and verbs.

The motionless sestet shows the child ineffectually questioned and, in the predestined style of runaways, giving no explanation. The contrast bathes the parent in sympathetic humor, by setting the act he must perform (in his daughter's theater) as a confident guardian against the glimpse we get of his inner uncertainty.

The octave also concentrates on the silence of the search, and the miscellaneity of objects the father sees—white, bright, and green against the darkness—ending with the steamer in port suggesting dangerous travel. The sestet shifts to the sound of the girl speaking, as she throws the father's query back at him (his "Why did you do it?"—I suppose; and her "I would prefer not to say"). Here the master of expression finds his voice absurdly ineffectual. The sestet also fixes on the single figure in black edged with red (suggesting terror) and then screened with virginal white. It ends in the affectionate picture of the quivering, stubborn deer, the child who, like an iceberg, is nine-tenths hidden from her parents:

> Discovering, discovering trees light up green at night,
> braking headlights-down, ransacking the roadsides
> for someone strolling, fleeing to her wide goal;
> passing blanks, the white Unitarian Church,
> my barn on its bulwark, two allday padlocked shacks,
> the town pool drained, the old lighthouse unplugged—
> I watch the muddy breakers bleach to beerfroth,
> our steamer, THE STATE OF MAINE, an iceberg at drydock.
> Your question, my questioner? It is for you—

crouched in the gelid drip of the pine in our garden,
invisible almost when found, till I toss a white raincoat
over your sky-black, blood-trim quilted stormcoat—
you saying I would prefer not, like Bartleby:
small deer trembly and steel in your wet nest!   (*SP* 220)

Pathos and comedy reach their mingled intensity of effect in Lowell's poems about the literary career. In these the self-ridicule depends on a double image: the man in his ambitious youth, planning to throne himself on Parnassus, and the older, established but dubious personage, only too conscious of the gulf between public recognition and true accomplishment. In one of his apostrophes to the girl in Mexico the poet saw himself as "humbled with the years' gold garbage, / dead laurel grizzling my back" ("Mexico" I; 201).

This was pointed enough. But in "The Nihilist as Hero" he goes further. Here Lowell faces the mutually incompatible desires of the modernist poet: to give us the experience of immediate, unrefined life, and to create something indestructible in its perfection: "to live in the world as is, / and yet gaze the everlasting hills to rubble." The poet says he wants "words meat-hooked from the living steer," and so opposes his own writing to the conventional idea of polished versification (201).

Yet the poem was obviously labored over to a degree remarkable even for Lowell, who has a compulsion to rewrite his verses both before and after publication. The outcome is vigorously but deliberately erratic in its rhythms, while hovering about the five-beat meter that the sonnet traditionally requires. The poet thus grimaces at the vision of formal perfection, a vision evoked by a quotation from Valéry which opens the poem.

On the same page is "Reading Myself," in which Lowell's patent mastery of form quarrels with the fear that he has not fulfilled his promise. The charming, witty imagery is related to that of the matching poem, and some of the lines are almost mellifluous. But the design elegantly reverses the old shape of a sonnet (i.e., description followed by reflection), for it has six lines of reflection followed by eight of the single, elaborate metaphor. In a triumph of expressiveness the sweetest lines deal with a honeycomb:

No honeycomb is built without a bee
adding circle to circle, cell to cell,
the wax and honey of a mausoleum—
this round dome proves its maker is alive;
the corpse of the insect lives embalmed in honey.   (201)

It seems plain that "The Nihilist as Hero" through its eloquent coarseness conveys one-half of the poet's ambition, while "Reading Myself"
conveys the other, and that Lowell illustrates by his technique a yearning to reconcile art as process with art as product.

Finally, there is "Fishnet," the opening poem of *The Dolphin,* in
which Lowell brings together the terms of love and art. The
lines carry a tribute to his present wife as not only the muse who
inspires him but also the dolphin who preserves him from drowning in
psychotic disturbance. By relying on metaphors from fishing, it touches
a current of autobiography, because that solitary pastime (as solitary as
writing) provided one of the constant pleasures of Lowell's boyhood
and some of the striking images of his poetry early and late. The reductive humor of writing conceived as a sport deflates the poet while
sparing his beloved and his art. The self-ridicule of "genius hums the
auditorium dead" has the same effect (*SP* 227).

So the poem opens with three unusually well-turned lines representing the wife as a muse in a dolphin's shape. The poet then breaks
in on himself, suggesting abruptly that he cannot capture the idea in
words eloquent or concise enough. The middle section of the poem
then voices dissatisfaction with his work in general, and contemplates
the approach of death as the end of a self-centered but hardly compla-
cent career.

To cut off the section, Lowell ingeniously employs a short line with
an implicit pun on that very word: "The line must terminate" (line of
verse, of fishnet, of life). Finally, in an expressive contrast to this brevity, he has four long lines (the last being the longest in the poem) on
poetry as salvation; it is the gift that rescues him from despair and

(through the permanence of art) from death—even as the dolphin does.

For all the free variations from traditional sonnet form, the poem clings to an underlying pentameter beat, and has a coherence of imagery that keeps it focused. Lowell added a line to the version published in *The Dolphin,* bringing the total up to the norm of fourteen. In design and in theme, therefore, the poem brings out his fundamental poise between liberty and determinism:

> Any clear thing that blinds us with surprise,
> your wandering silences and bright trouvailles,
> dolphin let loose to catch the flashing fish. . . .
> saying too little, then too much.
> Poets die adolescents, their beat embalms them,
> the archetypal voices sing offkey;
> the old actor cannot read his friends,
> and nevertheless he reads himself aloud,
> genius hums the auditorium dead.
> The line must terminate.
> Yet my heart rises, I know I've gladdened a lifetime
> knotting, undoing a fishnet of tarred rope;
> the net will hang on the wall when the fish are eaten,
> nailed like illegible bronze on the futureless future.
>
> *(SP* 227*)*

I ought to stop here, but cannot suppress an anticlimactic note on the choice of poems for this Bicentennial selection. Like Donald Davie, I think Lowell has been unfair to the splendid work in his volume *Near the Ocean.* I wonder how wise the poet was to destroy the symmetry of "Central Park." Its original sequence of young lovers, caged lion, exposed kitten, and old Pharaohs—its rhythm of poor and rich, of morning, afternoon, and night—satisfied my taste for complicated elegance. I wonder too whether he would not have done well to retain the passages now deleted from the compelling octaves of "Waking Early

Sunday Morning" and "Fourth of July in Maine" (renamed "Night in Maine"). And I wonder whether the vivid third stanza (now missing) of the poem "Near the Ocean" did not give that thorny composition a breadth and depth of reference enjoyed by others besides myself.[3]

3   Lowell replaced those excised passages in the Revised Edition of *Selected Poems* (1977). The page references used in this essay are all from that edition. [Ed.]

15

MERRILL

Anyone who wants evidence that James Merrill has held on to his formidable gifts as a poet should look at a few sections of his recent books, *Mirabell: Books of Number* (1978) and *Scripts for the Pageant* (1980). Merrill's versatility and inventiveness fill a description of the small town of Stonington, Connecticut, on Block Island Sound:

> White or white-trimmed canary clapboard homes
> Set in the rustling shade of monochromes;
> Lighthouse and clock tower, Village Green and neat
> Roseblush factory which makes, upstreet,
> Exactly what, one once knew but forgets—
> Something of plastic found in luncheonettes;
> The Sound's quick sapphire that each day recurs
> Aflock with pouter-pigeon spinnakers.   *(Mirabell* 53–54)[1]

Here, honest observation and smiling affection make themselves known through the clever rhymes, the exact epithets, and a witty mixture of colloquial with elegant phrasing. Later in the book, the rendi-

This essay was first published 22 Jan. 1981 under the title "Otherworldly Gods." Reprinted with permission from *The New York Review of Books.* Copyright © 1981 Nyrev, Inc.

1   *Mirabell: Books of Number* (New York: Atheneum, 1978).

tion of a storm in musical terms, supported by startling metaphors and (again) rhyming couplets, provides a tour de force of steady movement and shifting points of view (pp. 149–50). In *Scripts for the Pageant* the incantatory, expanded sestina "Samos" (87–88) will fill the auditory imagination of an attentive listener;[2] and the evocation of a moonlit red bedroom will delight connoisseurs of nightscapes.

> Woken—a bark? Night freshness and dazzle edging
> The room's pitch bright as day. Shutter flung wide,
> In streams moonlight, her last quarter blazing
> Inches above that wall of carbon mist
> Made of the neighbors'. Whereupon the bedside
> Tumbler brims and, the tallest story becoming
> Swallowable, a mind-altering spansule,
> This red, self-shuttered poverty and Heaven's
> Glittering oxygen tent as one conspire.
> *Dark dark the bogs do hark* . . . Instreaming, overwhelming
> Even as it pulls back, the skyward undertow
> Leaves, throughout city and countryside, wherever
> Somebody wakes and goes to his window, a glowing
> Tide-pool dram of bliss, diminuendo.   (208–9)

Normally, a critic pursues such articles of praise with the judgment that the separate bits of a long poem gain power from their relation to the whole. I am not inclined to say so much. It is true that some obscurities in the best-turned lines may be illuminated by other parts of Merrill's volumes. So also a reader may profitably recall earlier appearances (in either book) of themes, places, or characters employed in the marked passages. Still I think those passages might win strength if we read them independently.

Wallace Stevens once told Harriet Monroe that he wished to put everything else aside and amuse himself "on a large scale for a while." If he supposed the advice was good for American poets in general, I

---

2 *Scripts for the Pageant* (New York: Atheneum, 1980).

disagree. Our best poets came of age after extended narratives and lengthy works of exposition had deserted verse for prose. The so-called long poems of the last hundred twenty-five years (or since the first edition of *Leaves of Grass*) never represent a triumph of structure; the stronger the narrative, the weaker the verse.

Too many learned critics have wasted too many specious demonstrations on the effort to fit fragments together and show us a marble temple. Lowell could not make *Notebook* into one grand poem by mere fiat. As for the "long poems" of Wallace Stevens, they exhibit so many redefinitions of the same images, so many reconsiderations of the same points of view, that we should do well to call them sequences—collections of poems on related topics. They may have key words and themes in common; but they have little necessary order, little consistency of doctrine, and much material whose omission would leave no obvious gap.

In Merrill's recent books the burden of the author's ambition does not rest comfortably on the foundations of his genius. Merrill's early mature verse, collected in *First Poems* (1951), reveals a fascination with stanzaic design and with the extraction of subtle implications from a focused image or situation. The language is refined and musical; the meanings are obscure. The poet habitually works out his song in some form of aria da capo; and sometimes the observer and the image trade places.

Throughout these early poems Merrill displays the mastery of syntactic transition and verbal continuity that marks all his work. He indulges in some wordplay and in his compulsive habit of standing clichés on their heads. A pervasive feature of the poems is Merrill's avoidance of moral or social doctrine, a "chronic shyness / Vis-à-vis 'ideas'" (*Scripts* 137). The artist in his early twenties sounds unwilling to preach on any uplifting subject. He describes a peacock in language echoing the Sermon on the Mount; but opposing "beatitude" to "beautiful," he sets the fantasy of the peacock's gorgeous feathers against the mundane defects of ordinary birds: art against normality. The peacock lacks dignity and virtue; it suggests egoism, frivolity, van-ity, as well as painful effort. But the poet seems to prefer its fate to that of "merit / In body, word and deed" ("Peacock"; 55).[3]

At the same time Merrill almost flaunts a power of fitting his expression into difficult verse forms and strict patterns of images. As compensation, perhaps, he invites the reader to fit his mind into the cryptic paradoxes which the poems convey. Merrill gives riddling human traits to objects and landscapes; he turns abstractions into evasive persons. A reader who stays with the poet must decipher stone, animal, or landscape as an emblematic center around which surprising and absorbing associations cluster themselves: secret and painful recollections of the poet, memories of innocent early experiences which become symbolic anticipations of the deceits and disappointments to be suffered in later years. "Wreath for the Warm-Eyed" turns on a game of hide-and-seek which the poet as a young man played with children. Instead of following the rules, the children simply ran away and left their playmate with a vivid omen of the loneliness and childlessness that were to color his adulthood.

The habit of arriving at a meaning by cross-examining an image, or by inverting the usual relation of metaphor to implication, still dominates the poems collected in *The Country of a Thousand Years of Peace* (1959). For instance, the pregnant sister of the poet reminds him of a pendulum as she rocks in a hammock ("A Timepiece"). So he works out a poem on the clocklike aspects of a pregnancy. "The Doodler" seems to deal with the poet's scratchings on a pad as he talks to his friends by telephone. But Merrill draws a parallel between the speaker and God.

In "Hotel de l'Univers et Portugal," the poet and a lover, during their travels abroad, stay in one more bleak hotel room and find their affection deepened by the bleakness—which is of the world as well as the hotel. A lack of possessions or ties (luggage growing lighter as they travel) leaves them unfurnished and therefore open to each other. The analogy between place and person makes the poem; the lovers are a recurrent dream of the strange bed.

With no moral argument and no narrative line, the poems become

3 *First Poems* (New York: Knopf, 1951).

static and regressive. Although autobiography underlies them, the poet blurs and masks the original experiences: we learn what they are like, what they connote, but not what they are. At last in *Water Street* (1962), Merrill animates his stanzas by giving us anecdotes of the poet's life. The old refinement of language remains, but it slips into and out of colloquial slackness. Although the hero of the work is memory, the present keeps springing from the past and peering into the future.

Certain motifs, familiar from earlier works, begin to seem peculiar marks of Merrill's genius: fire and water, light playing on glass; houses, rooms, and their furnishings, especially mirrors and windows. Certain themes go with them: the poet's family, erotic adventures and disillusionments, foreign travel, death. Certain devices keep challenging us: personifications that create riddles (e.g., the five senses as demanding children in "From the Cupola"), metaphors that expand into scenes, perceptions that dissolve into symbols; pairs of juxtaposed images which reflect or become each other.

In works like "An Urban Convalescence" and "After Grace" the poet adds psychological depth and self-knowledge to his self-exploration: these poems are permanent additions to our culture. But in "Roger Clay's Proposal" Merrill still rejects any involvement in public issues; he still refuses to choose among conventional social philosophies.

Instead of moral principles, what he offers in most of his poems is a form of insight which gives meaning to the present by linking and contrasting it with clues from the remote past; and this activity in turn apparently gets the poet moving ahead after a lassitude of confusing emotions. When Merrill expanded his designs into sequential poems, he mixed narrative with meditation and analysis, holding the work together on a thread of place or time: the poet's surprising travels or the evolution of his psyche. The fascination of the poems derives in part from unconventional or scandalous material: exposures of family secrets and sexual deviations, frank narcissism, an anti-Puritan indulgence in dolce far niente (jigsaw puzzles, games of patience, doodling). But the brilliance of the wordplay, the ingenuity of the conceits, the expressive skill of the versification, all keep the style from appearing self-indulgent.

"The Thousand and Second Night" stretches the snip-and-tape design as far as it will go, skipping from place to exotic place while shuttling back and forth in time. Observation yields to memory; memory to symbolism and startling self-exposure. The poem comes to a focus in the themes of physical decay and death, and the need for the artist to triumph over both by incorporating them into his art. It is as splendid a work as Merrill has produced and occupies twelve pages in *Nights and Days* (1966).

In the same volume Merrill also tried a full-scale verse narrative, "From the Cupola." But he lost the shape in allegory and personification. The story of Cupid and Psyche transplanted to a New England village became an excuse for more emblematic and cryptic fantasy than most readers, however loyal, could absorb.

Other experiments with length include "The Summer People" (a narrative fantasy), the openly autobiographical "Days of 1971," and "Days of 1935" (supposed to be the nine-year-old Merrill's cinematic dream of being kidnapped by a thug and his moll).[4] Of these the weakest is the one farthest removed from experience, i.e., "The Summer People," which twists and turns as the poet infuses one or another dose of allegory into it.

The strongest of the three is the mock-travel diary "Days of 1971," told as an absurd sonnet sequence addressed to a former lover now serving as chauffeur. The miracle of this poem is the way the speaker conveys the most attractive side of his character through the cool sprays of analytic wit bestowed on his uncouth but inseparable companion. The paratactic, stop-and-go structure affords free expression to Merrill's verbal legerdemain; and the suggested link between irritation and the creative process is deeply characteristic of his genius.

 If I have managed to sketch the features of Merrill's accomplishment as his admirers would recognize them, it was a dangerous

4   In *Braving the Elements* (New York: Atheneum, 1972).

project for the poet to undertake an enormous opus dealing with me-
tempsychosis, theodicy, cosmogony, and (among other things!) escha-
tology. Yet this is what we have in *The Book of Ephraim, Mirabell,* and
Scripts for the Pageant. Each one, alas, is longer than its predecessor; and
they are all to be followed by an epilogue, "The Ballroom at Sandover,"
which closes with the poet beginning to read aloud the entire five-
hundred-page text to an audience of dead authors and friends.

At the center of the three-part enterprise we find a dissatisfaction
with the possibilities of human life today, a celebration of the world of
the dead, and a prophecy of a better race to come. These articles
naturally tempt us to wonder about the data that produced them.

The style of life evoked by Merrill's poems suggests few inhibitions
upon pleasurable activities. The poet's freedom to travel as he wished,
to love as he felt inclined, to accumulate possessions, and to yield to
moods has set him apart from ordinary men of talent. Yet the outcome
of so much accessibility to experience does not strike one as pure
felicity. The poems recall love affairs that did not gratify the poet's
ardor. They describe places he visited, scrutinized, and left. They can
suggest a disgust with himself at the same time as a disappointment in
others; "waste, self-hatred, boredom" (*Mirabell* 93). Whether these impressions are well- or ill-founded, the doctrines elaborated in Merrill's
three prophetic books do seem to spring from a profound discontent
with the normal grounds of moral stability, especially with traditional
religion.

The poet's attitude emerges both through innuendo and through
open statement. One reason for rejecting Christianity is evidently its
association with repressive morality. Another is the weakness, to the
poet's mind, of its revealed theology. Yet Merrill himself is not consti-
tutionally given to meditating on the principles of ethics, religion, or
philosophy; and he has never pretended to expert knowledge in those
fields of study. Like most amateurs of abstruse learning, he combines
diverse materials from sources that are not naturally harmonious.

In the course of his work the poet refers to the Book of Genesis and
to the version of that history which Milton supplied in *Paradise Lost.*
From time to time he evokes Dante, drawing parallels between his own
poems and *The Divine Comedy.* These parallels may be structural, or in
the adoption of themes and images, or simply in the use of terza rima.

Elsewhere, we hear echoes of Blake; and Merrill employs Blakean four-
teeners for the speech of many otherworldly beings. Yeats, both as a
poet and as author of *A Vision,* is another formative figure named or
echoed.

The result is not unpredictable. If a poet rejects Christianity yet
accepts materials from Christian texts, if he mingles these with
the teachings of quasi gnostics like Blake and Yeats, he can hardly help
sounding like a gnostic himself. Whether or not Merrill has studied
Nietzsche, whether or not he has read the work of Hans Jonas, he
presents us with inversions of biblical myth and Christian morality that
suggest the tradition of gnosticism. For him, however, matter is not
opposed to spirit; it is not identified with evil. Rather, it is the aspect
of reality which we owe to a benevolent creator, and which an evil
deity wants to dissolve. The poet's materialism and his attitude toward
pleasure suggest a refined epicureanism.

On these elements Merrill imposes some principles of modern science and some narrative motifs of science fiction or quack science:
DNA, the Bermuda Triangle, UFO's. He also has tastes or fantasies of
his own which color and shape the eclectic materials of the poems: a
passion for opera, a fascination with mirrors. As culture heroes Proust
and Auden seem omnipresent. Constantly, the poet intersperses his
otherworldly stuff with episodes of autobiography and images derived
from the house he lives in.

So we get a revelation delivered to Merrill and his friend David
Jackson by a cup which their cooperating hands move over a Ouija
board, with its arched alphabet, the digits from zero to nine, and the
words *Yes* and *No.* Because the board has no lower-case letters, the
otherworldly messages are transcribed for us in capitals. How lightly
should the reader take such a scheme of narration? Merrill's novel *The
Seraglio,* published in 1957, has a section in which the hero works suc-
cessfully with a Ouija board. In "Voices from the Other World"—a
poem which appeared about the same time—Merrill again reported
such success. At least once when he was asked about the trials, he said
they were serious.

We have strong American precedent for such occupations. Andrew

Jackson Davis, the "Poughkeepsie Seer," is known to historians of American spiritualism. While in a "magnetized" state, he delivered a course of lectures published as *The Principles of Nature, Her Divine Reve-lations* (1847). Here he traced the evolution of the universe and de-scribed the solar system, giving details of the planets' inhabitants. Thomas Lake Harris (1823–1906), a sometime Universalist minister, wrote volumes of "trance poetry" dictated by the spirits of Shelley and others. One assumes that Merrill would prefer a connection with Dante and Yeats. But his doctrines are not the sort one might sponta-neously expect from the creator of his best poems; and the land that invented spirit-rapping may claim him for her own.

To make a poem hold together when it is five hundred pages long, the poet must keep a large design in mind as he composes his verses and stanzas. But the shape of *Ephraim-Mirabell-Scripts* changes obstructively during the course of our passage through it. Characters who are introduced as important figures turn out to have little or no part in the story. Doctrines promulgated in one section are casually discarded in another. Spokesmen whom we are urged to trust confess themselves to be liars. Facts laid down in one place are contradicted in another.

Merrill tries to screen himself from such complaints. He expresses doubts concerning the very principles that his poem conveys—though he soon appears persuaded of them by characters in the work itself. He often treats the rebarbative material as symbol or allegory. Yet he also condemns allegory. At points we are told that the otherworldly beings can only draw (for their revelations) on the knowledge and imagination of the poet. Or Merrill simply declares that the whole work is a fiction he is trying to believe.

In *The Book of Ephraim* (1976), Merrill and Jackson open communi-cation with a person who entered the world as a Greek Jew in the time of Christ, was murdered (36 A.D.), and underwent a number of rebirths; during the reign of Louis XVI he became a French courtier.[5]

---

5   Published in *Divine Comedies* (New York: Atheneum, 1976), 47–136.

His name is Ephraim, and he teaches the Ouija boarders that each living person is the "representative" or protégé of a dead one, his "patron." There are nine stages of existence in the otherworld; and to qualify for the lowest, a soul must prove itself through a course of reincarnations. Once the poet has got into the habit, other spirits converse by Ouija with him and Jackson, especially spirits of old friends who are temporarily between bodies. He discovers that higher beings exist beyond the nine stages; and these powers break off the telegraphy when patrons try to reveal celestial secrets or to intervene in human affairs. Suddenly, Ephraim declares that he has met the souls of those who lived before mankind.

In *Mirabell* we too meet the creatures, who are, in fact, the higher powers. They appear human but black, winged, and batlike. While essentially good-natured, they also seem to be the original fallen angels and are themselves under the government of still loftier powers or regnant archangels. Above these in turn rises the God Biology, but even he is not the ultimate, supreme authority. Outside our system are other systems with their own suns and gods—a pantheon.

One of the batmen replaces Ephraim as mentor of the poet and his comrade. About the same time, two dead friends emerge as the steadiest, most informative human connections enjoyed by Merrill and Jackson in the otherworld. These are a late Athenian friend, Maria Mitsotaki, and the poet W. H. Auden. The group of two live and two dead humans make a quadruple alliance whose education is the theme of the book.

The four pupils grow fond of their master, and he returns the affection. As a result, he undergoes a metamorphosis into the shape of a peacock, to the delight of all five. Eventually, the poet names him Mirabell. Among many other revelations he teaches that the world we know is only the latest in a series of worlds, which were destroyed by various sci-fi events commemorated in well-known myths of universal catastrophe.

Some of the doctrines thrust upon the four friends (and the reader) have peculiar significance. We hear that as men die, the elements of their souls are extracted and refined in spiritual laboratories of the otherworld, to enrich a tiny proportion of creative minds—scientists, artists, and so forth—who elevate the condition of mankind while the masses remain in an animal state. All sorts of good and evil characters are required as material for these processes; and even animals and plants have souls whose ingredients may be employed to enrich the chosen few.

Yet conflicts arise from each stage of evolution and open the way to difficulties or dangers which the "vital laboratories" of the world must labor to control. Mind keeps organizing chaos, and chaos keeps resisting mind in an almost Manichaean rhythm.

In effect, traditional morality has little place in the poem. One reason is a kind of determinism. We hear that nothing in human events is accidental; for the genes of men are altered or "cloned" in the laboratories so as to change the institutions of mankind according to the wise desires of God Biology and the governors of the otherworld. Not only are all human actions predetermined, therefore, but the direction of history is ultimately benign; and it is hardly fair to blame people for misconduct that is imposed on them.

Sin, we are told, is only pain, given and received (*Scripts for the Pageant,* p. 173). The poet certainly does not admire those who abstain from hedonistic self-indulgence. And though he recommends devotion to others, the only self-discipline clearly praised is that of the artist.

These central doctrines float above a profusion of lesser principles concerning the evolution of the human species, the organization of life after death, the uses of the imagination, and so forth. It becomes clear that many of the propositions addressed to us are wholly or partly metaphorical and that the communications with otherworldly beings are derived from the poet's own fancy. But Mirabell continues lecturing in a rather telegraphic style until at the very end of the book he makes way for an archangel, Michael.

In *Scripts for the Pageant,* as in *Mirabell,* the scenes of earthly life and action shrink in scope while the range given to otherworldly wisdom expands. The body of the book is a set of question-and-answer séances in which Michael and his fellow archangels (Emanuel, Raphael, and Gabriel) explain various aspects of creation and evolution to the poet and his comrades. God Biology, we now learn, has a female twin in

Nature, personified as a young woman. But he is also pitted against a dark "monitor," who reverses time and annihilates matter. Among a stream of new characters two recently dead friends of the poet join the familiar foursome. They are George Cotzias, a medical research scientist, and Robert Morse, an amateur musician.

Besides the talk shows, Merrill provides scenes of preparatory dialogue leading up to them and scenes of reflective conversation commenting on them. He also affords us a number of masques in which familiar and unfamiliar characters take parts as embodiments of universal principles. Raphael, for example, is earth and wit; Gabriel is death and fire. There are performances by the nine muses and by the founders of great religions (Buddha, Christ, Mohammed). All the characters keep wavering between personality and symbolism, and the otherworldly action is heavily allegorical.

Because the doctrines set forth are numerous but fragmentary and inconsistent, it would be risky to attempt to expound them. Behind the whole assemblage, however, one detects attitudes that seem fundamentally revealing. For instance, the outcome of the process of selection and refinement that goes on in the spiritual laboratories—one that gives a benign aspect to the wars and plagues devastating mankind—is the development of a new race of men, "alpha men," about whom we are told little except that they will be healthier, longer-lived, happier, and more creative than our own lot.

Yet a third of the way through *Scripts for the Pageant* we hear the voice of God B singing in remote solitude to his far-off, unseen brothers of the pantheon and asking for a response from those gods. Referring to time as annihilation, he sings, "In my night I hold it back" (78). The song rings out again at the end of the poem. I cannot help relating it to the poet, who aspires to stave off annihilation by restoring lost time through art. Merrill seems to yearn to bestow immortality on his dead friends and ultimately on himself by celebrating them and grouping them with immortals of one sort or another.

 But at the same time one asks whether a subtler impulse may not be at work. Ephraim and Mirabell both lose their dignity in the course of the poems. We discover, gradually, that we cannot trust their information. Although they charm and love the poet, he does not finally respect them; and at moments they become contemptible. The slide from awed fascination to condescension suggests the way a man who has many love affairs comes to feel let down by each beloved. Looking for an idealized form of himself in the other, he is eventually disappointed because of an innate self-distrust.

"Mirabell" is suspiciously close in sound to "Merrill"; and when the batman is transformed into a peacock, the poet marks the occasion with a passage in the same form of stanza that he used for the early poem, in which a peacock seemed an emblem of his own gift and burden. So also the "alpha men," whose emergence—we are advised—will not be long delayed, might reflect a disillusionment with acquaintances of the poet who have failed, over the years, to satisfy his expectations from human society.

As he appears in his works, the poet strikes one as somebody with many friends who seek him out but few (if any) warm, long-lasting intimacies that he keeps close, season after season, day after day. When friends die, during the three long poems, they become, of course, manageable. The poet can summon them and ignore them as he turns to and leaves the Ouija board. With little emotional strain, he can thus preserve a circle of trustworthy and amiable chums.

Besides (we learn), the otherworldly friends may see one another only in the poet's light, and they have no life outside his imagination. Consequently, he controls them completely; they are always, lovingly, at his service. At the close of *Scripts for the Pageant,* Maria, Auden, and Cotzias leave the otherworld for new existences in our own, as if the poet were reluctant to let them continue together without him after he had finished his work. In a terminal ritual, Merrill and Jackson break a mirror into a bowl of water. It is through mirrors that the dead have the power to glimpse the living; so the poet is shutting them off from anyone else.

 Related to this will to control one's characters is a lack of straightforward narrative. It does not seem easy for Merrill's imagination to nourish independent, self-determined persons. He seldom allows a fiction to go its own way. If the characters are not versions of figures from his childhood and youth, they take on a weight of myth that cramps them into symbolic postures. Merrill's deeply autobiographical first novel, *The Seraglio,* has a life that his second, *The (Diblos) Notebook,* lacks. In the later story the author is too busy fitting masks on his creatures to let them work through an absorbing dramatic action.

In *Ephraim-Mirabell-Scripts* not only does the element of narrative fail us, but the poet also relies on arbitrary schemes to give an impression of order. He divides *The Book of Ephraim* according to the letters of the alphabet on the Ouija board, beginning each section with the appropriate letter and sometimes finding themes that are appropriate. In *Mirabell* the digits from nine to zero inherit the same function, and in *Scripts for the Pageant* the three words *Yes, &, No.* But these arrangements seem mechanical; they want inner meaning.

Merrill's versatility as a poet constantly shines before us. Again and again he wrings a sonnet from what look like random lines; or he moves gracefully through a ballade; or he adapts the meter to the person and occasion, as when God B sings in ten lines of ten syllables each. In a passage dealing with reincarnation, Merrill rhymes the penultimate syllable of the odd lines with the final syllable of the even. Musical effects, calculated enjambments, and other expressive devices will delight the careful reader.

A specimen of the ease with which Merrill moves among stages of emotion and levels of reality is an interlude of *Mirabell* when the poet is about to telephone his mother (138–39). The form is peculiarly elegant, because it occurs in Book Seven and there are seven stanzas in a difficult pattern of line lengths and rhymes. Effortlessly, Merrill associates the idea of mother with nature, reality, and earth, which he contrasts for a moment with the starlit sky—emblem of mind and artifice. Yet earth herself is of course an artist, and performs acts of imagination with her seasons and landscapes. As Merrill works the telephone dial, he feels suspended between the pleasures of imagination and those of sensuous reality. Then a sudden uneasiness, when his mother does not answer at once, dissolves the symbolism and leaves us with distinct human beings.

But the most satisfying passages are the few that deal with the poet's observation of the known world and its life. In *Scripts for the Pageant,* a detachable section called "The House in Athens" (148–52) gives us a witty record of the changes that Merrill and Jackson made in their Greek home. Puns, personifications, and brightly remembered details join to transform the ordeals of interior decoration and house repair into an affectionate comedy. The place grows into a patron goddess—cranky but maternal—of two friends' affections.

Reading such verses, one has a standard for judging the bulk of the three long poems. Surely the proportion of otherworldly business is misjudged in them, and it impedes rather than enriches the effective passages. The doctrines do not collaborate to give the poems direction; rather, they hold back the flow, and seem to fix us once more in the immobility of Merrill's first collections.

Other poets have reflected searchingly on ultimate questions. Richard Wilbur, in "Walking to Sleep," tells us, with fresh images and penetrating insight, about the darks and lights of human nature. But Wilbur was early and naturally drawn to religious and moral problems, and his poem is barely six pages long. Merrill's steady disinclination to immerse himself in "great ringing 'themes'" (*Scripts* 109) hardly prepared him for the challenge he courageously took up in his new books.

16

❈ ASHBERY and JUSTICE

❈ There is room in our literature for John Ashbery. The poems in his new book are seldom coherent, shapely, or intelligible; neither their sounds nor their rhythms go far to please the ear; they hardly convey the poet's character in the usual sense. Mr. Ashbery may hope to surprise us agreeably with the leaps or turns of his mind from image to insight and back again; and he may challenge us to make the brightest of these connections ourselves. But most of his work will tire nearly all his readers.

Yet this poetry has its design. Behind much serious writing of the last hundred years lives the belief that the highest use of literature is neither pleasure nor edification. We are hardly supposed to become better citizens by reading Mallarmé or Wallace Stevens. Neither are we supposed merely to titillate ourselves as we would be titillated by an evening of fireworks. The poems in the tradition that prepares us for Ashbery are serious without being conventionally moral. They may delight us, but we say they do more than delight. What then can they accomplish?

One answer is that they bring more of reality into consciousness.

This essay was first published 16 Oct. 1975 under the title "Boysenberry Sherbet" as a review of John Ashbery, *Self-Portrait in a Convex Mirror* (New York: Viking, 1975), and Donald Justice, *Departures* (New York: Atheneum, 1973). Reprinted with permission from *The New York Review of Books*. Copyright © 1975 Nyrev, Inc.

They enlarge the world, make us aware of the aspects that do not fit our purposeful careers or our selective view of usefulness. They remind us of the changes and chances of things, of the happy accidents that underlie so much that we claim for deliberate industry. They teach the rewards of passivity, of letting the life of sensation impose its order on us, of enjoying the designs that start up in spite of us, as we raise our eyes from a newspaper while smelling bread in the oven, hearing Brahms on the phonograph, and feeling the heat of a wood fire, all linked in the welcome surprise of a composition that fades at once.

Such poems restore the freshness and sharpness of preconscious impressions, the unclouded moments of pure feeling, like the first time one tasted boysenberry sherbet—before one knew about boysenberries. Language too should be restored by such poetry to the denseness and mystery of words without their primary meaning—the ugliness of "unction," or as James Schuyler said, "the sinuous beauty of words like allergy / the tonic resonance of / pill when used as in / 'she is a pill.'"

Schuyler, a more gifted poet than Ashbery, can accomplish these ends with verve and wit, a command of language, and a visual acuteness that engage the reader, delight him, opening his mind to the excitement of city landscapes, sounds and smells, to rural artifice, to the humorous charm of our objects, books, furniture, and emotions as they evoke and link up with one another, piercingly reminding us of human intimacies.

Ashbery's response to these things is different. He once described the existence of civilized men today as an effort to cushion themselves against the realities of "alienated life" with chosen objects, art, people, and attitudes. Man's fate, he has said, is boredom; we are "condemned to putter about the universe, halfheartedly trying to make sense of it." He has spoken of our "urban bleakness, both spiritual and architectural." He has called our time a "forlorn, transistorized age," and said this age seems to believe that "a lot of chance and a little organization reflect its temper." In art, he has said, "in a sense, any change has to be for the better, since it shows that the artist hasn't yet given in to the ever-present temptation to stand still."

For such a man, as for Mallarmé, obscurity is essential to poetry. The poem itself must become an exercise in reexamining the world from which the self has become alienated. We must confront its language with the same audacity that we want when confronting the darkened world within us and without. To offer a clear meaning would be to fix the reader in his place, to turn him away from the proper business of poetry by directing him to an apparent subject. It would be like saying the "subject" of a baroque quartet was the scene of dancing peasants that gave the composer one of his tunes. Instead, the act of reading must become the purpose of the poem.

Consequently, the poem must stand by itself as the world stands by itself. It must change as the world changes. It must offer the same challenge as the world. And therefore, the poet as a private person must not appear in it.

No poetry is less confessional than Ashbery's. He brings his impressions of phenomena into his poetry: the time of day, the changes in weather, the seasons, light and color, phrases overheard or picked out of newspapers. He brings in generalized emotions of disappointment, anxiety, apprehension, satisfaction, expectation. He refers to paintings, places, stories of which the phenomena remind him. He even offers statements and propositions, so long as they occur like events, detached sentences evoked by the phenomena, and not emerging from a private chain of reasoning. The poet becomes, like Newton's God, a hidden person for whom the universe is a sensorium.

So the impressions of the poet in the act of composing are precisely what define his work; the rain that is suddenly evocative for him, the music that drifts through the doorway. This shifting assemblage of changing sensations is his substance. He may well have a theme in mind—a person, an object—but he does not normally render or describe it. He merely supplies the phrases, images that reach him as he contemplates the theme, which of course the reader is not asked to discover.

Frank O'Hara thought of the color orange and wrote pages "not of orange, of / words, of how terrible orange is / and life." He produced twelve poems without mentioning "orange," and called the whole thing "Oranges." Sometimes, as in "Self-Portrait in a Convex Mirror," the last poem in Ashbery's new book, the theme is fully presented. Generally, it is to be thrown away after its job is done—after it has given the poet an occasion for focusing his impressions. The reader's responsibility might be to explain the poem to the author without reference to its germinal starting point.

So Ashbery tries to make us act out the division between workaday reality and those moments of transcendence that are like moments of love or of mystical communion. Up from the obscure, low-keyed passages arise lines clearly, lyrically conveying the sense of insight, comprehensive vision, that tantalizes from time to time with heavenly possibilities, "a glance, a ballade / That takes in the whole world, now, but lightly, / Still lightly, but with wide authority and tact" ("As One Put Drunk into the Packet-Boat"; *Self-Portrait* 1).

The danger in the low-keyed passages—a danger Ashbery seldom avoids—is that they will move dully as well as darkly. Their fragmentary, disjointed, or maddeningly evasive nature not only baffles but bores the reader. If a poet does find most of reality meaningless, he is ill-advised to proportion his verses accordingly, and to deal out lengths of murk as settings for brief illuminations. How does one keep the background alive and attractive without letting it overwhelm the foreground?

Ashbery does much with omens and foreshadowings, suspense and recollection. He gives us provocative broken images, references to time and mood, that lead away from transcendence. The moon of imagination goes up in the sky, and "a sigh heaves from all the small things on earth, / The books, the papers, the old garters and union-suit buttons / Kept in a white cardboard box somewhere" ("As One Put Drunk . . ."; 2).

He also gives parodic versions of the small talk of small people, or he catches the automatic gestures of mechanical lives. He works out funny allegories of the way routine traps us, deafening our ears to messages from the sublime, as when the angelic messenger urges the poet to communicate with him, but the poet goes on "looking at old-fashioned plaids" to dress up his dreary existence ("Worsening Situation"; 3).

Ashbery is not so solemn that he misses the absurdity of his enterprise. He knows the visions are illusory, and that his aims contradict one another. Often, therefore, he turns on himself and ridicules the view of the poet as the light of the world. In "As You Came from the Holy Land," he elaborates the comic parallels between the messianic bard (come to restore the dead self to imaginative life) and the passion of Christ. In "Soonest Mended" (from an earlier collection, *The Double Dream of Spring*) he compares the poet, rescuing the self from alienation (in ye olde "technological society"), to Ruggiero rescuing Angelica in Ariosto's poem; only it is not Ruggiero but Happy Hooligan.

Yet self-sacrifice is not enough to compensate for the limitations of Ashbery's work. When one has shown there is purpose in his method, one has not endowed the method with the attributes rightfully to be sought in poetry. Among the muddles of our critics is the assumption that if an author has persuasive theoretical grounds for his literary practice, the reader ought to be satisfied that what the man writes is good. There is no logical connection between these propositions; and in Ashbery's work the case collapses of its own weight, because so many readers are dismayed when they try (intelligently and seriously) to enjoy his poems. I find it sinister that the most successful one in his new book—the last and longest of the collection—deals with the theory behind it.

Donald Justice has some kinship with Ashbery. The master to whom both seem deeply related is Wallace Stevens. But there is some difference between the author of "Peter Quince at the Clavier" and the one whom Jarrell named "G. E. Moore at the spinet." Justice recalls the music, elegance, and passion of Stevens, not his devotion to aesthetics. In Justice's latest book, certainly his best, the poet keeps his old attachment to the community of vulnerable creatures—lovers, children, the old, the weak. And he bestows on them the richness of sound and cadence, the depth of feeling and subtlety of language that he displayed in his earlier collections.

What draws him to such people is not their dependence but their openness to affection and fantasy, to strong emotions and wild thoughts. For Justice, the receptivity of the artist feeds both his creative imagination and his human sympathy, two aspects of one impulse. Conversely, what seems to matter most to him, in the labors of art, is the chance the imagination offers us to keep in touch with those who share our world but not our neighborhood: the dead, the remote, those imprisoned by their frailty or foolishness.

Justice has marvelous poems about the way the creative process goes: the need to be tough, violent, and fearful at the same time ("ABC"); the difficulty of the effort and the littleness of the reward ("Sonatina in Green"). One that exemplifies his power to charm us is "The Telephone Number of the Muse." Here the poet feels his talent is dwindling; his muse has turned to other, younger lovers:

> I call her up sometimes, long distance now.
> And she still knows my voice, but I can hear,
> Always beyond the music of her phonograph,
> The laughter of the young men with their keys.   (15)

The unfashionable refinement of the syntax, like the unfashionable purity of the language, is typical of Justice. Both these features are touching contrasts to his pathos when Justice gives in to the elegiac mood and turns to his central concern. This is with the class of people who sink in the trajectory of their wayward natures, who leave the tribe sooner than alter their own essence. I suppose that for him the poets belong to this class.

The circular patterns that Justice loves sound appropriate to the solitary character of such people, turned back on themselves, shut in willingly or unwillingly, caught in irreversible cycles. No wonder he finds so much occupation for mirrors, guitars, pianos, repetitions of words and syllables. Such images and devices, such iterative and musical designs, suit the meditations and recapitulations of the solitary life.

The dead belong here, because our relation with them must be circular. They prepare us for their place, and we have taken it. The hushed tone that marks Justice's voice mounts to reverence as he evokes his relation to his father in "Sonatina in Yellow." Here, the ambiguities, continuities, and repetitions move parallel to memory and forgetfulness, in a sequence impressively like a musical modulation. Love for the dead suggests love for the past, the poet's desire to keep with him the beauty and awfulness of the filiation that he will hand on in his turn; and the imagination then seems our one genuine weapon against mortality:

> The pages of the album,
> As they are turned, turn yellow; a word,
> Once spoken, obsolete,
> No longer what was meant. Say it.
> The meanings come, or come back later,
> Unobtrusive, taking their places.   (44)

Solitude falls into loneliness, isolation decays to imprisonment, repression gives way to murder, as Justice travels across his land of self-enclosures. And we meet the neurotic in the sanitarium, longing to get back to the way of life that sent her there ("A Letter"), or the love-hungry poet (not Justice), reliving in his poems his love-hungry youth ("Portrait with Flashlight"). Because he has the habit of understatement and terseness in an era when overexpression is normal, Justice may sound too reserved. But the intensity of vision that directs his work will be evident to those who care to observe it, as when the poet admits his complicity in the terrors he conveys:

> You have no name, intimate crime,
> Into which I might plunge my hand.
> Your knives have entered many pillows,
> But you leave nothing behind.   ("The Confession"; 20)

In making these new poems, Justice discarded some of his old traits. He has given up regular meters for free verse. He has enlarged his allotment of dreamlike images and veiled meanings. But his ear and his sense of design are so reliable that the poems remain seductive in sound and shape.

He has not reduced his most engaging feature, the mixture of gentleness with power. The confidence Justice has in his own selfhood enables him to reach out to lives that would unsettle a thinner character; and he can obey his admonition in "ABC":

> Be the statue leaning out from the stone,
> > the stone also, torn between past and future,
> > and the hammer, whose strength we share.   (3)

17

POETRY
and
LANGUAGE
OPPEN | HILL | SNYDER

The criticism of poetry in this country has been rendered immobile by the history of American taste. Fifty years ago, writers who now *look* canonical were noticed with indifference or ridicule. Even Cummings—who, read aloud, charms one in a surprisingly traditional way—offended so many editors that he called one of his books *No Thanks* and dedicated it to a list of publishers who had turned it down.

To recommend or explain the new writing of the twenties, men of good will like I. A. Richards and R. P. Blackmur offered new principles of judgment. They argued that expressive rhythm was more effective than familiar meters. They justified erratic rhymes as appropriate to erratic states of mind. They analyzed obscure images and disclosed subtle meanings that depended on complexity of style. They took work that sounded anarchic and assigned a firm place to it in the traditions of American and European literature. Waldo Frank connected Hart Crane with "a great tradition, unbroken from Hermes Trismegistus and Moses."

This essay was first published 22 Jan. 1976 under the title "The State of Poetry" as a review of George Oppen, *Collected Poems* (New York: New Directions, 1975), Geoffrey Hill, *Somewhere Is Such a Kingdom: Poems 1952–1972* (Boston: Houghton Mifflin, 1975), and Gary Snyder, *Turtle Island* (New York: New Directions, 1974). Reprinted with permission from *The New York Review of Books*. Copyright © 1976 Nyrev, Inc.

Eventually, manuals came out (above all, *Understanding Poetry* by Brooks and Warren) that harmonized iconoclasts like Eliot and Pound with Whitman, Browning, and tamer authors. Definitions of literature and art were stretched radically; and effusions that would once have been called barbaric yawps came to be heard as grace notes of civilization.

But while the scope of poetry widened, the power of exclusion shrank. If free verse became acceptable, how could one reject any work merely because the verse sounded inept? If transitions were unnecessary, and the poet might hop freely from theme to isolated theme, how could any shape be condemned as disorganized? If obscurity no longer mattered, and Blackmur might praise a poem by Stevens while announcing that he did not understand it, how could profundity be distinguished from opacity?

The line that led from Eliot and Pound involved learning and allusiveness. A reader who felt unsure of their art might still appreciate their cultivation, and agree that whether or not the stuff was verse, it certainly was highbrow. But William Carlos Williams jettisoned the humanistic tradition and set up local history in the shrines of Virgil and Dante. When his epigones crowded into the little magazines, they contributed dubious regions of easy language and domestic experience to the territory of poetry.

For many persons, subversive ideology, esoteric learning, mysterious "deep" images, and scandalous self-revelation became sufficient marks of the lyric gift. To judge poetry, some critics relied less on analysis than on affiliation, and the praise of what might be called aesthetic heroism. If an author could be linked to Pound, his archaisms were vindicated, even though he might lack Pound's ear, eye, wit, and taste. If his pages resembled those of Williams, his triviality became tolerable, even though he wrote without Williams's humor, warmth, or accuracy.

At the same time, a heroic devotion to literature became a standard of merit. Instead of praising a man's accomplishment, advocates praised his devotion to art. A fearful number of poems (especially by Berryman) have celebrated men who crucified their bodies on the cross of the creative imagination; and a fearful number of critics have urged us to admire poems born of exemplary persistence in "making."

In the careers of several poets—Plath, for example—the whole question of literary judgment sank to a whisper because they had (we were told) sacrificed their very lives to their work; and critics who doubted the value of the actual writing seemed like barbarians rending the veil of the temple. Even survival has now become a source of panegyric. To have continued writing into old age, is for some critics, an achievement that makes any further achievement supererogatory.

This detachment of poetry from literary skills has ancient and modern causes. In part it derives from a simple idea of expressiveness, the belief that any parallel between style and meaning is a sign of excellence, and that the use of established forms must imply an adherence to the established social order. By this doctrine, whoever feels dissatisfied with things as they are must depart boldly from the formal expectations of his reader. Broken phrases, coarse words, awkward rhythms would then disclose one's sympathy with oppressed minorities.

The doctrine is not without its point. One of the good deeds of the older generation of modern poets—especially Stevens, Pound, and Cummings—was to report on the battles fought between "greeting-card morality" and the literary conscience. Our social and political institutions now depend for their health upon the sickness of language and taste. For the labor of dramatizing that opposition, no writers have taken more responsibility than the poets.

During the postwar years of prosperous conformity, it was natural that the rift between the nation and its poets should widen. From the administration of Eisenhower to that of Johnson, a dogma of our literary faith was the mutual exclusiveness of art and the public life. Lowell embodied the attitude in his poem "Inauguration Day," and Nixon finally reciprocated with an edict to his footmen: "The arts you know—they're Jews, they're left wing—in other words, stay away."

But the existence of such a dichotomy is not the same as the equivalence of innovative forms (or shapelessness) to revolutionary ardor.

Chaos is best conveyed not by chaos but by the order against which its nature becomes visible. The fragmentation of syntax can express madness, carelessness, or a loathing of the reader. Only a very innocent poet or critic believes that boring poems deserve to be read because they mirror the truth that life is boring. Yet even Donald Davie takes a step in this direction when he says that Pound's *Cantos* may mirror, in the *large,* unpredictable patterns, "the rhythms of discovery, wastage, neglect, and rediscovery that the historical records give us notice of."[1]

Today it might be more interesting for the reader to be offered an ironic contrast between rich, subtle technique and the ideology of protest. As a model, Baudelaire might be an alternative to the disintegrating line of Whitman, Williams, and Charles Olson. Some readers might prefer being charmed to being pummeled and frustrated by turns.

But at work with the shallow notion of expressiveness has been a shallow concept of democracy. In this country the rise of Andrew Jackson signaled the opening of a long era of distrust of careful speech. For 150 years, villainy and articulateness have been confused in the American mind. A number of poets have half-consciously bowed to the idol and imagined that by avoiding art they have been serving the people.

Yet humble, nonliterary men and women do not warm to the sound of free verse. Poetry belongs for them to the realm of ceremony, and they want it clearly set apart from workaday language. They look for hymnlike stanzas, metered and rhymed, delivering a measure of soothing morality—e.g., birthday verses and the words of popular songs. To give them what they seek is not a labor of democracy but of commerce.

To complicate the separation of poetry from art there is also the sheer difficulty of winning friends for most of what passes for poetry today. Those who are not determinedly sympathetic cannot easily be persuaded to turn page after page of ill-directed itemizations. We are sometimes told that it is undemocratic elitism to expect a poet

---

1   Donald Davie, *Ezra Pound* (New York: Viking, 1975), 86.

to possess either a special talent or a special training. We are implicitly advised that it is the reader and not the author who must submit to judgment. Some critics seem to hint that the prosperity of the literary commonwealth depends on the readers' not expecting too much pleasure from the writers—that it depends indeed on the full employment of voluntary poets.

But this is again an accursed idea of democracy. We have no duty to accept whatever is put before us. There is an obligation to be sympathetic, to allow the artist a second and a third chance, to give our attention to the excellent parts of his work and to set aside the disappointing. We have to encourage poets who sound promising, even if they fail to please us deeply. But not forever! We also have to declare our dissatisfaction with repeated efforts to exclude us.

For much of the violence of recent poetry is defensive. Unable to hold the reader who lives outside his circle, the poet defies him and hurls denunciations at his retreating back. As the habitual readers of new poetry abandon more and more of the field to the spontaneous writers and their advocates, an old Bohemian practice grows more common. Instead of trying to win an audience, the embattled poet appeals to others in his plight and joins forces with them to blame the community of unbelievers.

In the end, some turn against language itself. They feel uneasy because they cannot make it serve them, cannot capture their listeners or convey their own insights through speech. Rather than try to acquire expressive skills, they fall back on silences, white spaces, portentous gestures of inarticulateness.

Now it is perfectly true that all words taste stale to a unique genius, and that he feels they misrepresent the freshness and fury of his vision. But one does not master the problem by invoking the name of Rimbaud and spurning every kind of rhetoric or poetic. I wonder whether the best way for a creative mind to direct its energy is to exalt intuition above the rest of its faculties combined.

Meanwhile, the addicts of poetry are waiting. What they desire is fresh insights into the human condition, eloquent language, subtle forms, a true connection between the poem they read and the living tongue. Poets exist who satisfy the desire: Lowell, Elizabeth Bishop,

James Merrill, James Schuyler—and one could easily extend the list. Recently, Robert Penn Warren has stepped out of his familiar wrapping and produced moving, funny, daring poems that rise from the ashes of the old Fugitive.

The appearance of George Oppen's *Collected Poems* invites us to place his work in this context. Oppen was born in 1908 and his first book, *Discrete Series,* was published in 1934 with a preface by Pound. He deals with the process of making the self at home in the world— that is, the imaginative self in the world it must define. For him the work of the imagination is to naturalize us to our universe. In this activity the poet may seem to start from the way he sees particular objects or persons. But he is really following the reciprocal movement of the mind between the tangible, external reality and the reality of the self.

Frequently, therefore, Oppen considers places or creatures he loves, and meditates on the current of feeling or thought reaching from him to them and back. The order of his themes is seldom discursive, for he does not unfold a series of reflections leading rationally from one to the next. Rather, his themes emerge discretely, as the poet's attention reverts to the object to consider it again and yet again. So the poem is often less a sequence than a set of observations and insights stemming from a common center:

> A picture seen from within. The picture is unstable, a
> moving picture, unlimited drift. Still, the picture
> exists.

Although Oppen's language is plain, he heightens it with echoes. He alludes to Blake, Whitman, and other poets; the old quatrain "Western Wind" reverberates through the whole book. Oppen also draws on his friends' conversation, perhaps to less advantage. But a feature of his method (reminiscent of Pound's) is the constant reemployment of his own phrases. Sometimes whole poems turn up afresh in new settings. The long sequence "Of Being Numerous" includes nearly all of the earlier, eight-part sequence "A Language of New York."

This practice supports the main drama of Oppen's work, which is the effort of the mind to reach clarity of vision by turning always upon itself, traveling back and forth between things and words, reconsidering and correcting earlier impressions or ponderings. As one nears the end of the whole book, the force of the retrospection rises. One must admire the poet as he contemplates death and still affirms the supremacy of the imagination which transforms the world in the act of seeing it truly.

Oppen also takes up the difficulty of being true to one's unique vision without being disloyal to one's community. He fully understands the ambivalence provoked by the challenge. Yet he does not weaken his devotion to a wife, a sister, a daughter, a city, or to the entire class of "the small poor." Rather, by seeing them in the light of his imagination, he conveys his love. Merely by illuminating and thus celebrating intimate ties and humble people, Oppen's poems become a criticism of irresponsible luxury—"The great utensiled / House / Of air conditioners, safe harbor / In which the heart sinks" ("Guest Room"; 87–88).

Oppen's identification of himself with the poor leads directly into his practice of poetry. Here he rejects fullness, richness, abundance. So he shies away from the sublime, from rhetoric, from anything like role-playing. The poet, he says, must be "impoverished / of tone of pose that common / wealth / of parlance"—a phrase in which "parlance" is chosen for its absurd richness ("Song, the Winds of Downhill"; 213).

For Oppen the original impression of an experience upon the mind is not something to be worked up or elaborated but rather to be cut down: the process of eliminating does the work of shaping. For him a complete sentence has less integrity than a fragment which the reader can finish by himself. How elliptical may one be—he seems to ask—and still suggest a meaning that carries an emotional charge?

So he likes to imply his meanings by juxtaposing impressions and omitting interpretative links. In a poem called "Workman" he compares his own habit of seizing and shaping an epiphany with the performances of a hawk and a carpenter:

> Leaving the house each dawn I see the hawk
> Flagrant over the driveway. In his claws
> That dot, that comma
> Is the broken animal: the dangling small beast knows
> The burden that he is: he has touched
> The hawk's drab feathers. But the carpenter's is a
>   culture
> Of fitting, of firm dimensions,
> Of post and lintel. Quietly the roof lies
> That the carpenter has finished. The sea birds circle
> The beaches and cry in their own way,
> The innumerable sea birds, their beaks and their wings
> Over the beaches and the sea's glitter.   (41)

The poet's nature comes through his bare, simple, terse style as admirably modest and even self-effacing, determined not to interpose a flamboyant self between his reader and his world. Honesty, clarity, illumination, are his desiderata.

But sparseness has little power by itself. When Oppen rejects the common privileges of a poet, he not only adds little excitement to his language; he also risks bathos. The elliptical character of his style barely distinguishes it from the cryptic. When one receives his insights, they often sound like those of Pound and W. C. Williams, and though truly felt are unsurprising. Even humor is rare; Oppen sounds averse to wit or satire. I wonder whether by resisting the lure of abundance he has not been left with a style that is pinched and thin.

Geoffrey Hill, an English poet in his mid-forties, is easy to consider in American terms because he reflects the influence of American poets. Hill refers directly to Ransom and Tate. So one is not surprised that his early poems have something in common with those of the young Robert Lowell. Unlike Oppen, Hill finds no contradiction between witty writing and authentic emotion; and he desires richness of style. Like Yeats and Lowell, he seizes on intimate, private experience and tries to endow it with public meanings. Like Swift, he possesses a deep sense of tradition and community which is (as Hill has wisely observed of Swift) "challenged by a strong feeling for the anarchic and the predatory."

In most of his poems Hill tries to convey extreme emotions by opposing the restraint of established form to the violence of his insight or judgment. He uses savage puns, heavy irony, and repeated oxymorons. He uses bold, archetypal images and religious symbols while complaining of their inefficacy. He deals with violent public events—crusades, prison camps, civil wars—and denounces the hideous crimes performed by deluded men in the service of divinities (or ideals) which they clothe with their own vices.

But in his ambitions as a poet and his failings as a man he detects the sins that dismay him in others:

> I have learned one thing: not to look down
> So much upon the damned. They, in their sphere,
> Harmonize strangely with the divine
> Love. I, in mine, celebrate the love-choir.
>
> ("Ovid in the Third Reich"; *Somewhere . . .* 51)

Appalled by the moral discontinuities of human behavior, he is also shaken by his own response to them, which mingles revulsion with fascination.

Hill longs for moral coherence. He would like to close the gap between what he knows himself to be and what others see in him. So also the orders of family, society, and government show him a dispiriting view of possible goods corrupted by indeterminate evils. Though he wishes to find his own integrity, Hill dismisses the way of transcendence and the way of withdrawal from the world: he will not blame the devil for our villainy or look to the realm of pure spirit for salvation. Integrity is meaningless for him apart from experience, and experience must involve him in the corruption he loathes. Ideally he would be a priest-king-poet, one who could order the chaos, sanctify the routines of communal life, and celebrate the goods of the natural world.

In his poems on such subjects, Hill tries to stir the reader up with strong rhythms, a mingling of coarse and sublime particulars, and a tone of ridicule pierced by sorrow. He strains to be compact and explosive, gnarled and bruising. The effect is not fortunate. One gets the impression of muffled outcries rather than furious eloquence.

The domestic equivalent of civil wars is the ambivalence of sexual passion. On this topic Hill's self-mockery and irony are more appealing than on the grand themes of moral outrage. Giving himself the name of Sebastian Arrurruz (for St. Sebastian and the arrows of love), he has written a set of agreeably wry, stylized laments over the memory of lost love; and in the sequence he manages to smile ruefully at the very scheme he is executing:

> Oh my dear one, I shall grieve for you
> For the rest of my life with slightly
> Varying cadence, oh my dear one.
>
> ("The Songbook of Sebastian Arrurruz"; 83)

Hill's latest poems are a series of prose pieces devoted to an imaginary spirit of the English Midlands. This figure is the poet as reincarnation of King Offa, ruler of the British kingdom of Mercia in the eighth century; and it represents that union of private and public, history and immediacy, that Hill wants. The poems are called "Mercian Hymns," and ambiguously celebrate the poet's links with his own region as if they were scenes from a monarch's life.

The tone varies from mock-epic to elegiac, as sour memories of childhood and maturity mix dreamily with impressions of landscape and the artifacts of Offa's reign. Most of the hymns are too unsure of their direction to reach a significant goal, but a few capture the grotesque wistfulness of a talented boy's conceit.

So a quarrel with a classmate over a toy plane merges happily with the wars of an eighth-century king named Ceolred and with Offa's interest in coinage:

Ceolred was his friend and remained so, even after the day
    of the lost fighter: a biplane, already obsolete and
    irreplaceable, two inches of heavy snub silver.
    Ceolred let it spin through a hole in the classroom—
    floorboards, softly, into the rat-droppings and coins.

After school he lured Ceolred, who was sniggering with
    fright, down to the old quarries, and flayed him.
    Then, leaving Ceolred, he journeyed for hours, calm and
    alone, in his private derelict sandlorry named
    Albion.   (101)

Nobody who reads Hill's collection will doubt that he has the attributes of an excellent poet. But his desire to produce stormy emotions with a few calculated gestures seems wrong for his technical resources; the quasi-sublime rhetoric does not move one, and the poet probably knows it. I suspect that his anger and self-mockery are due as much as anything to the frustration he feels over his lack of an authentic voice.

Geoffrey Hill thoroughly understands the dialectic of good and evil within the self, and its relation to the moral ambiguities of history and society. He is well on the way to a moving poetic style—less powerful, I think than he would like it to be, but strong enough for his purposes. "Mercian Hymns" probably brings him to the edge of his best work, which is still to come.

Gary Snyder does not take Hill's road to moral coherence; and his new book represents not so much a development as a hardening. As usual he mixes Zen Buddhism and American Indian mythology with a dislike of urban industrialism and an exemplary concern for the wilderness. An attitude that might be called stoic primitivism dominates his social philosophy. Like most primitivists, Snyder assumes that human nature is essentially disposed to benevolent conduct. To account for social evils, the primitivist has to blame institutions that corrupt our native disposition.

If he were logical, he would then try to show how benevolent dispositions can give rise to evil institutions. But this problem is one the primitivist does not like to contemplate. He prefers to treat technology, urbanization, mass production as modern aberrations which people can be taught to abandon.

Yet there are good reasons for connecting those recent phenomena with gigantic improvements in the conditions of life of men below the station of the ruling class; and there are equally good reasons for believing that before the advent of those phenomena most lives were threadbare, uncomfortable, and nightmarishly dependent on the caprice of men in power. Mature and thoughtful minds hardly need to be informed of such truths.

Snyder's doctrines are more attractive to younger minds, to those who have given up the relations of necessary dependence—that of citizens to a half-corrupt government, or son to aged parents, husband to a disagreeable wife, or sibling to a dumb brother—and who are strong, bright, and attractive enough to make their way in a voluntary society of people like themselves. According to Snyder, human beings are "interdependent energy-fields of great potential wisdom and compassion—expressed in each person as a superb mind, a handsome and complex body, and the almost magical capacity of language" (*Turtle Island,* p. 99). He never explains how one is to care—joyously and spontaneously—for the old, the ugly, the frail, the stupid.

In his untrammeled free verse, Snyder supplies illustrations of the life spent in harmony with natural rhythms. He represents this as painlessly available to those who truly desire it. In the routines of Snyder's own family—healthy husband, devoted (and tireless) wife, two goodlooking infants—the chores and mutual responsibilities appear to be deliciously compatible with individual freedom. The relation between children is summed up by the boy's gesture of patting the baby brother on the head, when he is sad, and saying, "Don't cry." If there are jealousies, rivalries, quarrels in this family, the reader is never told. Perhaps there are none.

Yet when one examines it, the life of harmony with natural rhythms—and with the community of all living men—appears voluntary and without stress only for those who accept the doctrine of stoic primitivism, i.e., for the saving remnant. Talking about the wrong-minded others (i.e., nearly all of mankind), Snyder sounds less permissive. "Must" is the auxiliary he favors. The need for haste, in the face of nuclear bombs and the pollution of the environment, is too great for him to feel like waiting for gradual, voluntary conversions.

Those who like Mozart's operas, art museums, and cheap books may wonder just how these will be supplied when all the world is tucked away in places like Marin County. Snyder does not linger over these issues. He says that wastefulness, for example, "must be halted totally with ferocious energy." We have heard these impersonal verbs before, in the mouths of Robespierre and his benevolent descendants; and although the poet himself renounces the use of force, history tells us what his impatient followers may attempt. As Snyder puts it, "Nothing short of total transformation will do much good" (p. 99).

18

HEANEY | AMMONS | STRAND

Only the most gifted poets can start from the peculiar origin in a language, a landscape, a nation, and from these enclosures rise to impersonal authority. Seamus Heaney has this kind of power, and it appears constantly in his *Poems 1965–1975*. One may enter his poetry by a number of paths, but each joins up with the others. Nationality becomes landscape; landscape becomes language; language becomes genius.

For a poet, language is first; and in considering this, I may clarify my meaning. Speech is never simple, in Heaney's conception. He grew up as an Irish Catholic boy in a land governed by Protestants whose tradition is British. He grew up on a farm in his country's northern, industrial region. As a person, therefore, he springs from the old divisions of his nation.

At the same time, the theme that dominates Heaney's work is self-definition, the most natural subject of the modern lyric; and language, from which it starts, shares the old polarities. For Heaney, it is the Irish speech of his family and district, overlaid by the British and urban culture which he acquired as a student.

This essay was first published 8 Oct. 1981 under the title "Digging In" as a review of Seamus Heaney, *Poems 1965–1975* (New York: Farrar, Straus, & Giroux, 1980), A. R. Ammons, *A Coast of Trees* (New York: Norton, 1981), and Mark Strand, *Selected Poems* (New York: Atheneum, 1980). Reprinted with permission from *The New York Review of Books*. Copyright © 1981 Nyrev, Inc.

The outcome is not merely a matter of vocabularies and accents. Even the smallest constituents bifurcate. In the poet's ear, vowels are soft and Irish; consonants are hard and English. Heaney once said he associated his personal pieties with vowels and his literary awareness with consonants. So also the vocabularies and etymologies (sometimes fanciful) have their ground. For softness and hardness belong to the landscape of the poet's childhood, to its bogs and farms, its rivers and mountains. Consequently, we hear lines from poems translating sound into terrain and nationality:

> The tawny guttural water
> spells itself: Moyola
> is its own score and consort,
>
> bedding the locale
> in the utterance,
> reed music, an old chanter
>
> breathing its mists
> through vowels and history.
>
> ("Gifts of Rain"; *Poems* 103)

Instead of being hemmed in by the old divisions, Heaney lets them enrich his expression. Fundamental to his process of self-definition is a refusal to abandon any part of his heritage. The name of the family farm, Mossbawn, divides itself between the soft Irish bog and "moss" and a word meaning fortified farm, or "bawn," of a British settler. The Heaneys' farm actually lay between a "bog" of yielding peat and the cultivated "demesne" of Moyola Park—belonging to a peer who had served as head of the British establishment. It was bordered as well by townlands with malleable Gaelic names, Anahorish and Broagh. But it looked out on Grove Hill and Back Park, firm with the definitive consonants of a ruler's voice. What the poet means to accomplish is a union of the two traditions:

> But now our river tongues must rise
> From licking deep in native haunts

> To flood, with vowelling embrace,
> Demesnes staked out in consonants.
>
> ("A New Song"; *Poems* 111)

Heaney incorporates these subtle attitudes into a coherent literary self. He feels eager, as he says of some English poets, to defend a linguistic integrity, to preserve the connection of his own speech with "the descending storeys of the literary and historical past." Historically, therefore, he can identify himself with the English tradition and oppose it in turn to the Latin of the conquerors of Britain.

In "Freedman" (216), for example, he begins with Latinate diction and ends with short English words as he traces his evolution from a shy Northern Irish student of the master culture ("Subjugated yearly under arches") into a poet acknowledged by readers in New York and Melbourne ("poetry wiped my brow and sped me").

The same poem illustrates the characteristic, pervasive gravity of the poet's wit. He describes himself going through the streets of Belfast on Ash Wednesday with a touch of ashes on his forehead, and links the mark to the humble, earthbound status of the native Roman Catholic Irish before their Protestant governors:

> One of the earth-starred denizens, indelibly,
> I sought the mark in vain on the groomed optimi:
> Their estimating, census-taking eyes
> Fastened on my mouldy brow like lampreys.

The Latinate words go with the Protestant masters. The boy himself has a plain "mouldy brow," implying his ties with the soil. "Groomed" suggests "groom," which once meant an officer of the royal household. The Protestants are "estimating" because of their commercial pursuits. They are "census-taking" because they anxiously reckon the growing proportion of Catholics in the Six Counties. But the census is also a function of the overlords, and the word has the same root as "censor," which evokes the moral rigor of Presbyterianism. Lampreys are parasitic as well as clinging, and suck the blood of the fish to which they attach themselves. I am only hinting at the weightiness of Heaney's language.

The habit of digging into the history of the words he uses comes from the same impulse as a wish to tie the images of the poems to a racial past. In his writing as in his character, the poet tries to root the present age in the oldest, elemental patterns of his people, and then to relate the people to the countryside that fostered them, ultimately reminding us of the situation of all humanity in nature. Love for a woman must be like love for a region; and the features of the homeland call up the countryside the poet knows best. In "Polder" (from the recent book *Field Work*) Heaney speaks of embracing after a quarrel as a reclaiming of territory from the sea.[1]

Quite deliberately, the poet tries to describe elements of landscape in human terms and people he loves as reminding him of animals. The humor and wit convey affection, but they also suggest a wish to be at home in the world, to surmount the barriers between man and beast. If a stream turns into a woman ("Undine") and a woman into an otter ("The Otter"), Heaney implies that his own devotion to the countryside links up with his attachment to people. This is how he carries off a tribute to his wife, in a poem recalling a skunk he had seen in California:

> It all came back to me last night, stirred
> By the sootfall of your things at bedtime,
> Your head-down, tail-up hunt in a bottom drawer
> For the black plunge-line nightdress.
>
> ("The Skunk"; *Field Work* 48)

The yearning toward a racial past takes powerful forms. It is characteristic of Heaney that when he wished to find symbols adequate to the ordeal of his countrymen, he should have turned to an ancient

1   *Field Work* (London: Faber and Faber, 1979).

mystery which reaches toward the hidden aspects of human nature. This is the problem of the so-called "bog people," or bodies found in Danish bogs, where they were placed from the time of the early Iron Age. Heaney accepts the view that at least some are the remains of a fertility ritual. But he uses them in his poems to suggest that modern terrorism, rather than meaning a breaking with the past, belongs to an archetypal pattern. In a forceful passage, he indicates the strain on his character as he contemplates the national agony; for he too feels the yearning to be not a recorder or singer but a heroic actor in the terrible drama. Here, contemplating the body of a woman apparently hanged for a crime (perhaps adultery), he says,

> My poor scapegoat,
>
> I almost love you
> but would have cast, I know,
> the stones of silence.
> I am the artful voyeur
>
> of your brain's exposed
> and darkened combs,
> your muscles' webbing
> and all your numbered bones:
>
> I who have stood dumb
> when your betraying sisters,
> cauled in tar,
> wept by the railings,
>
> who would connive
> in civilized outrage
> yet understand the exact
> and tribal, intimate revenge.

("Punishment"; *Poems* 193)

The poet's triumph is to bring the ingredients of history and biography under the control of his music. Technique, says Heaney, "entails the water-marking of your essential patterns of perception, voice and thought into the touch and texture of your lines."[2]

Here again he accepts traditions that join England to Ireland; for his verse reminds us of the short lines (often octosyllabic), the couplets and quatrains of Swift, who liked to mix coarseness with idealism, humor with anger, observation with fantasy, and honesty with love. Heaney's expressive rhythms support his pleasure in reechoing syllables and modulating vowels through a series of lines to evoke continuities and resolutions. He has learned from Yeats without being suffocated by him.

> Our guttural muse
> was bulled long ago
> by the alliterative tradition,
> her uvula grows
>
> vestigial, forgotten
> like the coccyx
> or a Brigid's Cross
> yellowing in some outhouse
>
> while custom, that "most
> sovereign mistress,"
> beds us down into
> the British isles.   ("Traditions"; *Poems* 109)

Like Heaney, A. R. Ammons grew up on his father's farm; and like Heaney, he can remember the early death of a younger brother (another was stillborn). Fear and death are common themes of both

---

2 "Feeling into Words," in *Preoccupations* (New York: Farrar, Straus, & Giroux, 1980), 47.

men's poetry and keep appearing in Ammons's new book—one of his most impressive collections—*A Coast of Trees*.

But Ammons had a lonely, impoverished boyhood, and attached himself less to people than to the things around him. Landscape is what enthralls him; he seldom attends to personalities and hardly notices history. Often, Heaney writes in conventional forms. Ammons does not.

I think the difference between the two men exposes a difference between the literary culture of Irish or British writers and that of Americans. Poets in our country feel remote from their audience (such as it is); and outside a few great centers they are remote from one another. The American tends to confront the universe directly. As an artist, he gets little support from liturgical forms or from the songs and hymns that often provide patterns for Irish and British verse.

Robert Lowell, who influenced Heaney, was exceptional in his ties with the large community of the nation. He was exceptional for placing his family and friends in a historical frame even while he constantly employed landscape and animals to set humanity against the rest of nature. It may be significant that Lowell was at one time drawn to the Roman Catholic Church, for which mediation is far more important than it is for Protestantism.

Ammons deals with his world immediately. The macrocosm and microcosm of nature occupy his imagination, and he defines himself by his way of facing these ultimate challenges. In his engaging new collection he has some exquisite love poems and a couple of tender descriptions of old men trying to look after their frail wives. He also has an elegy on his own boyhood.

But as usual, nine-tenths of the poems invite us to stand with the speaker isolated in a landscape, sharply observing some particulars of the scene while responding with quasi-didactic reflections. The most densely populated of the poems is centered on a graveyard.

As if to make up for the lack of human agents, Ammons regularly personifies the features of landscape that hold his attention. Sometimes this habit can give sharpness to an image, as when the thawing brook "steps" down a ledge; and the effect is improved here because the lines themselves run over until the ledge, in a row of three slow beats, impedes the movement:

> the brook, the sky bright
> for days, steps lightly
> down ledge steps.

("Eventually Is Soon Enough"; 14)

But when the poet exchanges opinions with a mountain (as in "Continuing"), I balk.

✤ Selfhood, for Ammons, means the establishment of healing continuities in the face of unpredictable, often withering disruptions. So it is restorative for him to notice how the elements of landscape survive and establish a new balance after destructive assaults. On such images of change, loss, and restoration he concentrates an attention sharpened by scientific training.

Ammons's handling of free verse evokes the process he celebrates. One characteristic of the normally short lines is what might be called radical enjambment, or the ending of lines after words that demand an object or complement—adjectives, prepositions, transitive verbs, conjunctions. Another peculiarity is the repetition of a few key words, often three times or more. In spite of the apparent freedom of form of the whole poem, Ammons generally returns at the end to an image prominent at the start, to which he then gives new depth; and the poem often turns formally on the movement from observation to reflection. The effect of the enjambments, the repetitions, and the circular form is to suggest the disruptions, continuities, and resolutions of the flow of our emotions. The short poems of Ammons have more power than the long, because he tends to neglect shape and point when he becomes discursive.

An invitation to misread the poetry is the surface of calm in Ammons's work. Strangers may suspect him of complacency. But like Stevens and Bishop—two other poets obsessed with landscape—Ammons has only a slight hold on his hard-won moments of tranquillity. The bleakness of human life breaks out in phrases like "the many thoughts and / sights unmanageable, the deaths of so many, hungry or mad" ("Swells"; 3). The same bleakness is elaborated in "Sunday at McDonald's," which opens with an outcry against the American addiction to living in a detached present:

> In the bleak land of foreverness no
> one lives but only, crushed and buffeted,
> now: now, now, now every star glints
>
> perishing while now slides under and
> away, slippery as light, time-vapor.   (40)

The underlying sadness rises to anguish in "Easter Morning," the longest poem of the book. Here the lonely poet expresses his bitterness over the deformations produced in a child like himself by the imperviousness of adults who die before they can recognize and redeem their errors. Mourning for the person he might have been, the poet faces the graveyard in which are buried those people—teachers, relations, parents—who could have saved him from becoming a man more at ease with brooks and hills than with human society. The power of the poem springs from the central conceit of the isolated individual standing before the sociable dead.

But he does not see his crucifixion as unique:

> we all buy the bitter
> incompletions, pick up the knots of
> horror, silently raving, and go on
> crashing into empty ends not
> completions, not rondures.   (20)

In the last third of the poem, the theme of resurrection emerges, in the shape of two large birds seen flying together. When one veers from the straight way, the other notices and joins him. Then both return to the original route. The watcher admires their possession of free patterns which they may companionably leave and return to, unlike the rigidity of his own development; and he admires the beauty of the "picture-book, letter-perfect" morning (21).

The theme of Mark Strand's seductive poetry—amply represented in his *Selected Poems*—is the elusiveness of the self. We all assume by instinct that there exists in each of us a quintessential person separate from the physical appearance, separate from the clothes and actions, the thoughts and feelings, separate from one's history and expectations.

But how can we represent or even know this self when language can only render the visible, the tangible, the conceivable? We can try either to strip away the externals or to bring them into consciousness and so get beyond them. But the effort is defeated because the self we are defining changes during the process, and a new person displaces the old even while the old persists:

> I empty myself of the names of others. I empty my
>   pockets.
> I empty my shoes and leave them beside the road.
> At night I turn back the clocks;
> I open the family album and look at myself as a boy.
>
> What good does it do? The hours have done their job.
>   .   .   .   .   .
> Time tells me what I am. I change and I am the same.
> I empty myself of my life and my life remains.
>
>   ("The Remains"; 51)

Besides, the forces that change the self are not in one's control. They act mysteriously and capriciously. Especially is this true of other people. We are one person when alone but somebody else in the company of a friend. The force extends to the conception a friend or wife has of oneself. We change according to what others think we are, and our knowledge of them as quintessential persons is qualified by their view of us. We resent the process of decomposition, yearn for the old person, are deluded by the conviction that the inner self has not altered, will not change.

> These wrinkles are nothing.
> These gray hairs are nothing.
> This stomach which sags
> with old food, these bruised
> and swollen ankles,
> my darkening brain,
> they are nothing.
> I am the same boy
> my mother used to kiss.   ("Not Dying"; 78)

The poet is the man who does not merely submit to these questions. He studies them, and his imagination deliberately employs them to produce aesthetic forms of relationship, symmetrical analogues to the evolution of self from self, choreographies that will endure when the elusive performers are gone. In Strand's work what seem to be people are sometimes characters waiting for a poet to invent them. Or his people may create themselves by writing the story in which they will appear.

A self is the creation of one's memories. But since these cannot be verified, a poet may imagine a past and challenge recollection to oppose it. Indeed, since all memory is partly invention, we are constantly remaking ourselves. Let speculation move a step further, and we may say that to make up a story is to create a memory. Such paradoxes excite Strand's imagination in poems like "The Story of Our Lives" and "The Untelling" (both too long). He seems drawn to write parables of the act of literary composition.

In Strand's somewhat Proustian view of the human condition we are doomed to cling to evanescence. The world which the self loves decays as the self changes. The person yearns for an intimacy which is unattainable because each lover alters in the presence of the other. To understand and describe another human being, we must not render him as an independent figure but as conceived by a friend or son or wife, and preferably as himself facing the process of decay. In a fine poem about his mother, Strand places her in a carefully imagined landscape at sunset and attributes to her the thoughts that make one human:

> And my mother will stare into the starlanes,
> the endless tunnels of nothing,
> and as she gazes,
> under the hour's spell,
> she will think how we yield each night
> to the soundless storms of decay
> that tear at the folding flesh,
> and she will not know
> why she is here
> or what she is prisoner of
> if not the conditions of love that brought her to this.
>
> ("My Mother on an Evening in Late Summer"; 150–51)

The shape of a poem by him is almost always pleasing, with his favorite images and epithets (light, shadow, dark, moon, sun, water, rain, mirror, etc.) slipping easily into place, and with subtle rhyme schemes of patterns of assonance supporting the quiet repetitions and variations that lead to a sudden opening as the focus changes from something seen, remembered, or felt, to something still being written—the poem itself.

It is in fact this turning on itself, the movement toward solipsism, that weakens Strand's work. Many of the poems seem written to exemplify designs, to show how felicitously a dream or panic could be given satisfactory form but not to illuminate an experience so that readers might match it with their own. If I recommend the short lyric of self-definition as the proper modern poem, it is not because the character of a poet is the most important focus of a literary work. It is because through this frame the poet can describe human nature and the world.

Heaney's intimacy with landscape tells us not about the poet's aesthetic taste but about the world of parks and swamps. Heaney's relation to his friends tells us not about his peculiar adolescence but about loyalty and religious faith. The meaning of art and the character of the artist are noble subjects of poetry. They have been nobly treated by Dante, Baudelaire, and Yeats. But the lyric of self-definition has no special duty to concentrate its energies on these preoccupations. A poet who does so might well set himself in a community of artists and (as in the late poems of Wallace Stevens) might indeed conceive of creative imagination as an essential trait marking the whole human species.

For all his mastery of rhythm and music, Strand does not open the lyric to the world but makes it a self-sustaining enterprise. His forms tend toward the infinite regress of a mirror watching a mirror. In his realm you can realize your own self only by imagining another self which in turn is imagining you. That other may be a lover, a wife, a child. It may be your own old self which the new one has destroyed and replaced—after, of course, being imagined in advance. But the movement of all the profound self-awareness is toward decoration rather than abundance. Caught up in the subject-object relations, Strand sees the world as what the perceiver is not, and the perceiver as what the world is not:

> In a field
> I am the absence
> of field.   ("Keeping Things Whole"; 10)

19

PLATH

The habit of reading Sylvia Plath's poems biographically is so common that one forgets how many of them are dramatic monologues, how many are spoken by imaginary characters who have no obvious connection with the poet. The new, long-awaited edition of *The Collected Poems* brings together many such pieces, balancing the unmediated lyrics.

The most elaborate of the monologues is the highly effective *Three Women,* in which Plath interweaves the speeches of a mother, a secretary, and a university student all responding to the experience of pregnancy. Here the poet discloses the separate dispositions of the introspective women by steadily shifting images which convey the veering moods through subtle parallels and contrasts. What fascinates the author is the way each speaker wholly redefines herself in terms of the experience. With no external narrative, Plath manages to give haunting embodiment to three lives at the same, supreme turning point.

Reading and rereading the many monologues, one must be struck by the poet's genius for using physical bodies as emblems of inner character. Not through Balzacian physiognomy but through the manip-

This essay was first published 2 Feb. 1982 under the title "The Other Sylvia Plath" as a review of *Sylvia Plath: The Collected Poems,* ed. Ted Hughes (New York: Harper and Row, 1981). Reprinted with permission from *The New York Review of Books.* Copyright © 1982 Nyrev. Inc.

ulation of the body as an object, she expresses her preoccupation with selfhood and personality. In the monologues Plath regularly brings the speaker's thoughts to a focus on this theme. Not all the attempts come off. But in "Face Lift" it is plain that the woman hopes a new skin will produce a new person:

> Now she's done for, the dewlapped lady
> I watched settle, line by line, in my mirror—
> Old sock-face, sagged on a darning egg.
>
> (*Collected Poems* 156)

A secondary motif is that of self-control. Not only does the speaker delight in the pathetic hope that appearance will transform reality; she also preens herself on having taken hold of the situation and by an act of will accomplished what she desired. (I believe the laboratory jar is an allusion to jars in which miscarried foetuses are kept.)

> They've trapped her in some laboratory jar.
> Let her die there, or wither incessantly for the next
>   fifty years,
> Nodding and rocking and fingering her thin hair.
> Mother to myself, I wake swaddled in gauze,
> Pink and smooth as a baby.   (156)

In her best poems, Plath dramatizes, at perhaps the deepest level, the willed effort of the human identity to establish itself, to find a stable base, to grow and unfold. For there is a ferociously ambiguous environment standing against the hesitant first movements of the primitive personality. Things that look kind to it become cruel. Things that look dangerous become nourishing. Bewildered by the duplicity of people, clothes, food, domestic furniture, the infant self wavers between expansion and shrinkage.

At the same time, the tentative person suffers the pressure of its inner, overwhelming moods and instincts. Hurting what it loves, grasping what it detests, the self learns anxious diffidence. Its multiple, conflicting desires threaten to frustrate the yearning for coherence. In

America, where homogeneous cultural patterns are rare, and the individual must forge the conscience of his race along with his own, the problem is aggravated. Plath carried further the experiments of Eliot and Lowell in handling the theme.

In fact, she created a vocabulary of images and gestures to convey the primal condition. For instance, she uses hooks, again and again, to suggest the mixture of seduction and menace offered by apparently neutral stimuli. In "Tulips" (160) a hospital patient, sinking into a drugged nonentity of exhaustion, feels troubled by a family photograph which still requires her to be an individual. The smiles of the husband and child in the picture seem like "little smiling hooks." But the image is quickly adaptable to other contexts. In a poem about picking blackberries, the curves of an inviting but sinister path, going down to the sea, are also "hooks" ("Blackberrying"; 168).

Nets are another form of the image. They are hidden traps that work with deceptively pleasing sensations. In "Purdah" (242), a betrayed wife thinks of herself as wearing veils because she hides her true feelings from her husband. Moonlight is dangerous, for it encourages her to reveal emotion. So the moon rises with "cancerous pallors," illuminating trees which in turn act like "little nets," since the poet must evade the softening effect of landscape and not expose her "visibilities."

The word *glitter* also belongs to this pattern of moral ambiguity, because, like the Latinate equivalent, *specious,* it suggests allurement and falsehood at once. In "Death & Co." (254) the poet combines the word with another, *plausive,* a rare adjective that can mean approving or specious. She implies that the person described is concealing real hostility and pretending to like somebody whom he wishes to make use of for his own purposes. Wearing hair that is "long and plausive," he is "masturbating a glitter."

Less precise imagery can generalize the effect. For Plath, any blank, shimmering, or curtained appearance attracts sinister implications. Baldness, the gleaming whiteness of the moon, call up dangerous ambiguity. One can too easily project hopes and fears upon a tabula rasa. In "A Life" (150) the poet draws a contrast between a work of art representing a contented family, and the reality of a woman cut off from relations, dragging her shadow around "a bald, hospital saucer."

On a bleak day in February, another woman, recovering from a miscarriage, looks out and sees that the new year "hones its edge" on a bald hill, "faceless and pale as china" ("Parliament Hill Fields"; 152). Both images refer to a way of life that combines isolation with loss of meaning.

Syntax, figures of speech, and modes of expression enrich Plath's double vision of moral reality. Often she frames questions to bring out the doubtfulness of the signals from the environment, or the anxiety of the self trying to get a secure footing. So the brilliant colors of poppies in July trouble the poet. "Do you do no harm?" she asks ("Poppies in July"; 203); for if she lets down her guard and warms to the blossoms, she will be hurt. In "Getting There" (247) the misery of holding the fragmented self together until the final release into death is conveyed by the allegory of a hideous journey in wartime, punctuated by the frantic question, "How far is it?"

To combine the various effects is not difficult. In "Mystic" (268) Plath faces the irrational spasm of hopefulness which often strikes one during a season of well-earned despair. "The air is a mill of hooks," says the poet as she considers the many, confusing stimuli that make life seem not only endurable but (perhaps!) promising. The hooks, however, turn at once into questions, partly because question marks look like hooks. The movement from ambiguous hope to uncertainty slips over into images of menace as the air-filling questions become flies, that kiss and sting at once. After a central section on religious experience, the poet closes with the world regaining significance. The sun blooms like a geranium, and she can say, "The heart has not stopped."

Menace implies intention. It is easy therefore to attribute motives and minds to the things that encroach upon the self. In Plath's work a radical sort of personification indicates a transfer of vitality from human beings to objects or abstractions. It is typical of the poet that in her language the hooks which threaten one should smile maliciously as they do so. But more striking personifications are available. In "Insomniac" (163) the sleepless man dreads the approach of dawn: "Already he can feel daylight, his white disease, / Creeping up with her hatful of trivial repetitions."

This brilliant poem also brings out the fragmentation of the isolated, introverted personality. Rather than being strong and continuous, the self is a bundle of memories and painful feelings which the insomniac cannot organize. One thinks of the helpless panic of an infant child at his failure to withstand the mysterious strength of an unpredictable rage. Here the transformation is from vital to mechanical: the person is reduced to a set of mirrors producing an infinite regress:

> His head is a little interior of gray mirrors.
> Each gesture flees immediately down an alley
> Of diminishing perspectives, and its significance
> Drains like water out the hole at the far end.

Sometimes the interrogative mood determines the whole form of a poem, and Plath composes the riddle. Instead of providing a resolution which satisfies the reader, however, she replaces suspense with a new, more concrete uneasiness: we are asked, "What is this disturbing presence?" The poem "Mirror" (173–74) seems like an undemanding enigma: "I am silver and exact. I have no preoccupations," says the reflecting surface; and then it tells us about the room it watches. But in the second half of the poem a woman tries to define herself by her appearance; and the mirror says,

> Now I am a lake. A woman bends over me,
> Searching my reaches for what she really is.
> Then she turns to those liars, the candles or the moon.
> I see her back, and reflect it faithfully.
> She rewards me with tears and an agitation of hands.
> I am important to her. She comes and goes.
> Each morning it is her face that replaces the darkness.
> In me she has drowned a young girl, and in me an old
>   woman
> Rises toward her day after day, like a terrible fish.

The shape of the poem imitates the search for and achievement of selfhood: it moves in an accelerating advance from the leisurely calm of the mirror's self-portrayal to the quick, sinister precision of the close-up of the fish.

Certain themes recur in the poems, to enlarge the meaning of the images and technical devices. Dismemberment suggests the difficulty of putting or keeping together the personality. The self can disintegrate, fly apart, or merely flake off. In the poem "In Plaster" (158–60) the soul-body relation takes the shape of a fantasy in which the poet finds a plaster replica in the bed beside her. Although at first this new, "absolutely white person" takes care of the older one, gradually she alters and grows critical: "She let in the drafts and became more and more absentminded. / And my skin itched and flaked away in soft pieces." Under the impact of moral self-scrutiny the person loses shape; character dissolves in doubt.

In an equally astonishing poem, "Event" (194–95), a husband and his embittered wife are in bed, back to back. Disillusionment has changed her view of him and of herself. As she lies there, she senses her angry feelings emanating from the creatures and things of the house and neighborhood. The moonlight is a "chalk cliff / In whose rift we lie." Coldness and whiteness loom against the heat of private emotions. The wife imagines herself walking around like a needle in the groove of a record, as she goes over and over the suppressed recriminations. She has been transformed by the "event"—i.e., his treachery. Even more—in her eyes—has his nature been changed. "Who has dismembered us?" she asks, referring both to their falling out and to the disintegration of their separate characters.

During such crises the role of the will grows important. The person fears that any relaxation of control will leave the components of the self without cement. To hold them in place, when forces within and without are tearing them apart, requires constant effort. Even death must be arranged ahead of time. In a faultless monologue, "Last Words" (172), the speaker is an ancient Egyptian planning her own

burial. Through the instruction she indicates the self she means to
become in death; and the poem ends,

> They will roll me up in bandages, they will store my
> > heart
> Under my feet in a neat parcel.
> I shall hardly know myself. It will be dark,
> And the shine of these small things sweeter than the
> > face of Ishtar.

"Things" here refers to the domestic objects that will accompany the
body: cooking vessels, rouge pots, etc.—more reliable than the spirit.
Plath's poetry abounds in such articles. She sets her tremendous agons
in humble locations, often indoors—kitchens, bedrooms, offices.

It is a short step for her imagination to replace parts of the self by
equivalents or by things. In "The Applicant" (221), one of Plath's masterpieces, prosthesis suggests a lack of authenticity—false, incomplete,
corrupt character—along with dependence. It suggests the inter-
changeability of the meaningless parts of abortive personalities. In the
poem a monstrous marriage broker is bringing together a token man
and an inchoate woman. It opens unforgettably:

> First, are you our sort of person?
> Do you wear
> A glass eye, false teeth or a crutch,
> A brace or a hook,
> Rubber breasts or a rubber crotch.

The poem brings out the risks faced by true selfhood. Here a male
nonentity is given vital substance through his connection with a chosen
female who exists only to serve him. By implication, the social order
that saw fit to join them would move against a woman who was authentic, a person in her own right. This danger in turn has an under-
side; for a number of poems carry the further hint that society may

not be quite mistaken in its reaction, and that to assert one's own identity is in truth to menace or destroy others.

In "The Stones" (137)—a controlled triumph of nightmare vision—doctors make prosthesis their occupation. The hospital or factory (a mental institution) is a "city of spare parts," and health here means a surrender of intrinsic personality. Almost like Frankenstein's monster, the individual is reassembled, newborn into the fake harmlessness of compliant normality: "My swaddled legs and arms smell sweet as rubber." The theme emerges more lightly in "Tulips" (160), as the speaker, drugged in a hospital bed, loses her hostility along with her character: "I am nobody; I have nothing to do with explosions." Here Plath hints at the ruthlessness of authentic personality. The tulips trouble her because they induce her to respond as a person, and she is afraid of the destructiveness that may be released if she gives way.

At this stage the principle of the double, or total prosthesis, moves into the foreground of Plath's imagination. Instead of letting the split between dangerous and benign impulses remain an internal affair, the poet sometimes represents it as opening between herself and a shadowy figure, created to receive blame. There is a communal aspect to the concept. Socially or politically, the victim of oppression is linked to a tyrannical community or government just as a mistreated wife is bound to an unfeeling husband. Yet sufferers may teach cruelty to the masters. The victim can be a prosecutor too, once she embodies the regime or the spouse in Another.

The speaker of "In Plaster" (158–60) first accepts the humble ministrations of her new, white companion, who seems a benignly blank version of herself. But since the replica is only a projection, she has the underlying defects of her original; and these soon appear. For the white figure tires of good works, turns censorious, and at last reveals malice. The speaker then complains, "She wanted to leave me, she thought she was superior." However, instead of being tolerant and good-natured, the speaker reacts with a plan to collect her own strength and abandon the Other first. "And she'll perish with emptiness then," says the poet vindictively.

Drawing out the implications, we may say that the martyr invents a torturer in her own image. Neither could exist without the other. (One thinks of a daughter requiring a father to be childishly enraged so she may complain of his injustice.) Eventually, therefore, the parts of oppressor and oppressed become reversible, like Lucky and Pozzo in *Waiting for Godot*.

Such a confusion of roles between victim and persecutor is barely intimated in "Death & Co." (254–55). Here the poet is visited and feels threatened by two evil men. One has the "scald scar of water" and reminds her of a condor. The scar suggests a victim, and recalls the scars of Lady Lazarus. But the condor is certainly a bird of prey. The second man "wants to be loved," and is a helper in the mysterious, criminal enterprise.[1] But the poet refuses to be taken in; she will not "stir." Yet she ends with the words, "Somebody's done for." Is it the poet, or one of the dangerous but vulnerable men, who is done for? Is she destroying them, or are they destroying her?

Possibly, then, the tormentor was correct all along? It is a masterstroke of irony for the poet to join the opposed characters of victim and avenger in one. That is the accomplishment of "The Applicant." Again, in "Lady Lazarus" (246–47), deservedly the best-known of Plath's poems, the two roles are united. Here the victimized speaker shows her rage at first only by her tone. But at last she drops the disguise of passive sufferer and turns into nemesis. The doctors who have revived her are persecutors, Nazis, even Lucifer. Now, therefore, the tyrant, the social order, the male state that tortured the victims of the Holocaust, are themselves savagely threatened.

The poet becomes her own prosthesis. Instead of imagining an Other on whom to smear the hostilities and inadequacies of her inner

---

1   Sylvia Plath explained this late poem (written near the end of 1962, a few months before her suicide) in an unbroadcast interview: "This poem . . . is about the double or schizophrenic nature of death—the marmoreal coldness of Blake's death mask, say, hand in glove with the fearful softness of worms, water, and other catabolisms. I imagine these two aspects of death as two men, two business friends, who have come to call" (quoted by Edward Butscher in *Sylvia Plath: Method and Madness* [New York: Seabury Press, 1976] 391). [Ed.]

nature, she will die as the outer, beguiling social person and be reborn as the vengeful "true" self. The role of martyr gives way to that of assassin. Like a phoenix, the speaker will come back:

> Out of the ash
> I rise with my red hair
> And I eat men like air.

APPENDIX
LETTERS TO THE EDITOR OF
THE NEW YORK REVIEW

Talk about Ashbery

To the Editors: February 19, 1976

Because I am a reader I am a bit unnerved by Irvin Ehrenpreis telling me, in his review of John Ashbery's *Self-Portrait in a Convex Mirror* (*NYR,* October 16), what, as a reader, my responses to an Ashbery poem are: "his work will tire nearly all his readers." "So many readers are dismayed when they try (intelligently and seriously) to enjoy his poems." "Their fragmentary, disjointed, or maddeningly evasive nature not only baffles but bores the reader." I think it would have been clearer if instead of "readers" Professor Ehrenpreis had said "my students," because ultimately what he conveys to us in his review is not that Ashbery's poems are boring to read, but that they are boring to teach, boring to talk about. They don't have much in the way of *themes.* There is so little meat to leave one's teeth marks on.

"There is room in our literature for John Ashbery," he says. I'll go along with that. But then in talking about poems such as Ashbery's, Professor Ehrenpreis says, "They teach the rewards of passivity, of letting the life of sensation impose its order on us, of enjoying the designs that start up in spite of us, as we raise our eyes from a newspaper while smelling bread in the oven, hearing Brahms on the phonograph, and feeling the heat of a wood fire, all linked in the welcome surprise of a composition that fades at once." This is a chillingly self-satisfied listing. And it is what an Ashbery poem is *not* and does *not* do.

An Ashbery poem is not an evanescent composition of sensations. It is a composite of images so exact that they instantly strike us as God's truth. As Eliot pointed out in his Preface to Perse's *Anabasis,* "There is a logic of the imagination as well as a logic of concepts. People who do not appreciate poetry always find it difficult to distinguish between order and chaos in the arrangement of images"; and later, "such an arrangement of imagery requires just as much 'fundamental brainwork' as the arrangement of an argument." But Professor Ehrenpreis shrewdly quotes none of the imagery. Instead, he searches out those lines that come closest to fitting into his preconceived idea of what poetry should be: "A glance, a ballade / That takes in the whole world, now, but lightly, / Still lightly, but with wide authority and tact." These are lines that could have been written by anyone being pushed around the room by a lyrical urge. But they are the kind of lines that please Ehrenpreis and give him a chance to say, "So Ashbery tries to make us act out the division between workaday reality and those moments of transcendence that are like moments of love or of mystical communion."

Ashbery does no such thing. The lover may drop in to say goodbye to us in a few of the poems, and some of the poems may seem to have been written just at that moment the towels are beginning their trip to the laundry, but there are no requests for us to "act out a division" and we are never asked to imagine what is not shown to us. I am not so sure that a book by Ashbery shouldn't be given to an art critic to review instead of to an English professor.

The astonishing imagery that is so visually right and so carefully eschewed by Ehrenpreis does not need to be quoted here. Any reader who has tried ("intelligently and seriously") to read Ashbery's poetry cannot help but claim a few for himself. (I who slop varmints every day of my life often accuse them of being "sullen fecundity to be watched over," and I now find it impossible to stare down a row of diminishing white fenceposts without thinking "nudity.")

But it is not the remarkable images in isolation that is Ashbery's achievement. It is the connotative methods he has devised to organize them. One of these methods, the one that is so exhilarating, is the tremendous distances that are traveled between the poems' opening and closing lines. But Professor Ehrenpreis says, and this statement scares me to death: "When one has shown there is purpose in his method, one has not endowed the method with the attributes rightfully to be sought in poetry." The major of these rightful attributes, it is implied, is shapeliness. "If a poet does find most of reality meaningless, he is ill-advised to proportion his verses accordingly, and to deal out lengths of murk as settings for brief illuminations."

Murk as background. I cannot think of one poet, Dante included, who has given me one good murky background, and I went back to *Self-Portrait* to see if I could find some lengths of murk. There were none, of course, but there were some awfully nice backgrounds such as this: "Nameless shrubs running across a field / That didn't drain last year and / Isn't draining this year to fall shod / Like waves at the end of a lake, / Each with a little sigh, / Are you sure this is what the pure day / With its standing light intends?" I could be looking at a landscape in the background of a Renaissance painting.

Professor Ehrenpreis has another complaint about the poems: "I find it sinister that the most successful one in his new book—the last and longest of the collection—deals with the theory behind it." In other words, how dare the poem claim dibs on a domain that is rightfully the critic's. But I think that Professor Ehrenpreis is issuing a warning here: Ashbery's work is going to be slim pickings for the exegesis freaks. At least for those who seek rightful attributes.

Robert Brotherson
Andes, New York

Irvin Ehrenpreis replies:

I don't know why Mr. Brotherson should give himself an air of integrity while attributing to me attitudes and conduct that have never been mine. I do not lecture to any class on the poetry of Ashbery; I do not assign it to students or discuss it in a classroom. My comments on the usual responses of most sympathetic readers were based on conversations over a period of five years with young poets or habitual readers of poetry, including a number who had heard Ashbery read his poems aloud, a few who had met him, and several who admired his work. The sentence Mr. Brotherson derides ("They teach," etc.) does not, as he implies, deal with the form of a typical poem by Ashbery; it is an attempt to suggest the kind of imaginative response to routine life that lies behind the poems, and it is based to some extent on hints supplied by Ashbery himself in published remarks. In my experience, directly contrary to what Mr. Brotherson asserts, Ashbery's poems are indeed more exciting to talk about than to read, and it is precisely this quality that gives them much of their reputation. It ill becomes the supporters of literature to sneer at university teachers. An American must live far out of the world if he imagines that in this country poets like Ashbery would be better known and better appreciated if there were no place for their work in our colleges of arts and sciences.

AOI!

To the Editors: September 30, 1976

Irvin Ehrenpreis should reread his own *Literary Meaning and Augustan Values,* in which he demands of critics scrupulous common sense in handling allusions and sources, and insists that we must not disregard a poet's "explicitness of statement and purpose." He wonders "what we gain by diverting a reader from the text to a reminiscence," and demonstrates how insisting on ingenious allusion "beats up awkward references." In his long article on Pound (*NYR,* May 27) he abandons his own principles for an inaccurate, flashy, meanly reductive review of Pound's work.

The kind of biographical criticism he suggests as a clue to Pound's "most private feelings" is unproductive. Determining whether the poet was "inspired" at this point or that by any of the many women in his life helps us read his poems no more than finding another name for Lucy makes more public the feelings of "She dwelt among the untrodden ways."

(1) He suspects that Pound translated the *Trachiniae* "because it reminded him of the occasion when he asked his own wife to share a home with his mistress," as the Germans forced the Pounds from Rapallo. For this, he ignores everything Pound wrote about the play, most importantly the note he added to the dying Herakles' speech, "what / SPLENDOUR / IT ALL COHERES." For Pound, "this is the key phrase, for which the play exists." It was upon that phrase that the poet, preparing

for the end of his poem and the end of his life, drew to present his private feelings—if Ehrenpreis insists on distinguishing between private feelings and what gets written: "And I am not a demigod, / I cannot make it cohere." For a sliver of imprecise parallel, Mr. Ehrenpreis ignores the overall feeling of the play and most of its plot, where no parallels can be discovered. His interest in *Women of Trachis* springs from the coarsest available way of reading literature.

(2) Concerned with Pound's love life, he misreads the great cry of "AOI" which forms the "turn" of Canto 81, makes no effort to look at its context, nor recognizes it as the heroic refrain that echoes through the *Song of Roland*. Rather, he naively accepts an unfounded remark by the poet's daughter that the cry expresses the stress of being pent up with two women who loved him. The cry marks a heroic effort by the poet / prisoner to return to his true calling as an artist, after which he produces, masterfully, the formal and "traditional" lyric passages that end the canto. Only unjustified guesswork allows reading the "AOI" as an expression of stress produced by living with two women.

(3) Mr. Ehrenpreis next "leaves it to specialists" to decide how Pound's "relations with the two devoted women influenced his treatment of Penelope and Circe in the *Cantos.*" Again, for a crude biographical parallel, he is willing to cheapen the poem and ignore all the narrative and psychological implications where common sense says there are no parallels. He "beats up awkward references," for Pound did not have to take *moly* to protect himself from Miss Rudge's charms; she did not delay his return to any Ithaca, etc. Must we also wonder how Pound's domestic affairs influenced his treatment of Beatrice and Francesca da Rimini?

(4) The paraphrase from Mary's letter in Canto 76 is not "framed in such a way that the implications can hardly be grasped unless one realizes the nature of the source," nor leads to Pound's domestic affairs. The words are there for what they say, not for who said them: it would make little difference if the source was a letter from *X* rather than from Mary. They refer to a young Italian soldier blinded in the war, and are related to the long meditation on war in the *Pisan Cantos*.

(5) Mr. Ehrenpreis complains that Pound "tried to embody his ideals not in lucid reasoning but in suggestive images" (!), and was "unable to make an argument," lacking "powers of intellectual synthesis." If we

imagine a poet whose virtue is lucid reasoning, and who does not work through suggestive images, would we want to read him? The ways in which the *Cantos* makes sense cannot be explained here—but surely Ehrenpreis is suppressing everything he knows about poetry for the sake of his argument.

(6) He believes the "best parts" of Pound's longer poems "would gain power if they were isolated. . . . 'Medallion,' for instance, has been misinterpreted largely through its place in *Mauberley*." But it was never anything else than part of *Mauberley*: it has intricate connections with the rest of the poem. It's like arguing that "Out, out, brief candle!" has been misinterpreted largely through its place in *Macbeth*.

(7) After a blurred discussion of "concepts of culture" he slides towards the conclusion that Pound confused "an intellectual elite with a racial elite." What race this is is hard to know, since the *Cantos* draws positive or "paradisal" insights from so many traditions, including the Chinese, Japanese, African, Hebraic, and Egyptian. The *Cantos* is the "tale of the tribe" and the tribe is the human race. Pound believed in a "conspiracy of intelligence" (*not* of intellectuals) open to anyone, and having nothing to do with class or race.

Pound at times displayed enormous errors as a poet and as a man. His worst, he admitted, was "that stupid, suburban prejudice of anti-Semitism." His fictional, selective "Mussolini" has little to do with Mussolini. When he fell from his own ideals his language coarsened incredibly, and, as he said, he lost the law of Confucius. Like many intellectuals, he became frustrated in the role of *unacknowledged* legislator, and the results were disastrous. Yet he thought that "the only chance for victory over the brainwash is the right of every man to have his ideas judged one at a time." We need not claim that Pound's virtues *outweigh* the specific politics we detest, for such things cannot be quantified.

Yet Mr. Ehrenpreis does not begin to suggest the scope of Pound's vision; the energy and wit with which he collected the "record of the top flights of the mind"; nor the power of his dramatization, within a tragic view of history, of the "attempt to move out from egoism and to establish some definition of an order possible or at least conceivable on earth." He does your readers a disservice in his inaccurate summation and in the suggestion that Pound's domestic life is a key to the *Cantos*. But then, since the time of Joseph's brethren, there have been those who are willing to slay the dreamer to see what will become of his dreams.

George Kearns
Rutgers University
New Brunswick, N.J.

Irvin Ehrenpreis replies:

The first question a reviewer of poetry, film, or ballet must face is whether he represents the audience or the artist. Some critics, especially of contemporary painting, suppose it is their job to explain the intentions of the artist and encourage the reader or spectator to sympathize with them. Critics of television programs are more likely to report the experience of a spectator and to tell in what ways a program delighted or instructed them. Reviewers of poetry sometimes sound as if they had a duty to educate the poet and tell him how to do better next time.

I take my job to be helping people decide whether or not to read a book, especially by suggesting the kinds of pleasure they may expect from it. If an author is young or his work is obscure, and if in addition I believe a knowledge of his intentions and peculiar techniques will open the pleasures of his work to those who might otherwise miss them, I try to elucidate those intentions and techniques while recommending the work. But when I deal with an established author, I do not try to win readers over to his inferior work by asking them to let his intentions make up for flaws in the accomplishment.

Pound's poetry is often obscure. But he had the highest poetic gifts. I think his best accomplishments are found not in the large design of the *Cantos* but in the shorter, independent poems. The reason, I think, is that he ignored his own genius when he chose to produce a modernist long poem.

In revolt against models like *Idylls of the King* or *In Memoriam*, but sympathizing with the kind of judgment that Poe delivered on conventional long poems, Pound had incompatible aims. He inherited the Romantics' high esteem for brief, intense, lyric effects; and he wished to embody that beauty in a poem which also had the powers of cumulation, foreshadowing, and retrospection to be gained from length. What he (like his successors) would not admit is that length holds most readers only through coherent narrative or coherent argument.

A long poem may have a unified narrative plot like the *Iliad;* it may have a series of interlocking actions like *Orlando Furioso;* it may have an instructive or persuasive argument like *De rerum natura.* Otherwise it separates into passages which are perhaps linked by various motifs but which lack the impetus to carry most readers across the gaps.

Pound wished to live like Homer on Horace's income. He wished to convey lyric intensity by the direct representation of heightened moments of awareness. He wished to avoid the moral didacticism and dull informativeness of expository poems; and he rejected the obvious, ponderous shape of epic narrative (which was already, of course, splendidly managed by novelists in prose). As he went on with the *Cantos,* he admitted the need for edification after all, yet would not supply it through coherent exposition or firm, implicit design. Instead, he relied on extracts from documents, on teasing aphorisms, and on the ideograph.

I tried indeed to see the *Cantos* in Pound's terms. But after I took his definitions and statements of purpose back to the experience of reading the poem, I discovered they did not fit. Why should I substitute the poet's commentary for my own response?

As for the cry of "AOI," although I knew it came from the *Song of Roland,* I also knew scholars were unsure of its meaning there. Mr. Kearns is as ungracious in suggesting I overlooked its origin as I should be if I faulted him for not knowing the cry occurs outside the *Cantos* in Pound's "Phanopoeia," which I regard as deeply erotic. In other words, the meaning Mr. Kearns attributes to the cry is not to be found in an external source, as he implies, but in Pound's peculiar application; and to clarify that, its context in "Phanopoeia" seems of crucial significance.

As for the poet's daughter, since she was familiar with the *Cantos* from childhood, translated much of the poem under her father's correction, and provided material for several passages, I am inclined to credit her explanation against that of Mr. Kearns.

A quite different issue is the use of biography in criticism. I don't see why one should not search a man's life for clues to obscurities in his writing. Neither do I see why one should not satisfy the normal human instinct to connect a man's work with his life, so long as the one is not confused with the other.

For example, *The Women of Trachis:* according to the consensus of learned judges, the Greek original is deeply flawed. Certainly, this is my experience of it. Pound's version sounds unsuccessful to me as either translation or independent composition. So I did not discuss it as a literary work but only observed that the choice of the play for translation puzzled me. I then tried to account for the choice and remarked that the central situation would have attracted Pound.

Mr. Kearns replies with an exposition of Pound's doctrine. But I found no such doctrine in the Greek original; so I could not believe this was the basis of Pound's choice. Nor did I think his own play rose to the level of deserving an elaborate interpretation. Besides, I had a further reason for making so much of the central situation. Before Pound took to *The Women of Trachis,* the Greek tragedy he singled out for praise was the *Agamemnon,* which has the same central situation.

Another example: Pound often paired poems to show contrasting treatments of the same motif; he often grouped poems to illustrate various responses to the same scene. If I try to link a lyric called "Doria" with his wife, and from the biographical clue can infer that a number of poems the poet liked to keep together seem to make a sequence dealing with a crucial experience, the attempt does not seem to me wasted.

Another example: suppose that a poem keeps evoking parallels with the *Odyssey;* yet it has many references to Circe and hardly any to Penelope. If neither the *Odyssey* nor the modern poem tells one the cause of the lopsidedness, a reader may be pardoned for seeking an explanation elsewhere—not only of the lopsidedness itself but also of the alert poet's failure to anticipate one's natural bafflement.

Finally, there is the relation of culture to race and class. Pound's own career is an example of how a high, aesthetic culture can reach across the differences of race and class; and I agree that Pound urged his readers to accept insights which he claimed to draw from many traditions. Yet in his poems Pound also relieved certain classes—the rulers, the creative elite—of common moral obligations; and he granted them various privileges (such as the infliction of suffering) that he withheld from other folk. In his poems he opposed certain races and classes to his vision of the best life, except as they occupied the humble place he might assign them in that hierarchical vision.

"Fictional" is a curious epithet for the Mussolini of the *Cantos.* The character was not invented by the poet; he has Mussolini's name, his life, his mistress, his death. The poet represented him as possessing attributes of Pound's ideal ruler. Did he thereby create a fiction or make a mistake? According to the poem, this man was the historical figure. Incidentally, I knew that Pound as an old man tried to recant some of his doctrines; but that is a fact of his biography: the poetry remains.

These are the chief issues between us. The reader who would like to follow up Mr. Kearns' other points had best go back to the works under discussion and test our reasoning against independent responses. As for my recent book on English literature 1660–1760, since the main effort there was to show that the practice of modernist writers like Pound is fundamentally different from that of "Augustan" writers like Dryden, it would be awkward for me to apply exactly the same principles to both.

Lowell's Irony

To the Editors: November 25, 1976

Professor Irvin Ehrenpreis (*NYR,* October 28) stresses the comic element in Robert Lowell's *Selected Poems.* One comic aspect of this recent collection that Ehrenpreis missed is that not all the poetry published in the volume is original with Robert Lowell. Specifically, the poem the reviewer quotes in its entirety, "Will Not Come Back," is a good and almost literal translation by Lowell of one of the Spanish language's most famous and frequently quoted love lyrics (school children memorize it in Spain and Latin America, and an undergraduate Spanish major from an American university who couldn't identify the poem would be either a surprise or a mediocre student). The poem is "*Rima LIII*" by Gustavo Adolfo Bécquer (1836–1870), a Sevillian post-Romantic writer whose lyric verse was published in book form as *Rimas* a year after his death. Because Lowell's volume places "Will Not Come Back" at the end of a section called "Nineteen Thirties," I selected an English translation of the Bécquer poem from 1924 for comparison with Lowell's version (the following is from *The Infinite Passion,* translated by Young Allison, Chicago: Walter M. Hill, 1924):

> Dusky swallows again will come
> Upon thy balcony their nests to swing,
> And tap their wings upon thy window-panes
> In playful fluttering;
>
> But those which slackened in their flight,
> Thy beauty and my fortune their concern;
> Those which even came to know our names . . .
> Those . . . will ne'er return!
>
> Twining honeysuckle will come
> Again thy garden wall to clamber o'er,
> And spread again upon the air its blossoms,
> Fairer than all before;
>
> But those, bediamonded with dew,
> Whose drops we two were wont to watch aquiver
> And fall, as they were tears of limpid
>   morning . . .
> Those . . . will come back never!
>
> Burning words of love will come
> Again full oft within thine ears to sound;
> Perchance thy heart will even be aroused
> From its sleep profound;
>
> But mute and prostrate and absorbed,
> As God is worshipped in His holy fane,
> As I have loved thee . . . undeceive thyself:
> Thou wilt not be thus loved again!

Clearly the Lowell version of "*Rima LIII*" shows the hand of a translator who is also a good poet; it is much better than the earlier translation. And he has modified the softness of Bécquer's first image, preferring instead the harshness of "Dark swallows will doubtless come back killing / the injudicious nightflies with a clack of the beak." Lowell's version on page 192 of *Selected Poems,* carries a bracketed subtitle, the word "Volveran (*sic*)," that contradicts the English title (it means "will come back"), but his translation makes no attempt to imitate the metric pattern or the rhythmic stresses of the original. He does reproduce Bécquer's imagery, language, and internal structure.

One cannot expect, perhaps, that Ehrenpreis, a professor of English literature, be familiar with nineteenth-century Spanish poetry. But Robert Lowell's failure to identify "Will Not Come Back" as not his own work but a translation, leaves a very bad taste in the mouth. Lowell's lapse has made Ehrenpreis look slightly foolish in his attempt to relate the imagery of the Bécquer poem to Lowell's other poetry. He calls this poem, in fact, "one of the simplest poems Lowell ever wrote," and links it to the poet's life experiences and to Lowell's *Benito Cereno.* The reviewer deserved better treatment from the poet / translator.

Certainly we might look to Robert Lowell for a greater degree of artistic integrity and a bit less condescension (did he think none of us would recognize the original?). Or is he working from a strange definition of translation-as-creation that does not give credit where credit is due?

Constance A. Sullivan
Department of Spanish and Portuguese
University of Minnesota
Minneapolis

Irvin Ehrenpreis replies:

I am grateful to Professor Sullivan for identifying the source of "Will Not Come Back." When I described the poem as far simpler than Lowell's usual style, I did not suggest that it was his most characteristic work. The line I drew attention to was not derived from Bécquer and comes close indeed, in its imagery and tone, to the line quoted from *Benito Cereno.* The connection with the episode in Cuernavaca was made by the poet in *Notebook;* for in the third American edition "Volveran" appears under the heading "Eight Months Later"—following a summer sequence—while the earlier, Cuernavaca sequence is dated "midwinter" and follows "Christmas and New Year." I suppose one reason Bécquer's poem attracted Lowell is that the images were reminiscent of his own: the swallows of "Das ewig Weibliche," the leaves across the barn window in "Our Twentieth Wedding Anniversary," are among the many parallels one might cite.

Professor Sullivan's remarks about Lowell's integrity trouble me. In my review I drew attention to the poet's well-known habit of adapting the materials of other authors to his own purposes. Nobody familiar with the humanistic tradition (or merely with the practices of Dryden or Pound) should be puzzled by the phenomenon. Lowell himself, in the "Afterthought" to *Notebook,* said that the poems in the book often depended on borrowings, and he identified a number of his own sources. As for the title "Volveran," it does not sound like condescension to me but like a reminder for those who might know Bécquer's poem. "*Nunc est bibendum*" and "*Dames du temps jadis*" are other titles with such a purpose.

When Lowell published *Imitations,* many critics savagely attacked him because he referred the poems to their original authors. The attackers blamed him for representing his versions as faithful translations, even though the poet used the term *Imitations,* and declared in his introduction that he had been "reckless with literal meaning." As Professor Sullivan says, Lowell has not preserved the versification of Bécquer's poem. I myself find that though Lowell has kept the images and their sequence, he has also reduced six stanzas to a rough sonnet in which two of the lines are not from the Spanish; he has toughened the tone and touched the poem with irony; and if he had offered it as a translation, he would have opened himself to the old complaints.

I should like to add a note on a quite different part of my review, the comments on "No Hearing (Discovering)." I have it on excellent authority that the poem does not deal with a poet's daughter.

"Will Not Come Back" Returns

To the Editors: January 20, 1977

Professor Constance Sullivan, writing about Robert Lowell's poem "Will Not Come Back" (*NYR*, November 25), rather insultingly asks "did he think none of us would recognize the original?" On the contrary, he thought everyone would. The point that this poem is based on a Spanish poem by Gustavo Adolfo Bécquer was raised in *The Listener* of December 10, 1970. Lowell wrote in reply, in the same number: "The poem is meant to be read in the context of the book as an original poem. But the source is indicated by the Spanish title, 'Volveran.' The Bécquer poem is as well-known in Spanish as 'Tears, idle tears' is in English."

Derwent May

Eliot's "Headland"

To the Editors: April 6, 1978

At the end of his thoughtful essay-review entitled "Mr. Eliot's Martyrdom" (*NYR*, February 9), Irvin Ehrenpreis objects to a claim made by Derek Traversi in his *T. S. Eliot: The Longer Poems*. "Traversi," Professor Ehrenpreis writes, "assumes that the headland in *The Dry Salvages*, Part I, is the same as the 'promontory' in Part IV. But as it happens, the first is on the coast near Gloucester, Massachusetts; the other is at Marseilles."

How Ehrenpreis arrived at this determination I should like to know. Throughout *The Dry Salvages*, Eliot compares modern secular existence to an endless voyage, a random journey with no apparent destination. Hence it seems likely that, in writing Part IV of the poem (a prayer addressed to the Holy Virgin, asking her to guide and protect sailors), Eliot had in mind the Church of Our Lady of Good Voyage, which overlooks not Marseilles, but Gloucester harbor. A noteworthy feature of this church, particularly relevant to Eliot's poem, is its statue of the

Virgin, who stands between two spires and cradles in her arms not the infant Jesus, but a sailing ship.

David L. Simpson
English Department
Northwestern University
Evanston, Ill.

Irvin Ehrenpreis replies:

Eliot said that when he wrote, "Lady, whose shrine stands on the promontory," he had in mind the Church of Notre Dame de la Gard, overlooking the Mediterranean at Marseilles. (See William Turner Levy and Victor Scherle, *Affectionately, T. S. Eliot,* p. 121).

It could not matter less which church the poet was thinking of; neither the meaning nor the value of the poem depends on the fact. What I drew attention to was Traversi's assumption that *The Dry Salvages* would be a better poem if the reader took the "headland" and the "promontory" to be the same.

I am uneasy because of the principle implied, one widely accepted by academic critics, that coherence of this sort is a mark of good writing. It is time to stop invoking such a principle, because a number of great masterpieces can be made to seem aesthetically coherent only through acts of interpretive legerdemain.

There is an unavoidable coherence in practically any extended discourse uttered by a single person. Inevitably, themes, words, and classes of imagery will reappear. A child complaining about his parents' mistreatment of him, or an ill-educated septuagenarian writing to his daughter about his illness will produce a "coherent" discourse.

To praise great poets for that sort of unity seems to me to destroy the idea of literary merit. Precisely by seeking it, Traversi led himself (here and elsewhere) into unnecessary, unilluminating error. Eliot characteristically altered the reference of his poems from point to point. Just as Mr. Eugenides is not a Phoenician sailor, and Tiresias is not a young man carbuncular, so also the Lady of *Ash Wednesday* II is not the "veiled sister" of section V. In *The Dry Salvages,* Eliot, who was a master of repetition, would not have changed "headland" to "promontory" if he had wished to dwell on the identity of the two locations.

Mr. Eliot's Motives

To the Editors: May 4, 1978

I found Irvin Ehrenpreis's essay of appreciation of T. S. Eliot (*NYR,* Feb 9) interesting, and many of his views quite compatible with my own, even though they are supported by "reasoning" that could only be termed "fragile" or nonexistent. I was in general agreement when he observed that in Eliot's poetry, "the old poignancy of evasive moments and missed opportunities kept returning . . . in patterned lines"; that in many of his poems, it was "the squalor of the poet's own mind and the lusts of his own eye . . . that he excoriates"; that "the satiric impulse died after he wrote *The Waste Land*"; that he "might have used a mask" in some of his poems. Imagine my surprise when I discovered appended to his essay a distorted summary of my book, *T. S. Eliot's Personal Waste Land: Exorcism of the Demons.*

I made it quite clear in my book that my reading of the *Waste Land* manuscripts reconstructing the psychic origins of the poem, did not hinge on establishing an overt relationship between Eliot and Jean Verdenal in the Paris Pension in 1910–11. Why Ehrenpreis feels he must spend most of his space on my book proving that there were no "homosexual relations sixty-five years ago" between Eliot and Verdenal is beyond my comprehension. That Eliot returned to Harvard in 1911, that he "became attached" to Emily Hale between 1911–14, that no one has yet documented another "homosexual relationship" in Eliot's life—these "facts" bear little relevance to what Eliot might in retrospect have made imaginatively out of the relationship with Verdenal: compare, for example, Tennyson's grief for Hallam in *In Memoriam.* Among the "sparse" details of the relationship relayed by his review, Ehrenpreis fails to include Eliot's 1934 outburst in a *Criterion* "Commentary": "My own retrospect [of the Paris of 1910–11] is touched by a sentimental sunset, the memory of a friend coming across the Luxembourg Gardens in the late afternoon, waving a branch of lilac, a friend who was later (so far as I could find out) to be mixed with the mud of Gallipoli."

And when Ehrenpreis refers readers who find my "path through *The Waste Land* enticing" to John Peter's earlier essay, he also fails to point out Eliot's legal move to suppress the Peter essay, especially the curious intensity of Eliot's overreaction to a reading of his poem which (when Eliot read it in 1952) was discreetly nonbiographical. Of course Peter did not have in 1952 nor on the essay's reappearance in 1969 the *Waste Land* manuscripts with all their rich resources for the psychosexual interpretation.

Ehrenpreis passes over the bulk of the material present for my reading and focuses on Part IV of *The Waste Land,* "Death by Water." He ignores entirely the highly suggestive sexual context this brief segment had in its original setting in Eliot's poem, "Dans le Restaurant" (where it is a glowing memory), and instead quotes Grover Smith's essay pointing out, among other things, that "Phlebas" means penis in Greek (I summarized this admirable essay in my book). Ehrenpreis assumes that Grover Smith's 1946 essay is incompatible with identification of Phlebas the Phoenician, however subterraneously, as Jean Verdenal. I cannot see why. I summarized the Smith essay because its speculation on the sexuality implicit in "Death by Water" reenforced my own reading of the lines as rooted in the anguished memory of Verdenal. To see it thus obscurely rooted, it is certainly not necessary to read "Death by Water" as Eliot's literal "tribute" to or "celebration" of his dead friend!

Moreover, in the latest edition of Grover Smith's book, *T. S. Eliot's Poetry and Plays* (1974), he adds a footnote (p. 321) connecting Phlebas the Phoenician with Jean Verdenal. Since Ehrenpreis says that he has relied heavily on Grover Smith to formulate his own point of view on Eliot, is he willing to accept Smith's conclusion if not mine?

James E. Miller, Jr.
University of Chicago

Irvin Ehrenpreis replies:

By rooting Part IV of *The Waste Land* in an "anguished memory" of Verdenal, Miller directs us away from the tone, meaning, and value of the passage. Anguish is precisely what does not characterize Part IV, which is peculiarly calm. It represents death as a release from the strains of an existence preoccupied with material gain. In it, the merchant seaman who has drowned does not face the alternatives of salvation and damnation. Unlike Lazarus (see "Prufrock," line 94), he suffers no resurrection. His body returns to its elements; and the "whispers" of the fish nibbling it (*The Waste Land,* line 316) suggest a contrast with the fate of Christ's body alluded to in "Gerontion" (line 23). The last three lines of Part IV sound like a pagan elegy from *The Greek Anthology.* But this prospect of death as peaceful dissolution seems unavailable to the spiritually torn poet; he must find another Way.

To this account of "Death by Water," I oppose what we know of Eliot's attitude to Jean Verdenal. When Eliot explicitly commemorated his friend, he identified him as having died in a military campaign. For an epigraph, he chose to quote from a poem devoted to the fate of Christians after death. Again, in the tribute to Verdenal in *The Criterion,* Eliot dwelt on his friend's part in a military campaign. How painfully the First World War disturbed Eliot, we know from letters written at the time. We know that he disrupted his life and quit his job in an effort to serve in the war, an effort which failed. His guilt over the failure, and his employment in a bank, would have complicated his devotion to a friend who perished nobly in a hideous battle. To imagine what Eliot himself made of Verdenal's memory, I think we had better look not at "Death by Water" but at the ideal of Christian heroism which Eliot praised when he wrote about Péguy in 1916.

As for the issue of covert or overt homosexuality, the biographical implications remain the same either way. From the evidence, it looks as if Eliot chose Vivien Haigh-Wood not over Jean Verdenal but over Emily Hale. If he later recoiled emotionally from the marriage, he presumably returned in his thoughts to the woman whose continuing importance for Eliot is amply documented. And regardless of covert or overt behavior, if the friendship with Verdenal had the qualities alleged by Miller, one would have expected the poet to stay with him longer and to return to him sooner. On Miller's innuendoes concerning Eliot's legal action against John Peter's essay, I have two comments. First, it does not puzzle me that the leading layman of the Church of England should wish to protect his own moral reputation and that of a cherished friend; secondly, it seems a leap in logic to presume that if a man tries to suppress a libel, there must be some truth in it.